Ministry Is...

How to Serve Jesus with Passion and Confidence

DAVE EARLEY AND BEN GUTIERREZ

Ministry Is...

How to Serve Jesus with Passion and Confidence

ACADEMIC

NASHVILLE, TENNESSEE

Contents

Part 4. The Manner of Ministry

Part 5. The Methods of Ministry

Introduction

We love ministry!

After God and our families, there is nothing we cherish more than the privilege of serving the Lord in ministry. We rejoice in ministering to people through evangelism, teaching, disciple making, praying, preaching, administrating, and leading. We also find great fulfillment in helping prepare others for ministry. We have served for many years in church ministry as church planters, pastors, professors, administrators, and authors; and we would not trade it for the world. Therefore, we jumped at the opportunity to create this practical guide to church ministry.

We don't claim to be special.

We assume that Paul was speaking to us when he wrote that God called us in spite of the fact that we are nothings and nobodies apart from Jesus Christ (1 Cor 1:26–31). As missionary hero C. T. Studd would say, we are "Christ's insignificants and etceteras." Our only boast is in God.

We do have some experience.

We have given our adult lives to church ministry. In our journeys we have tried anything we thought might help. We have made plenty of mistakes and have won many victories. We have read the books and attended the conferences. We have trained thousands of students, laypersons, and pastors across America and in many foreign nations. As a result, we have culled our combined 50 years of hard-earned church ministry experience to give you what we believe are the 31 most important lessons to grasp in order to serve Jesus with passion and confidence.

We are incredibly proud of you.

Anybody who has the courage to read a book with the word *ministry* in the title is our kind of person. Effective church ministry can be one of the hardest yet most fulfilling challenges you can accept. Often it demands immense patience and perseverance. At times it feels like the enemy is fighting you every step of the way. You need encouragement in strong doses. That's why we wrote this book.

We deeply desire to help you.

We want you to be the type of minister whose heart is on fire for God and who will give headaches to the Devil. So we have crafted 31 chapters of high-octane equipment, empowerment, and encouragement for any potential difference maker. In it we cover church ministry from just about every angle possible. Great for beginners, it also offers practical guidance for the most seasoned veteran. Each of the 31 chapters is written as a stand-alone article, yet they tie together to train, teach, and encourage any potential world changer.

We think this is more than "just another book."

This book is your guide to the great adventure of doing your part to change the world for Jesus Christ. We believe these 31 chapters are positively potent. They will transform your life so you can be used of the Lord to revolutionize the lives of many others.

You won't get it all at once.

Learning to serve Jesus with passion and confidence can seem a little like eating an elephant. You don't get it all down in one bite. You have to eat it one bite at a time, learning a little more each week.

Chew it slowly.

This book was not designed to be rapidly read and quickly forgotten. It was prayerfully put together with the goal of changing your life. It will explain the what, why, and how of church ministry. Read it with a pen in hand to mark it up and make notes in the margin. Personalize it. Let it mark your life by making it *your* book.

At the end of every chapter you will find "What Now?" challenges to help you apply what you have just read. There also will be a summary about the nature of ministry and some good quotes to encourage and motivate you.

Read it all.

We want to encourage you to read all 31 chapters. We saved some of our best ideas for the final section. If you are reading this book outside of the classroom, you may want to read one a day for the next month. You will want to make it a regular appointment in your schedule.

Get a cup of coffee, grab a pen for note-taking, and dive in.

We pray that this little book will become a big book in your life. May it become your coach, equipping encourager, and idea catalyst for a lifetime of making an eternal difference for the glory of God in the lives of others.

—Dave Earley and Ben Gutierrez

Part 1

The Meaning of Ministry

Ministry Is . . .

Leaving a Trail of Dust

Dave Earley

*True greatness, true leadership is achieved not
by reducing men to one's service, but in giving
oneself in selfless service to them.*

—J. Oswald Sanders[1]

When I (Dave) was a little kid, I loved to read the cartoons in the Sunday paper. One of my favorites was *Peanuts*. First printed in 1950, *Peanuts* is one of the most popular syndicated cartoons of all time and is still in Sunday papers today. One reason it is so well loved is because it has such a fascinating collection of characters. This cast of characters includes Charlie Brown, the ever-unfortunate boy; Snoopy, his beagle dog; Linus, the boy with his blankie; Linus's mean sister, Lucy; the piano playing boy named Schroder; and Pig Pen, my favorite. The thing I especially loved about Pig Pen was that wherever he went he was followed by a cloud of dust.

Real ministry is not about being so dirty that a cloud of dust follows us. But it is about being so busy getting our hands dirty serving God that we leave a trail of dust in our wake.

Leaving a Trail of Dust

The most common Greek term used in the New Testament for the verb "to minister" is διακονεω (22 times, plus 10 times it is rendered as "to serve"). *Diakonos* is the most common Greek term used in the New Testament for the noun "minister" (20 times as "minister," plus eight times as "servant," and three times as "deacon"). In Phil 1:1 and 1 Tim 3:8–13 it denotes an office in the church. But almost everywhere else the word is used in a more general sense.

It indicates not just "work" in general but primarily "work that benefits someone else." Paul used the word *diakonos* to describe himself as a servant of the Lord (1 Cor 3:5), "God's ministers" (2 Cor 6:4), "ministers of a new covenant" (2 Cor 3:6), "a servant of this gospel" (Eph 3:7), and "a minister of the church" (Col 1:25).

Paul noted that many of his coworkers were also servants: the woman Phoebe (Rom 16:1) and the men Tychicus (Eph 6:21; Col 4:7), Timothy (1 Tim 4:6) and Epaphras (Col 1:7). Jesus said that His followers should be servants (Matt 20:26; 23:11; John 12:26). All Christians must do the work of a servant or minister. We are all servants or ministers of Christ, servants of His message and servants of one another.

While we are not certain of its origin, it could be the product of compounding the words δια ("spreading") and κονις ("dust"), to mean, properly, "raising dust by activity." Hence, being a "minister" is not merely having the title "minister" or "deacon" or "servant" but "serving so actively that a trail of dust follows in our wake." It is about doing what needs to be done. It is not about the title we are given but rather the work that we do—we serve. It is about getting dirty in order to make others clean. Wasn't that what Jesus was all about anyway?

I once spoke at a church that was exploding in growth by reaching public university students with the gospel. I was somewhat surprised to see several obviously postcollege age adults diligently serving the students as they arrived. The pastor of the church pulled me aside and commented that the cheerful man carrying the chairs was the city manager, the smiling gentlemen at the door welcoming every guest was a downtown lawyer, the grinning man taking the offering was a distinguished professor, and the happy lady running the nursery was a nurse. Each was also a member of the leadership team.

Unlike some churches that nominate and vote on deacons in a sort of popularity contest, they had a different approach. They chose those who were the greatest servants. The pastor said that they looked for "a cloud of dust" and selected the ones who were so actively serving that they left "the cloud" in their wake.

Real Ministry Is Getting Dirty for God

After my freshmen year in college, I spent a summer with Teen Missions International. Their motto was, and still is, "Get Dirty for God." We spent our first two weeks outside Merritt Island, Florida, living in pup tents in the jungle. The days were long, hard, and muddy.

I had heard about Teen Missions because the founder, Bob Bland, spent many years as a Youth for Christ director and as the recruitment director for the Christian Service Corps in my hometown. He founded Teen Missions with a group of men and women who were passionate about getting youth involved in missions. He wanted to get young people plugged into ministry before they had completed their college degree.

His innovative idea of involving teenagers in missions continued to develop from a single trip to Mexico and now boasts of more than 40 teams that travel to 30 countries each year. The goal of Teen Missions is to awaken teenagers to the needs in missions, acquaint them with the reality of life on the mission field, and give them an opportunity to serve the Lord through work projects and evangelism. The success of Teen Missions the last 40 years lies in the fact that teens get to experience real ministry.

My summer with Teen Missions was one of the most difficult in my life. The adventure of being far from home, sleeping on an air mattress in a church hallway, eating tomato soup, and bathing and shaving out of a bucket lost its novelty in a few days. Ten straight weeks of tough, draining ministry got tiring. Yet it was worth it because I had the opportunity to work with God and others in His kingdom. I was able to "get dirty for God" in order to clean others up for God. I led several young men to Christ and discipled them. It changed their lives . . . and mine.

Real Ministry Is Serving Others

Jesus' disciples were competitive young men. As they traveled together, I imagine that they joked a lot, argued about many things, and jockeyed for position. One day James and John let their competitive natures get the best of them.

Then James and John, the sons of Zebedee, approached Him and said, "Teacher, we want You to do something for us if we ask You."

"What do you want Me to do for you?" He asked them. They answered Him, "Allow us to sit at Your right and at Your left in Your glory." . . .

When the other 10 disciples heard this, they began to be indignant with James and John. (Mark 10:35–37,41)

Whoa! Did you catch that? James and John were seeking high positions, asking to be the number-one- and number-two-ranked spiritual leaders in the kingdom of God. They wanted to be great in God's kingdom.

Also notice that they totally left the other 10 disciples out of the discussion. When the other 10 found out about it, they were not thrilled. Neither was Jesus.

Sometimes young leaders assume that Christian leadership is about titles and positions (sometimes older leaders do as well, for that matter). They assume that success is measured by the size of their office, or their paycheck, the name on their door, and how many people report to them. They think the trappings of success equal greatness. But they are wrong.

Jesus called them over and said to them, "You know that those who are regarded as rulers of the Gentiles dominate them, and their men of high positions exercise power over them. But it must not be like that among you. On the contrary, whoever wants to become great among you must be your servant, and whoever wants to be first among you must be a slave to all." (Mark 10:42–44)

Notice that Jesus said real greatness comes from being a "servant" (διακονος) and a "slave" (δουλος). Jesus wanted His young followers to understand that unlike the world system, when it comes to Christian leadership, the measure of real success is service. It is being willing to get dirty in order to benefit others.

Real Christian ministry is not about being over people and bossing them around. It is about getting *under* people and lifting them up. It is not about getting but about giving. It is not about being served; it is about serving and sacrifice.

If Jesus' words were not enough, He wanted them to consider His example. After all, if Jesus Himself left His high position to serve and sacrifice for us, shouldn't we, as His disciples, do the same?

For even the Son of Man did not come to be served, but to serve, and to give His life—a ransom for many. (Mark 10:45)

Jesus is God. Prior to coming to Bethlehem, He had existed in heaven throughout all eternity. As God, He was the richest, most powerful being in the universe. Angels served His every need. Yet, when He came to earth, He did not come to be served but to serve.

Jesus did more than come to serve. He also came to give, and not just a convenient, comfortable amount. He gave it all. He gave His life in order to provide a ransom for our sins.

Real Ministry Is Doing Your Part

The first century Corinthian Christians were not known as spiritual giants. In Paul's first letter to them, he tries to help them sort out several questions and issues. He rebukes them for their carnality, envy, strife, and divisiveness. Then he scolds them for their childish practice of choosing sides and lining up behind various Christian leaders.

> Brothers, I was not able to speak to you as spiritual people but as people of the flesh, as babies in Christ. I fed you milk, not solid food, because you were not yet able to receive it. In fact, you are still not able, because you are still fleshly. For since there is envy and strife among you, are you not fleshly and living like ordinary people? For whenever someone says, "I'm with Paul," and another, "I'm with Apollos," are you not typical men? (1 Cor 3:1–4)

Paul was a man who understood real ministry. He lived the life of a servant (διακονος—Eph 3:7; Col 1:23,25) and a slave to God (δουλος—Rom 1:1; Gal 1:10; Phil 1:1; Titus 1:1). To him the Corinthians' futile attempt to rank him and Apollos was foolishness. After all, God is the ultimate author of spiritual life and fruit. He and Apollos were merely ministers (διακονος) carrying out their assignments.

In your life in church ministry, you may have the title "lead pastor." You may be called "youth pastor" or "worship leader." You may serve as "children's ministry director" or "women's ministry director." Or you may have no title at all. That's not the point.

You might be paid a ton of money, have a large staff, enjoy a nice office, get many weeks of paid vacation, and have a bunch of benefits. Or you may receive no compensation at all. It ultimately will not matter.

What will matter is whether you have faithfully carried out the assignment God gave you. Real ministry is simply doing your part.

Real Ministry Is Not for Cowards

Paul described his ministry (διακονια) as blameless (2 Cor 6:3) and himself as a minister (διακονος) who was commendable to God (2 Cor 6:4). Why? Did he have a large church? Did he pack out concert arenas? Did everyone download his podcasts? No way!

It is stunning to read what made Paul's ministry acceptable to God. Reading Paul's words is extremely challenging to us who have accepted the call to be a servant of God. Note what Paul writes:

> We give no opportunity for stumbling to anyone, so that the ministry will not be blamed. But in everything, as God's ministers, we commend ourselves: by great endurance, by afflictions, by hardship, by pressures, by beatings, by imprisonments, by riots, by labors, by sleepless nights, by times of hunger, by purity, by knowledge, by patience, by kindness, by the Holy Spirit, by sincere love, by the message of truth, by the power of God; through weapons of righteousness on the right hand and the left, through glory and dishonor, through slander and good report; as deceivers yet true; as unknown yet recognized; as dying and look—we live; as being chastened yet not killed; as grieving yet always rejoicing; as poor yet enriching many; as having nothing yet possessing everything. (2 Cor 6:3–10)

Did you catch that? In order to carry out his assignment and be a real minister doing real ministry, Paul was ready to face any consequence of serving God—good and bad. Real ministry is not for cowards or wimps. It can be excruciatingly hard and extremely costly. But according to Paul, it is ultimately worth it as the real minister is known by God, is fully alive, is full of joy, is eternally rich, and ultimately possesses all things (see vv. 9–10).

Real Ministry Is Serving No Matter What

In his second letter to the Corinthians, Paul adds further to the picture of what it might mean to be a minister (διακονος—2 Cor 11:23) of Christ. The Corinthian Christians were being led astray by some false apostles. Paul wanted them to understand what a real servant of Christ was like so he listed some of his ministry credentials. Yet, instead of listing his academic achievements, or the books he had written, or the number of churches he had planted, or his other incredible successes, Paul talked about what it meant to be a servant of Christ. His description demystifies the concept of serving Christ and helps us see that there is no earthly glamour or glory in it.

According to his testimony in 2 Cor 11:23–31, Paul as the minister of Jesus Christ faced labors, imprisonments, and "far worse beatings, near death many times" (v. 23). He worked hard, regularly went without sleep, was often homeless, and suffered hardships most of us only experience in our nightmares. Serving Jesus meant dishonor and being regarded as a fraud. Being a servant was not about convenience or comfort but rather dying to self and giving up all rights to a comfortable life. Yet Paul considered his ministry a privilege.

Paul makes it crystal clear—the real servant of Christ serves in spite of difficulties and dangers. Servants of Christ are to expect calloused hands and broken hearts. Significant pain, serious perils, and severe persecutions are part of the territory. Scars and prison bars may be involved. The true servant of Christ will serve no matter what.

Paul does not talk of big salaries. He does not mention fame and fortune or prestigious assignments. Instead Paul said that he experienced exhausting labor, frequent imprisonments, severe physical persecution, and outright torture—all in order to serve Jesus no matter what. He said that his life was one of constant danger, never-ending toil, and extreme deprivation. Forty lashes! Being beaten with rods! Being stoned to death!

Go into ministry with your eyes wide-open. Yes, serving Jesus has its high points and rewards, but some days it's little more than hard work. It could lead to misunderstanding, rejection, oppression, and outright persecution. Real ministry often leads us out of comfort and convenience into dangerous situations. It is serving no matter what. But no matter what, serving Jesus is always ultimately worth it because He is worth it.

Now What?

What activities are you doing that mark you as a servant of Jesus? Who are you serving? When are you serving? What is your assignment?

What is your attitude as a servant? Are you in it for what you can give or for what you can get? Do you place limits on your service, or will you serve no matter what?

Ministry Is . . .

1. Leaving a trail of dust.
2. Getting dirty in order to make others clean.
3. Serving.
4. Fulfilling your assignment and doing your part.
5. Not for cowards.
6. Serving Christ, no matter what.

☞ Quotes ☜

*If you don't want to serve, you don't
want to be in the ministry.*

—DAVID AND WARREN WIERSBE[2]

*You say you're a servant of Jesus Christ,
show me your scars.*

—JOHN MACARTHUR[3]

*God is not necessarily looking for leaders, at least not
in the sense we generally think of leaders. He is looking
for servants (Isa 59:16; Ezek 22:30). When God finds
men and women willing to be molded into his servants,
the possibilities are limitless.*

—HENRY AND RICHARD BLACKABY[4]

Ministers are servants who lead and leaders who serve.

—DAVID AND WARREN WIERSBE[5]

Notes

1. J. O. Sanders, *Spiritual Leadership* (Chicago, IL: Moody Press, 1967), 13.

2. D. and W. Wiersbe, *Making Sense of the Ministry* (Chicago, IL: Moody Press,1983) 35.

3. J. MacArthur, "The Hardship of Paul: 2 Corinthians 11:22–25," Grace to You, http://www.gty.org/Resources/Sermons/47–79.

4. H. Blackaby and R. Blackaby, *Spiritual Leadership* (Nashville, TN: B&H Publishing Group, 2002), xi.

5. D. Wiersbe and W. Wiersbe, *Making Sense of the Ministry*, 35.

2

Getting Your Ears Pierced for Jesus

Dave Earley

Sometimes when I (Dave) read the Bible, a word or phrase jumps out at me like it is printed in italicized, bold, neon print. This happened recently when I picked up my Bible to read the book of Romans. "Paul, **a slave of Christ Jesus**, called as an apostle, and singled out for God's good news" (Rom 1:1, bold added for emphasis).

As I read those words, I was struck with the thought that Paul, the amazing apostle, first considered himself "a slave of Christ Jesus." Paul was the author of half of the books of the New Testament. He was one of the greatest missionary church planters in history. He was arguably the most influential man born after Jesus Christ. Yet how did Paul choose to identify himself? "Paul, a slave of Christ Jesus." He *first* called himself a "slave" of Jesus Christ and *second* called himself an "apostle."

Then I looked at the cross references in the margin of my Bible. I saw "Philippians 1:1; Titus 1:1; James 1:1, 2 Peter 1:1; and Jude 1:1." This is what I read.

- Paul and Timothy, **slaves** of Christ Jesus—Phil 1:1
- Paul, a **slave** of God—Titus 1:1
- James, a **slave** of God and of the Lord Jesus Christ—Jas 1:1
- Simon Peter, a **slave** and apostle of Jesus Christ—2 Pet 1:1
- Jude, a **slave** of Jesus Christ, and brother of James—Jude 1:1

- The revelation of Jesus Christ . . . to His **slave** John—Rev 1:1 (bold added for emphasis)

I was stunned. Here was a listing of the most powerful men in early Christianity—Paul, James, Peter, Jude, and John—and they all had the same perspective. They each gave themselves the same title—*slave*.

James was the lead pastor of the first church of Jerusalem, which had tens of thousands of members. More impressively, he was the half brother of Jesus Christ, a son of Joseph and Mary. Yet how does James choose to identify himself? "James, **a slave of God**."

Simon Peter was Jesus' right-hand man. He was the big guy who preached the first sermon of the first church and 3,000 souls were saved! He was one of the stones Jesus said He would build His church upon. How does Peter choose to identify himself? "Simon Peter, **a slave** and an apostle **of Jesus Christ**."

As the son of Mary and Joseph, Jude was the full brother of James and the half brother of Jesus Christ. How does Jude choose to identify himself? "Jude, **a slave of Jesus Christ**."

John was the disciple whom Jesus loved. He was one of the three disciples invited to witness the amazing events on the Mount of Transformation. He wrote five books in our New Testament. In his Gospel and three epistles John refused to identify himself. But when he finally identifies himself at the opening of the letter of Revelation, what does he call himself? His "**slave**," John.

Doulos

If we do a quick Greek 101 lesson, we'll see that the word used in these verses for "slave" is δουλος (*doulos*). Of all the words Paul could have used to describe himself—"apostle," "ambassador," "saint," "missionary," "church planter," "author," "disciple," "rabbi," "revolutionary," Paul chose to call himself the "slave of Jesus Christ."

Several words in the Greek language describe various types of individuals whose task or station is to provide service for others. For example:

- *Paidos*, as used in Acts 3:13, describes Jesus as the Father's servant.
- *Diakonos*, as used in Rom 16:1, describes Phoebe as a servant to her church. It is also the word for "deacon."

Paul chose to use the word *doulos*. This word has been described by Greek scholar Kenneth Wuest in the following manner:

The word is *doulos*, the most abject, servile term used by Greeks to denote a slave, one who was bound to his master in chords so strong that only death could break them, one who served his master to the disregard of his own interests, one whose will was swallowed up in the will of his master.[1]

When we think of "servants," we think of "butlers" or "maids," but Paul, James, Peter, and Jude chose to call themselves "slaves"! Of all the terms for servant, *doulos* was the lowest scale of servitude.

For those of us called into a life of ministry, we need to recognize that ministry means being the slave of Jesus Christ. We come to find that ministry often only makes sense when we see ourselves as the slaves of Jesus Christ.

A slave is owned completely by his or her master.

In the first century slavery was common. An estimated one out of every four individuals in the Roman Empire was a slave. Slavers were known to follow the Roman Army so they could take possession of all the people Rome wanted sent back to their country as slaves. Often tens of thousands of slaves would be rounded up in a single day. These men, women, and children would be escorted to cities that would conduct public auctions. Sometimes slaves would be presented with signs hanging around their necks that listed such things as the slave's age, health, and education. A slave was viewed as a piece of property. The *doulos* owned nothing. Slaves and everything about them all belonged to the master. This is why the defeated foes of Rome sometimes chose suicide over slavery. A Christian in the early church was aware of the life of a slave. Yet he or she chose to be a slave of Christ.

In order to live as a slave of Jesus Christ, you must recognize the truth that God owns you. He created you. Every part of your mind, soul, and spirit was made by the creative breath of God.

Not only that. When you illegally sold yourself into spiritual slavery through sin, Jesus came along and saw you in your wretched state. He wept for your pain and hurt for your shame. There you were—naked, filthy, broken, blind, and all but dead with the shackles of sin around your ankles, wrists, and neck. The Devil himself was jerking your chain however and whenever he wanted.

But one day Jesus Christ rode into the slave market and redeemed you with His own blood. He took upon Himself your filth and your sin. He bought you with His blood. Then He declared that you are free, free at last, free at last!

Being a *doulos* was not the slavery of compulsion and law, but the willing and glad slavery of love. This was the voluntary attitude of Paul, Jude, Peter, and James. Jesus had won them by love. Jesus is the Great Servant of Love who came not to be served but to serve, to minister to others, to give His life a ransom for all.

Christian slaves are people who recognize that they owe Jesus an amazing debt and voluntarily sign up to serve Him. He is their rightful owner.

Most of us try to live the Christian life backward or upside down. Too often we ask God to take care of *our* things instead of living as faithful managers of *His* things. We think that we choose to use our gifts, abilities, time, or money to serve God. But the truth is that because He owns us, our gifts, abilities, time, and money already belong to Him.

One day, when Jesus was ministering on the earth in the flesh, He did an odd thing. He watched what people gave in the offering. In doing so, He pointed out someone who was living as one of His slaves.

> Sitting across from the temple treasury, He watched how the crowd dropped money into the treasury. Many rich people were putting in large sums. And a poor widow came and dropped in two tiny coins worth very little. Summoning His disciples, He said to them, "I assure you: This poor widow has put in more than all those giving to the temple treasury. For they all gave out of their surplus, but she out of her poverty has put in everything she possessed—all she had to live on." (Mark 12:41–44)

Jesus commended this widow because she did more than give God the extras in her life. She gave all she had. Realizing that God owned her made it possible for her to give all she owned back to God. This is the heart of a slave.

Often I think I am really spiritual because I give Him 10 percent of my money. Often as I do so, I am secretly expecting Him to give it back to me. A *doulos* does not give Jesus 10 percent or even 90 percent. They give it all. Everything belongs to the Master.

A slave is one whose will is in full submission to the master.

Too often my will is surrendered to God *as long as* His will is something I like. But when His will is something I do not like, that becomes a different story. I get mad at Him, or I pull away from Him, or I pout.

This attitude is the opposite of living as a slave of Jesus. A slave lives with the mind-set that:

- I serve *where* He wants.
- I serve *when* He wants.
- I serve *how* He wants.
- I serve *who* He wants.
- I serve *only if* He wants.
- I serve Him *no matter* what.

Being a slave is not selective service when it is convenient or comfortable. Being a slave is not serving only when it looks good, or when everything is going my way, or when it advances my agenda, or if others notice, or if I am being paid. Being a slave is a lifestyle of total surrender to Jesus and to His will.

A slave is one whose will and capacities are actively engaged at the service of another.

Being a slave of Jesus Christ is an active, not a passive venture. Slaves serve. They *do* something. Sometimes we spend so much of our time and energy focused on avoiding and eliminating the evil from our lives that we miss the opportunity to do good. I agree with Erwin McManus when he writes:

> I am convinced that the great tragedy is not the sins that we commit, but the life that we fail to live. You cannot follow God in neutral. God created you to do something.[2]

"You cannot follow God in neutral." Too often we just sit there waiting for something to happen and wondering why it never does. Someone observed that there are three types of people in the world—those who make things happen, those who watch things happen, and those who wonder, "What just happened?" God only promises to bless the first type, those who make things happen.

"God created you to do something." Do it. If you sense God is in something, pursue it. Put it in gear and go for it. Act. Move. Reach. Do something.

Do It Now

As a young man, David could have stood with the rest of the nonsoldiering soldiers when Goliath and the Philistines tormented the Israeli army day after day. He could have stood around with the others waiting to see what would happen. He could have stood back with the others hoping someone else would make things happen. He could have laid back and told how he had killed a bear and a lion in the past. But that would not have done anyone any good. He was a slave of God. He had to act. So he took confidence from his past and launched out into the present.

David determined that he had to do something and do it now. He went out onto the field of battle trusting God to help him as he faced the giant Goliath. God honored his active faith, and a great victory occurred.

Past success is often the cause of failing to experience God in the present. We try to hold on to what we already have and miss what could be. God exists in the moment. He lives in the here, the now. Theologians will tell you that God lives outside the realm of space and time. He does not exist in the past or future but as a never-ending present. If we want to experience God, we must embrace the opportunities of the now.

In spite of doing what some have viewed as crazy, my friends Jamal and Ed launched a church at Ohio State University among secular university students. In a place of radical godless thought, wild drinking, and rampant sex, they were convinced God was passionately at work with their generation at that time and at that place. As a result, a vibrant church exists today because they *did something*.

My friend Ken believes God loves the urban poor, the lonely, the homeless, the forgotten, the gays and lesbians, the prostitutes, and the alcoholics of the inner city. Among the tattoo parlors, vulgar gift shops, tiny art galleries, and in trendy restaurants staffed with gay waiters, Ken believes God is waiting to bust out in the now. As a result a church was launched that is making a difference because he *did something* for God.

I am a professor in a Christian university and teach a class called "Evangelism and the Christian Life." One semester, on the next to last day of class, a student named Katie came up to me and asked me to pray for a lady to whom she was witnessing. Katie said that she worked with this lady and the lady had not been open to Christ. But the lady told her that she was behind on her payments and was going to lose her house if she could not come up with a large sum of money by the end of the week.

I told Katie that I was not going to pray about it, but we were going to *do something* about it. I told the class about the situation, and some of the students with baseball hats passed them around like offering bags.

Within minutes the hats were filled with dollars. Katie counted it, and the total was $735!

The last day of class Katie came in with a big smile on her face. Then she told me that when she gave the lady a card with the money in it the lady started to cry. When the lady saw the $735, she turned white. It blew her away because she needed exactly that amount to make the rent payment and get groceries.

On top of that, Katie led the lady to Christ! This only happened because Katie and our class *did something* for God.

A slave finds his or her greatest and only real freedom in serving the master.

Over a hundred years ago, Salvation Army Captain Samuel Logan Brengle wrote a great little book on Christian ministry called *Love-Slaves*. Brengle wrote the book because he could not get out of bed. Let me explain.

Samuel had been on the fast track to become one of the best-known preachers in America, but his Master called him to give it up. The Master assigned him to go to the streets and preach to the down and out, the poor and helpless, the drunks and the whores. In fact, while he was preaching, some drunks hit him in the head with a brick and crushed his skull. After that, all Samuel could do was lie in bed and write.

In speaking of the freedom found in the "love slavery" of Paul, James, Jude, and Peter, he wrote:

> They had seen Him "wounded for our transgressions, . . . bruised for our iniquities, . . . chastised for our peace, and stricken that we might be healed, and their hearts had been bowed and broken by His great love; henceforth they were His bond-slaves, no longer free to come and go as they pleased, but only as He willed, for the adamantine [brilliant] chains of love held them, and the burning passion of love constrained them." Such bondage and service became to them the most perfect liberty. Their only joy was to do those things that were pleasing in His sight. Set at liberty to do this, their freedom was complete, for he only is free who is permitted to do always that which pleases him. The love slave has no pleasure like that of serving his master. This is his joy, and his very 'crown of rejoicing . . . this is the joy of the slave of love, and this he counts his perfect freedom."[3]

A slave finds his or her identity in the master.

In an entitlement era even Christians live with an ungodly focus on their rights and privileges. Too often we ask, "What is in it for me?"

If anyone had reason to feel entitled, it should have been the apostle Paul. He was the author of much of the New Testament. He had received special revelations of heaven. He was a Roman citizen and a well-trained scholar. He was one of a handful of living apostles. Yet he lived as a slave of Jesus. As a slave, he approached life with a strong sense of identity instead of entitlement.

> Paul calls himself the slave of Jesus Christ. The case classification is genitive possessive. The apostle is proud of the fact that he is a slave belonging to his Lord. There are certain individuals in the Roman empire designated "Slaves of the Emperor." This was a position of honor.[4]

When the Corinthian Christians were clamoring about position and prestige, Paul was above and immune to their attempts to draw him into a discussion of his entitled authority. Notice his response.

> So, what is Apollos? And what is Paul? They are **servants** through whom you believed, and each has the role the Lord has given. (1 Cor 3:5, bold added for emphasis)

What a powerful and liberating statement! Paul did not have to be drawn into arguments about titles and position. He knew *who* he was and more importantly, he knew *whose* he was. He was a slave *of Jesus Christ.*

A slave is devoted to the master by choice.

A *doulos* was the lowest scale of servitude. Yet, when transferred to Christian service, it expresses the highest devotion of one who is bound by love   a love slave. It describes one who becomes a slave by choice, not by force.

For example, when Jesus came to earth, He could have been just about anything He wanted to be. He demonstrated many skills and abilities that would qualify Him to excel in many occupations.

He certainly could have set up quite a prosperous medical practice. He was the consummate healer. Or He could have been a world-renowned fisherman (see John 21). Another occupation He could have done extremely well is food catering. He knew how to stretch resources to feed everyone (especially for picnics). No doubt many companies would have paid top dollar for Him to be their personnel director. He had special skills in motivating and working with people. Without a doubt He would have been the ideal travel agent. He could book people on truly heavenly trips.

His many talents were recognized by even the master of worldly endeavors—the adversary (see Matt 4). No wonder the Devil tried to recruit Him!

Undoubtedly Jesus could have been the best in many fields of endeavors. But the occupation He chose was to become a servant.

Make your own attitude that of Christ Jesus, who, existing the form of God, did not consider equality with God as something to be used for His own advantage. Instead He emptied Himself by assuming the form of a **slave**. (Phil 2:5–7, bold added for emphasis)

Jesus chose to serve us because He unconditionally and unreservedly loved us. We become the slaves of Jesus as we unconditionally and unreservedly love Him.

Note that a person was not born a slave. A person was not forced into becoming a slave. Christ's slave is a slave *by choice*. Brengle wrote:

There was a law among the Hebrews that for sore [great] poverty or debt or crime one man might become the servant of another, but he could not be held in servitude beyond a certain period. At the end of six years he must be allowed to go free (Exod. xxi, 1–6; Deut. xv, 12–17). But if he loved his master and preferred to remain with him as his slave, then the master, in the presence of judges was to place the man against a door or door-post and bore a hole through his ear, and this was to be the mark that he was his master's servant forever.[5]

In other words, for the *doulos*, the love-slave, the steel pierced ear was a symbol of a love-pierced heart. Our desire is that everyone who reads this book would embrace this type of commitment. Of course we are not talking about the literal piercing of your ear. We are talking about the spiritual piercing of your heart and will. We are talking about viewing yourself as the slave of Jesus Christ by choice out of love for Jesus. We are talking about a decision to serve Him for the rest of your life.

Now What?

Has the love of Jesus pierced your heart? Are you willing to "get your ears pierced for Jesus"? Do you live each day as if Jesus owns all of you? Do you find your identity in Him? Do you allow Jesus actively to own your time, money, and possessions? Does He own your heart, your thoughts, and your will? Are you using your gifts and abilities actively to serve Him?

Ministry Is . . .

1. Getting your ears pierced for Jesus.
2. Finding your identity in your Master, Jesus.

3. Discovering your greatest freedom in serving your Master, Jesus.

4. Doing something for Jesus.

☙ Quote ❧

It is deeply instructive to mark that although our Lord said,
"No longer do I call you bondservants, but friends yet,
successively, Paul, Peter, Jude and John name themselves
bondservants—and that with great delight. It is the service
of perfect freedom"—deepest of all devotions, that of realized
redemption and perfected love.

—WILLIAM NEWELL[6]

Notes

1. K. Wuest, *Wuest's Word Studies: Romans in the Greek New Testament for the English Reader* (Grand Rapids, MI: Wm. B. Eerdmans Publishing, 1956), 11.

2. E. R. McManus, *Seizing Your Divine Moment* (Nashville, TN: Thomas Nelson, 2002), 34–35.

3. S. L. Brengle, *Love-Slaves* (Salem, OH: Schmul Publishing, 1996), 8.

4. Wuest, *Word Studies*, 12.

5. Brengle, *Love-Slaves*, 7.

6. W. Newell, *Romans, Verse by Verse* (Chicago, IL: Moody Press, 1938), 2–3.

Mission Is . . .

A Mission of Mercy

Ben Gutierrez

*I will sing about the LORD's faithful love forever; with my
mouth I will proclaim Your faithfulness to all generations.*
—PSALM 89:1

A Man in Need of Mercy

God can make a minister out of anyone! Regardless of the mistakes, missteps, regrets, or past reputation of any person, the mercy of God provides a second chance. You may have been a blasphemer, scoffer, atheist, agnostic, doubter, or blatant sinner in your past; God can still use you to be a minister of the gospel.

But why would God use a person with such a sordid past? Why doesn't He deploy only those who have seemingly never made any mistakes in their lives? Why does He not mind that His spiritual army is full of people who have once demonstrated such horrible spiritual actions against Him?

The answer is simple: Who better to deliver the message of mercy than those who have personally experienced God's mercy!

This is vividly testified in the life of a man named Sosthenes. He was considered a spiritual and social leader in the city of Corinth. He was responsible to facilitate not only religious training for the Jewish people in the first century but also the social activities that take place regularly in the synagogue. Even though he had been a student of the Old Testament and Jewish culture, he unfortunately did not accept the message of Jesus Christ as the true Messiah. When he heard of a minister named Paul who felt called by the living God to preach this gospel in his city, Sosthenes became outraged.

> After this, he left from Athens and went to Corinth . . . . Then the Lord said to Paul in a night vision, "Don't be afraid, but keep on speaking and don't be silent. For I am with you, and no one will lay a hand on you to hurt you, because I have many people in this city." And he stayed there a year and six months, teaching the word of God among them. (Acts 18:1, 9–11)

In Sosthenes's desire to protect his tradition and beliefs, he grew hostile to the message of Jesus Christ and to those who purported such a "heretical message," especially Paul. Believing that this message would not only convert the people of Corinth to a belief system contrary to his own but also would alter their social activities, Sosthenes's hatred for Paul escalated to the point that he physically detained Christians and pursued legal prosecution against them.

Sosthenes was passionate about putting an end to the propagation of the Christian message even if it meant the interrogation and castigation of the messenger, Paul. But just as Gen 50:20 reminds us, God can take what some mean as evil and use it for good.

> And as Paul was about to open his mouth, Gallio said to the Jews, "If it were a matter of a crime or of moral evil, it would be reasonable for me to put up with you Jews. But if these are questions about words, names, and your own law, see to it yourselves. I don't want to be a judge of such things." So he drove them from the judge's bench. Then they all seized Sosthenes, the leader of the synagogue, and beat him in front of the judge's bench. But none of these things concerned Gallio. (Acts 18:14–17)

God protected His minister during the attack of Sosthenes. And it appears that after this event God turned His mercy on Paul's enemy. We are not told why this crowd in Corinth decided to beat the leader of the synagogue who brought Paul to Gallio for punishment. We do know that Paul mentions a Sosthenes in 1 Cor 1:1 as someone dear to him in the faith. If Sosthenes is the same man in both instances (and we believe he is), then at some point after this incident, the ruler of the synagogue became a Christian.

A Man Who Received Mercy

Assuming them to be the same man, could it be that Paul ministered to Sosthenes after his beating and that Paul's act of mercy convinced Sosthenes that Paul's Lord is truly the Messiah? Maybe somehow underneath the pile of angry people, he got some spiritual sense knocked into him and he began to run toward the truth of Christ—sort of a spiritual "hit and run"!

I find it ironic in a way that the Lord brought the apostle Paul and Sosthenes together. For wasn't Paul himself a blasphemer to the tenth degree? So why is a former persecutor of Christians (Paul) openly receiving a man who persecuted him? Answer: Paul extended mercy to Sosthenes because he personally experienced God's mercy. In Paul, Sosthenes experienced a bond that transcended human emotions and sense of fairness. Paul exhibited mercy and was able to continue to minister with a man who at one time was his enemy and tried to have him thrown in prison.

A City in Need of Mercy

Let's not stop with Sosthenes. Consider the entire city of Corinth to which Paul devoted over three and a half years of his life and to whom he wrote some of his longest and most detailed letters (1 and 2 Corinthians). The testimony of Sosthenes seems tranquil compared to the lifestyle of the citizens of Corinth. Still, God wanted to see these people come to Him and for them to experience His great mercy.

Corinth was not a godly city but rather a cesspool of sin and debauchery. In the first century Corinth was a city known for immorality. Even their name became synonymous with living an immoral life. They worshipped false gods and involved themselves in inappropriate sexual activity all in the name of worship to their gods. Corinth was positioned on major travel routes; thus it attracted many transient people who were here today and gone tomorrow. This only added to the temptation to indulge in immorality with the feeling of little to no consequence. Corinth harbored those whose lives were far from the Lord.

A City That Received Mercy

God loves sinners. He honed in on Corinth and instructed his ministers to infiltrate its society because He desired for these people to come to Him. In fact, God specifically mandated Paul to go to Corinth to reach those people with the gospel. As we read earlier, the Lord spoke to Paul by a vision and sent Him specifically to Corinth (Acts 18:9). God desired that sinful men and women would experience His mercy! Knowing this about the city of Corinth makes Paul's second verse in 1 Corinthians an even more magnificent testimony of God's mercy:

> To **God's church** at Corinth, to those who are **sanctified** in Christ Jesus and called as **saints**, with all those in every place who call on the name of Jesus Christ our Lord—theirs and ours. (1 Cor 1:2, bold added for emphasis)

Did you catch the words used to describe these people? Sanctified! Saints! Better yet, God's church! And now they are part of the body of Christ—"with all those in every place who call on the name of Jesus Christ our Lord—theirs and ours." Our churches are full of people who need God's mercy and who have graciously received His forgiveness and cleansing. Therefore it seems reasonable to conclude that the mission of every minister in the body of Christ should be a mission of extending God's great mercy to the world!

Some of You Were like This

All of us are sinners (Rom 3:23), and all of us deserve death and hell (Rom 6:23). Mercy is God's way of withholding the punishment and judgment we deserve. God emphasizes this point: we never forget where we came from. In the same letter to the church at Corinth, Paul provides us with this profound reminder of our past spiritual state:

> Do you not know that the unjust will not inherit God's kingdom? Do not be deceived: no sexually immoral people, idolaters, adulterers, male prostitutes, homosexuals, thieves, greedy people, drunkards, revilers, or swindlers will inherit God's kingdom. Some of you were like this; but you were washed, you were sanctified, you were justified in the name of the Lord Jesus Christ and by the Spirit of our God. (1 Cor 6:9–11)

This reminder was not unique to the city of Corinth. Paul records this same message to other churches under his care. Notice his words to the people who lived in Crete. In the first century, Cretans were synonymous with barbaric behavior, brash and abrasive character, laziness, and habitual lying. Their culture was steeped in sin and depravity. Yet God offered great mercy to these people.

For we too were once foolish, disobedient, deceived, captives of various
passions and pleasures, living in malice and envy, hateful, detesting one
another. But when the goodness and love for man appeared from God
our Savior, He saved us—not by works of righteousness that we had
done, but according to His mercy, through the washing of regeneration
and renewal by the Holy Spirit. This [Spirit] He poured out on us
abundantly through Jesus Christ our Savior, so that having been justified
by His grace, we may become heirs with the hope of eternal life.
(Titus 3:3–7)

Consider Paul's letter to yet another church, Ephesus. Here he stresses the
fact that all believers have received insurmountable levels of mercy from God:

We too all previously lived among them in our fleshly desires, carrying
out the inclinations of our flesh and thoughts, and by nature we were
children under wrath, as the others were also. But God, who is abundant
in mercy, because of His great love that He had for us, made us alive with
the Messiah even though we were dead in trespasses. By grace you are
saved! (Eph 2:3–5)

God, Who Is Rich in Mercies

To emphasize that mercy is at the heart of His kingdom, the Holy Spirit
does something interesting within the pages of the Bible. When the Holy Spirit
desires to convey the truth that God is merciful, the Scriptures will occasionally
pluralize the word (mercies). Scripture writers do this to emphasize that God's
mercy is *inexhaustible*!

Pluralizing a word for this purpose is not uncommon in Scripture. Often
when biblical writers wanted to show that the source of something was vast, massive, or inexhaustible, they pluralized unique words. For example, if the writer
wanted to convey a large body of water, he would pluralize the word related to
the source of water. Consider Psalm 1 where the psalmist wanted to show that
the believer who delights in the law of the Lord will never wither up and die like
chaff but will be connected to an inexhaustible source of nourishment, he wrote
that the believer will be "like a tree planted beside streams of water"!

In many other instances in God's Word, we find reminders of the depth
and breadth of His mercies (see Ps 51:1; Lam 3:22–23; Rom 12:1; 2 Cor 1:3;
Col 3:12–13).

You will be a merciful minister if you remain evermindful that you once stood in the place of desperation requiring God's mercy. A Spirit-led minister never forgets this reality. Real ministry cannot begin and cannot be sustained without this perspective.

Needed: Mercy-Minded Ministers

Our God is characterized by mercy. Mercy is at the heart of His kingdom. As the Lord Jesus Christ dwelt among people on the earth, His mercy and compassion were made evident to everyone with whom He came in contact. In fact, the biggest complaint the Pharisees had about Jesus Christ was that He was too compassionate and merciful toward the downcast of society. Our God is a merciful God!

So what is real ministry? It is expressing God's vast mercy to others. Our mandate as servants of Christ is to be *merciful* ministers. If our Leader, Savior, Creator, and Head of the church (Col 1:18) ministered with a heart of mercy, how much more should we be characterized as merciful ministers as we serve His people? If we as ministers are to be imitators of our leader Jesus Christ, then we must also be known for our deep commitment to express mercy to those in need of forgiveness and salvation. Just as our Lord was known for being a merciful God, we must have a reputation among the community of believers and the unbelieving world as people who are rich in mercy and willing to share the wealth!

Do You Love Mercy?

If those who live and work closely to you were asked to describe the way you disciple and discipline them, would they say your actions are performed out of compassion and for their betterment? Or would the question be met with feelings of frustration, unfairness, and an absence of sincere mercy?

Do people come to you willing to accept your tender words of correction and instruction because they believe you will deliver those words in a merciful spirit? Or have you grown to appreciate uninterrupted office hours and a weekly schedule devoid of visits and phone calls from fellow believers? I encourage you to pause right now and do some self-evaluation.

Ask God to reveal any hesitation on your part to show mercy to others. Then take a moment to ask significant people in your life (i.e., roommates, close friends, wife, husband, children, coworkers, etc.) to evaluate you. Provide them the opportunity to speak freely and uninterruptedly about how they perceive you, your actions, your counsel, and your responses to them. Tell them that you welcome their honesty in order to become a better minister of mercy. If you do this, I'll make this prediction—you will witness in their replies to you a true demonstration of tender mercy.

I also encourage you to memorize some or all of the Scripture passages in this chapter. Display the verses so you see them every day. Review them on your way into class or to work, before you return home, and as you prepare to minister to those under your care. Rehearse their teaching during a busy season of your life. Recount their truths right in the middle of a conversation with a loved one that has all the makings of becoming heated. Place them in the frame of a mirror that you frequent during the mornings and evenings at your home. Teach them to those around you so that they can help you live the way our Lord lived. But most of all, make these truths the deep desire of your heart as a minister.

Ministry Is . . .

1. Remembering that you are a recipient of God's mercy.
2. Conveying God's vast mercy to others.
3. Performed by mercy-minded ministers.
4. A mission of mercy.

❧ Quotes ❧

*The hallmark of Paul's experience with God
can be summed up in one word—mercy.
Someone has said that mercy is God's
ministry to the miserable. So it is.*
—CHARLES SWINDOLL AND GARY MATLACK[1]

*And if our zeal for the glory of God is not a reveling in his
mercy, then our so-called zeal, in spite of all its
protests, is out of touch with God and hypocritical.*
—JOHN PIPER[2]

Notes

1. C. Swindoll and G. Matlack, *Excellence in Ministry* (Fullerton, CA: Insight for Living, 1996), 21.

2. J. Piper, *Let the Nations Be Glad,* 2nd ed. (Grand Rapids: Baker Academics, 2003), www.wordsearchbible.com/catalog/product.php?pid=3040.

4 Giving Headaches to Hell

Dave Earley

Oh that God would make us dangerous!

—Jim Elliot

Jim Elliot was a Christian college student in the middle of the twentieth century. Reading Eliot's journal, I was impressed that even as a college student, he understood that we have already been enlisted in a war that is much bigger than any war that has ever been fought on any political map. He believed that you are either going to fight or be left in the wake of destruction. His journal contains some challenging quotes, including this one.

> We are so utterly ordinary, so commonplace, while we profess to know a Power the Twentieth Century does not reckon with. But we are "harmless," and therefore unharmed. We are spiritual pacifists, non-militants, conscientious objectors in this battle-to-the-death with principalities and powers in high places. Meekness must be had for contact with men, but brass, outspoken boldness is required to take part in the comradeship of the Cross. We are "sideliners"—coaching and criticizing the real wrestlers while content to sit by and leave the enemies of God unchallenged. The world cannot hate us, we are too much like its own. Oh that God would make us dangerous![1]

Jim's prayer was answered. He became so dangerous to hell that the enemy killed him. After college Jim became a missionary to Ecuador. He was martyred with four other men in 1956 while attempting to evangelize the Waodani people through efforts known as Operation Auca. You may have seen the movie, *The End of the Spear*, which tells the story of these men who sacrificed their lives for the gospel message.

Certainly these men were heroes of the faith. But they are not unique. The Bible is full of accounts of men and women who made great sacrifices for the sake of the gospel (see Hebrews 11). Such people are always known by the enemy and are dangerous to hell.

Are the churches in North America as effective as we could be? Could it be that we, the ministers, have gotten caught up in careers and convenience? Are we looking for fame and fortune from this world instead of the next? Does the enemy consider us a threat?

Charles Thomas (C. T.) Studd

I pray that when I die, all of hell will rejoice that I am no longer in the fight.

Charles Thomas (C. T.) Studd was the most outstanding cricket player in England at the end of the nineteenth century. By 1882 he was considered one of the best cricket players in the world. He was probably the best known athlete of his day in England. However, in 1884 after his brother George became seriously ill, C. T. was confronted by the question, What is all the fame and flattery worth when a man must face eternity?

As a result of this experience, C. T. gave his life fully to God. He later stated, "My heart was no longer in the game; I wanted to win souls for the Lord. I knew that cricket would not last, and honor would not last, and nothing in this world would last, but it is worth while living for the world to come."[2] His heart was forever changed, and C. T. decided to serve the Lord through missionary work in China, against the wishes and persuasions of his family. Along with six other students from Cambridge (together they became known as "the Cambridge Seven"), C. T. served as a pioneer missionary under Hudson Taylor with the China Inland Mission. Of his missionary work he boldly proclaimed,

Some want to live within the sound of church or chapel bell; I want to run a rescue shop within a yard of hell.[3]

He also said, "Real Christians revel in desperate ventures for Christ, expecting from God great things and attempting the same with exhilaration."[4] Truly this man gave hell headaches. On his twenty-fifth birthday C. T. inherited $145,000—a vast fortune in that day. He had already determined it would go into the work of the Lord. He sent out huge checks to such dedicated ministers as D. L. Moody and George Muller, among others. He gave the rest to his new wife, Pricilla. She also viewed herself as a soldier in the Lord's army and refused the gift. She said, "Charlie, what did the Lord tell the rich young man to do?" "Sell all." "Well then, we will start clear with the Lord at our wedding."[5] They proceeded to give the rest of their money away for the Lord's work.

After 10 years in China, C. T. and his family began ministry in India, hoping the climate would be better for Charles's asthma. The Lord used them greatly as people were converted to Jesus every single week.

After nearly a decade in India, Charles heard about the urgent need for missionaries in the wild, unexplored interior of Africa. He was compelled to go where no Christian had ever been before. So he went into the fiercest place on earth in order to take the gospel to those who needed to hear. Alfred Buxton, C. T.'s friend and colleague during his ministry in Africa, summarized Studd's life with these words:

> C. T.'s life stands as some rugged Gibraltar—a sign to all succeeding
> generations that it is worthwhile to lose all this world can offer and stake
> everything on the world to come. His life will be an eternal rebuke to
> easygoing Christianity. He has demonstrated what it means to follow
> Christ without counting the cost and without looking back.[6]

Studd was bold, brash, intense, and fearless, and he fully expected every other believer to be just like him. When he spoke, he challenged his audience with these words:

> Come then, let us restore the "lost chord" of Christianity—
> HEROISM— to the world, and the crown of the world to Christ. Christ
> Himself asks you, "Will you be a malingerer or a militant?" To your
> knees, man! And to your Bible! Decide at once! Don't hedge! Time flies!
> Cease your insults to God. Quit consulting flesh and blood. Stop your
> lame lying and cowardly excuses. Enlist![7]

Studd would then prod his audience to sign a contract with God that in part read:

For me to live is Christ to die is gain.
I'll be a militant or a man of God
A gambler for Christ
A Hero[8]

C. T. Studd believed and practiced aggressive, militant, courageous faith. He said, "We are frittering away time and money in a multiplicity of conventions, conferences and retreats, when the real need is to go straight and full steam into battle." He continued, "Difficulties, dangers, disease, death or divisions don't deter . . . from executing God's will. When someone says there is a lion in the way, the real Christian promptly replies, 'That's hardly enough inducement for me; I want a bear or two besides to make it worth my while to go.'"[9] C. T. summarized his own aspirations and ambitions with these words: "I pray that when I die, all of hell will rejoice that I am no longer in the fight."[10]

The man who at one time was a famous athlete traded his earthly fame for eternal glory. He said good-bye to being known by man and became known by the enemy and as a result, truly dangerous to hell. Ministry is much more than a mere career choice. It is enlisting in a battle and giving headaches to hell.

Dangerous in the First Century

Jesus and Paul had wide and powerful ministries. Wherever they went, people's lives were wonderfully changed. Many took note of what the Lord was doing and wanted to get in on it for all the wrong reasons. This desire for fame and influence are nothing new. Paul also encountered the same passion for popularity and power while serving in Ephesus.

> God was performing extraordinary miracles by Paul's hands, so that even facecloths or work aprons that had touched his skin were brought to the sick, and the diseases left them, and the evil spirits came out of them. Then some of the itinerant Jewish exorcists attempted to pronounce the name of the Lord Jesus over those who had evil spirits, saying, "I command you by the Jesus whom Paul preaches!" (Acts 19:11–13)

Note how they referred to Jesus. He was the one "whom Paul preaches." That was unfortunate for them, and they soon discovered that a second-hand relationship with Jesus is not enough when encountering the dark spirits of the Devil. Merely saying the words was not enough. In an instant the man who was demon possessed overpowered all seven of them and sent them running from the house "naked and wounded."

Ouch! Dealing with the Devil is not fun and games. For Jesus and Paul it was not a matter of fame and fortune. Ultimately it led to their executions! Dealing with the Devil is serious business that requires a mature relationship with Jesus Christ. Look again at Acts 19:15. Before provoking the severe beating of the sons of Sceva, one of the evil spirits asked a profound question. The evil spirit answered them, "Jesus I know, and Paul I recognize—but who are you?" (Acts 19:15).

Jesus I Know

One of the evil spirits declared, "Jesus I know!" The name of Jesus was and is certainly well known in hell. Satan knows the name of Jesus. Satan tried to have Jesus killed as an infant in Bethlehem (Matt 2:13–18). Satan personally tried to tempt Jesus in the wilderness (Luke 4:1–13). The Devil tried to have Jesus thrown over a cliff at the beginning of His ministry (Luke 4:28–30). Of course, Satan prompted Judas to betray Jesus to be crucified (John 13:27–30; 18:1ff).

Demons know the name of Jesus (Mark 3:11; Luke 4:4). Even after He ascended into heaven, His name alone was so powerful that the sick were healed (Acts 4:10), and demons were cast out in the name of Jesus (Acts 16:18). As a result, the authorities were scared when the apostles even spoke the name of Jesus and commanded them to stop doing so (Acts 4:18; 5:40).

Paul I Recognize

The name of Paul was also well known in hell. Before the evil spirits prompted the man to beat the sons of Sceva, one of them declared, "Jesus I know, *and Paul I recognize!*" When Paul, as a leading persecutor of the church, switched sides and converted to Christ, the news certainly would have been coldly received in hell (Acts 8:1–3; 9:1–22). Hell certainly took angry note that Paul's ministry of taking the gospel to the Gentiles was so powerful that he was accused of turning the world upside down (Acts 17:6)!

As we read earlier in this chapter, while in Ephesus Paul had developed a known ministry and a reputation. The sons of Sceva wanted the power he had. They tried to cast out demons using the names of Jesus and of Paul, but they failed and were humiliated.

Merely mouthing the words did not work. A life given in full surrender to Christ was necessary to combat such foes. Paul lived such a life. His life was a perpetual gamble for God. Daily he faced death for Christ. Again and again he stood fearless before crowds thirsting for his blood. He stood before kings and governors and refused to give an inch. He did not even flinch before Nero, the Roman instrument of hell. He endured extreme suffering, pain, and persecution for the cause of the gospel. No wonder he was known in hell!

In his classic book *Why Revival Tarries*, Leonard Ravenhill explains why Paul was well known in hell. Building on the theme of Paul viewing himself as crucified with Christ, Ravenhill writes:

> He had no ambitions—and so had nothing to be jealous about. He had no reputation—and so had nothing to fight about. He had no possessions—and therefore nothing to worry about. He had no "rights"—so therefore he could not suffer wrong. He was already broken—so no one could break him. He was "dead"—so none could kill him. He was less than the least of the least—so who could humble him? He had suffered the loss of all things—so who could defraud him? Does this throw any light on why the demon said, "Paul I know"? Over this God intoxicated man, hell suffered headaches.[11]

Why Paul's Name Was Known in Hell

If we dissect Ravenhill's assessment of Paul, it helps us see why he was dangerous to hell. It also helps us evaluate our own lives.

He had no ambitions—and so had nothing to be jealous about. Paul's only ambition was the name of Jesus and the will and the kingdom of God. Do you get jealous, envious, frustrated, or hurt when others are elevated over you? Chosen instead of you? Recognized in place of you? Blessed more than you?

He had no reputation—and so had nothing to fight about. He called himself the slave of Jesus Christ. As such his reputation was that he was a man submitted to the cause of Christ. His identity was lost in the majesty of his Master. He could face slander, gossip, innuendoes, and outright lies. How do you feel when you are misunderstood and misrepresented? Are you willing to be lied about? Can you be slandered without defending yourself?

He had no possessions—and therefore nothing to worry about. He had brought himself to the place in this life where he literally possessed nothing. Money, things, titles, positions, gifts, talents, and abilities had been given to God. His only possession was Christ. Are you willing to forfeit everything for the sake of Christ? Are you more concerned about losing your possessions or losing your testimony?

He had no "rights"—so therefore he could not suffer wrong. Even as an apostle and author of Scripture, he claimed no right to be obeyed, respected, revered, or appreciated. Before God he claimed no right to be spared from suffering or sorrow. He claimed no right to comfort, convenience, pleasure, or prosperity. What rights do you claim before God?

He was already broken—so no one could break him. By being broken at the foot of the cross, no amount of persecution from without or problems caused from within the family of God slowed him down. In what ways was Paul broken? How did this affect how he lived?

He was "dead"—so none could kill him. He was dead to fame and fortune, health and wealth, comfort and convenience. He was dead to his will, his words, and his ways. Jesus said that we must first lose our life if we want to save it. When you examine your life, in what ways is it evident that you have lost your life for Christ?

He was less than the least of the least—so who could humble him? He had suffered the loss of all things—so who could defraud him? Do you view yourself as the least of the least? How would you respond if the government took all of your things because of your Christianity?

Does this throw any light on why the demon said, "Paul I recognize"? Over this God intoxicated man, hell suffered headaches. We need more men and women who will give hell headaches. Will you be one of them?

Who Are You?

Our discussion circles back to the main issue. The demons asked the sons of Sceva a revealing question, "Who are you?" Hell was unfamiliar with the sons of Sceva. None of them had distinguished themselves by their commitment or their courage. They were saying, "We have never heard of you. Your faces do not hang on the walls of hell's post office as: *"Most wanted! Most feared! Approach carefully, considered armed and very dangerous."*

Obviously the sons of Sceva did not have much of an answer. As we have read, the lone man possessed by the demons beat all of them up and sent them running for their lives.

What Now? Does the Devil Know Your Name?

We may not have the amazing power of the Lord Jesus Christ or the apostle Paul. But you and I can and must live positively dangerous lives for

God. We must live so completely for God's kingdom that we are well known by some in the kingdom of darkness. We need to be armed with an experiential knowledge of the Word, a powerful prayer life, and bold faith. We must be ministers who give hell a headache.

Let me ask you, if an evil spirit questioned your identity, what would you say? How would you be able to answer? Are you becoming a dangerous Christian? Are you famous in hell? Do demons shudder at the mention of your name? What are you doing to ensure that your face is on the walls of hell's post office? In the arena of spiritual warfare and on the playing field of eternal destinies, who are you? Does the devil know your name? What will you do to give hell a bigger headache? What will you do to become a more dangerous Christian?

Ministry Is . . .

1. Being dangerous to hell.
2. Spiritual warfare.
3. Giving hell a headache.
4. Being so committed and courageous for God that the enemy knows your name.

Notes

1. J. Elliot, quoted by E. Elliot, *Shadow of the Almighty: The Life and Testament of Jim Elliot* (Grand Rapids, MI: Hendrickson Publishers, 2008).

2. C. T. Studd, quoted in Norman P. Grubb, *C. T. Studd: Cricketeer and Pioneer* (Fort Washington, PA: Christian Literature Crusade, 1985), 34.

3. Ibid., 166.

4. C. T. Studd, "The Chocolate Soldier or Heroism—the Lost Chord of Christianity" on Wholesome Words, www.wholesomewords.org/missions/msctserm.html.

5. P. Studd, quoted in Grubb, *C. T. Studd*, 66–67.

6. A. Buxton, ibid., 5.

7. Studd, "The Chocolate Soldier or Heroism."

8. Ibid.

9. Ibid.

10. Studd, quoted in Grubb, *C. T. Studd*, 13.

11. L. Ravenhill, *Why Revival Tarries* (Minneapolis, MN: Bethany House Publishers, 1986), 186.

5

Joining the Jesus Discipleship Academy

Dave Earley

Are you open to the possibility that there is one who created you to be who you are and calls you to be who he alone knows you can be? Then listen to Jesus of Nazareth and his two words that changed the world—"Follow me."

—Os Guinness[1]

Jesus Was Jewish

That seems obvious enough, but often when we read, study, and teach the Bible, we leave out that one simple fact: Jesus was Jewish. Jesus grew up in a Jewish culture, ate Jewish food, and memorized the Jewish law. He frequently visited the Jewish temple in Jerusalem. He was raised in Galilee, a province of Israel. He frequently visited Galilean synagogues using their traditions as a platform for His ministry. Of all the times and places Jesus could have chosen to come, Jesus lived and taught in the religious communities of first-century Galilee.

The Jewish society that Jesus grew up in provided children the opportunity to learn the Torah, major sections of the Old Testament (if copies were available), and what is often referred to as "The Commandments." The Torah is the collection of the first five books of the Old Testament, and the Commandments are the biblical principles of law, ethics, and service to God found in the Torah. By learning these commandments, Jesus was taught what these Scriptures meant and how they applied to life. Those who instructed Jesus were called rabbi, which we generally interpret as "teacher." Such a person was greatly respected in this culture. They were also the teachers of the masses. They answered difficult questions about God's Word, they offered counsel, and sometimes they represented the people to the Gentile courts. This is the title that was most often used of Jesus throughout His ministry. At the end of his life, Jesus commanded His disciples not to allow anyone to call them rabbi. His reason was that they had one Teacher, which was Himself (see Matt 23:8).

As a rabbi, Jesus had disciples called *talmidim*. But these disciples were not the quiet, middle-aged men we often imagine today. Jesus' disciples were probably devout and extremely passionate young people who were at the edge of beginning their careers. In the first century it was common for gifted students to approach a rabbi and asked, "May I follow you?" in effect, saying, "Do I have what it takes to be like you?" The rabbi either accepted the student as a *talmid* (disciple) or sent him away to pursue a trade. Yet Jesus the Jewish rabbi broke this pattern when He chose His own talmidim.

Follow Me

Jesus' public teaching ministry had been in gear for about a year. Several young men had been interested in His ministry and teachings (see John 1:35–50). While they had been investigating Him, He also had been evaluating them.

> As He was passing along by the Sea of Galilee, He saw Simon and Andrew, Simon's brother. They were casting a net into the sea, since they were fishermen.
>
> "Follow Me," Jesus told them, "and I will make you fish for people!" Immediately they left their nets and followed Him. Going on a little farther, He saw James the son of Zebedee and his brother John. They were in their boat mending their nets. Immediately He called them, and they left their father Zebedee in the boat with the hired men and followed Him. (Mark 1:16–20)

Jesus pursued them and issued a potentially powerful invitation. Imagine the Son of God coming to the place where you were working and extending to you this offer. Like all invitations, this one could either be accepted or rejected. Andrew, Peter, James, and John all jumped at the summons. They literally dropped what they were doing, left their lives behind them, and followed Him.

The Jesus Discipleship Academy

When Andrew, Peter, James, and John saw Jesus that day and heard His invitation to follow Him, they understood that this was a summons into a serious and significant apprenticeship of discipleship. To say yes and follow Him was to enroll in what I call "The Jesus Discipleship Academy." This was a call to a much deeper relationship. No longer would they be spectators as Jesus taught and performed miracles. They would now literally "be with Him" (Mark 3:14). Jesus did not say "follow a set of rules" or "follow a series of rituals." He said, "Follow *Me*." To be the disciple of a rabbi was an intensely personal relationship. They would literally live with Him for much of the next few years.

This was also a call to a much greater commitment. The decision to follow a rabbi as a talmid meant total commitment in the first century. They would have to memorize His words and replicate His lifestyle. By following Him, they were choosing to be with Him, to learn from Him, and to become like Him. Just as they were making a significant commitment to Him, He was making a weighty commitment to them. He would give the next few years of His life— living with them and training them to become "fishers of men," i.e. disciple-makers or teachers in their own right.

Disciples Receive and Recite the Teachings of Their Rabbi

Memorization was a prime learning technique of the first century. Beginning at age five, Jewish children would memorize large portions of the Torah. As they grew, older boys went on to learning key chunks of the Old Testament, and girls learned the Psalms. At age 12, boys would begin to apprentice to learn their father's trade. Girls would learn homemaking skills in preparation for marriage. Between the ages of 12 and 18, a boy could begin an apprenticeship to become a rabbi. He would memorize the Torah, much of the Old Testament, *and* the teachings of his mentor.

Memorization was especially important in the first century because most people did not have their own copy of the Scripture so they either had to remember it or visit the synagogue to read the copies of the Scriptures the village owned. Being such an oral culture, memory was enhanced by reciting aloud. As disciples in the Jesus Academy, the disciples were essentially "rabbis in training." Therefore, memorizing of the Law, the key portions of the rest of the Old Testament, and their rabbi's words was essential.

> Among the Jews, rabbis were encouraged to memorize entire books of the OT, indeed the whole OT. All of Jewish education consisted of rote memory. . . . Disciples in early Jewish settings were learners, and, yes, also reciters and memorizers. This was the way Jewish educational processes worked. In fact it was the staple of all ancient education, including Greco-Roman education.[2]

In the Jewish culture in which Jesus and His disciples moved, the students of a rabbi had to memorize his words. Hence, Mishna, Aboth, ii, 8 reads: "A good pupil was like a plastered cistern that loses not a drop."

The present-day Uppsala school of Harald Riesenfeld and Birger Gerhardsson analyzed Jesus' relationship with His disciples in the context of Jewish rabbinical practices of c. AD 200. They discovered that Jesus, in the role of the authoritative teacher or rabbi, trained His disciples to believe in *and remember* His teachings. Because their culture was so strongly oriented toward oral transmission of knowledge, they could memorize amazing amounts of material by today's standards. This culture's values emphasized the need of disciples to remember their teacher's teachings and deeds accurately, then they would teach others [3]

When I was a freshman in college, one of our teachers encouraged us to memorize 60 verses of Scripture to use in evangelizing others. That summer I was on a student evangelistic team that shared the gospel in street meetings, schools, and jails in England. The verses I had memorized made my sharing so much more effective than it would have been otherwise. I saw the power of the Word of God unlock hard hearts time and time again. Also, because I knew so many Scriptures, I was selected as the lead speaker for our team. The next year I memorized the book of Philippians and the book of James. Several years later when I was super busy starting a church, the first two books of the Bible I preached through were—you guessed it—Philippians and James.

Disciples Replicate the Lifestyle of Their Rabbi

The followers of a rabbi not only memorized his words; they imitated his life. In speaking of the disciple/rabbi relationship, Jesus said, "Everyone who is fully trained *will be like* his teacher" (Luke 6:40, italics added for emphasis).

One ancient rabbi, Ben Sirach (d. ca. 175 BC), stated that the goal of a rabbi is to train his student to such an extent that "when his father [teacher] dies, it is as though he is not dead. For he leaves behind him *one like himself*" (Wisdom of Ben-Sira, 30:4, italics added for emphasis).

> There is much more to a *talmid [disciple]* than what we call student. A student wants *to know* what the teacher knows for the grade, to complete the class or the degree or even out of respect for the teacher. A *talmid* wants to be like the teacher, that is to become what the teacher is. . . . As the rabbi lived and taught his understanding of the Scripture, his students *(talmidim)* listened and watched and imitated so as to become like him. Eventually they would become teachers passing on a lifestyle to their *talmidim*.[4]

For the disciples, following Jesus was much more than reading the Scriptures. It was even more than memorizing the Bible. Following Jesus meant that they lived out His teaching in His presence so He could comment and evaluate their conduct. To follow Jesus meant that they had to become like Jesus. They were so much like Jesus that when anyone observed their conduct or listened to them teach they would immediately know who their Rabbi was. How about you? Is it obvious to everyone around you that Jesus is your Rabbi?

Disciples Reproduce the Life of the Rabbi in Others

The call into the Jesus Academy occurred at the Sea of Galilee. It is really more of a lake than a sea. It is only 7½ miles wide and 13½ miles long, not big enough to be a "sea" by our standards today. It is oval, wider at the top than at the bottom. It sits about 618 feet below sea level in one of the most fertile areas in the world. The water is clear and clean.

In Jesus' time, there were nine populous cities on its shore. The sea was thick with fishing boats in the first century. In fact Josephus writes of one fishing fleet that numbered 240 boats. That's a lot of boats on one lake. The Sea of Galilee was/is known for the vast number of fish that live in its clear, clean waters. As Andrew, Peter, James, and John fished on this lake, Jesus issued His invitation into discipleship. "Follow Me," Jesus told them, "and I will make you fish for people!" (Mark 1:17).

The call to follow Jesus was also a call to "fish for people." While Simon and Andrew would not have grasped the full meaning of these words of invitation from Jesus, as seasoned fishermen surely the metaphor was not entirely mysterious to them.

> They knew that fishing was not a life for the weak. They knew all about working yourself into exhaustion, yet coming away with nothing in the nets. They knew about being at the mercy of the elements in a sudden storm on Galilee. But they also remembered those magical moments when all the exhausting toil resulted in payback—a payback that put food on their tables and renewed motivation in their hearts. Now, this offer of a life "fishing for men" most certainly captured their imaginations. Jesus presented them the possibility of seeing their hard work pay off in eternally tangible results. The longing to have their lives matter in the epic story of redemption was just too strong to resist. They hit the beach and walked away from those nets, toward the adventure of a life following the Master.[5]

Ever the gifted teacher, Jesus tied what they knew, "fishing," with what they were to learn, catching people with the gospel. As followers of Jesus, the disciples' task was to become fishermen for the kingdom. Seeking people to follow Jesus would take the same care, dedication, and skill they needed in fishing. As members of the Jesus Academy, the disciples were to develop the compassion for lost people that characterized their rabbi, Jesus. What they were to learn from Him was not to stop with them. It must press out and impact others. If they were to be His disciples, they were to become disciple makers.

> When the teacher believed that his talmidim [disciples] were prepared to be like him he would commission them to become disciple makers. He was saying, "As far as is possible you are like me. Now go and seek others who will imitate you. Because you are like me, when they imitate you they will be like me." This practice certainly lies behind Jesus great commission (Matt 28:18–20). . . . As the rabbi lived and taught his understanding of the Scripture his students (talmidim) listened and watched and imitated so as to become like him. Eventually they would become teachers passing on a lifestyle to their talmidim.[6]

Disciples Replace Their Previous Life with the New Life of Their Rabbi

While it is important to note that Jesus called His disciples to follow Him and fish for people, it is equally significant to observe how they responded to

His invitation. Andrew and Simon "immediately . . . left their nets and followed Him" (Mark 1:18). James and John "left their father Zebedee in the boat with the hired servants, and went after Him" (Mark 1:20 NKJV).

Understand that leaving their nets was not a simple late-afternoon act of calling it a day. It meant they were leaving their nets for a lifetime! In order to say yes to discipleship, they were saying good-bye to their careers as fishermen. Because the text mentions that there were hired servants in the boat with James, John, and their father, this means that James and John would have been leaving what must have been a prosperous family business that used big boats and large nets. By leaving their nets to follow Jesus, they were turning their backs on the familiar, the comfortable, the convenient, the safe and secure. To follow Jesus as their rabbi and they as His disciples, James and John were also saying farewell to their father, with whom they had a special bond. Yet they left all to follow the Rabbi and become like Him. Their commitment and sacrifice were total and enormous.

When I was wrestling with the call to discipleship and disciple making, I changed my major. When I obeyed the call by planting a church and becoming a pastor, I was turning my back on what had become my father's prosperous insurance business. From the outside it probably seemed a foolish decision. But as any real disciple will tell you, it was easily worth it to follow our Rabbi, Jesus.

When the disciples left their nets to follow Jesus, it was not only for the rest of their *lives*; but in the case of Andrew, Peter, and James, it was to their premature *death*. James was the first to die, being beheaded for his faith in Jerusalem (Acts 12:12). Church tradition holds that Peter was crucified upside down on an X-shaped cross because he told his tormentors that he felt unworthy to die in the same way Jesus Christ had died. Tradition also says that Andrew was crucified on an X-shaped cross in Patras, Greece. After seven soldiers severely whipped him, they tied his body to the cross with cords to prolong his agony. His followers reported that when he was led toward the cross, Andrew saluted it in these words: "I have long desired and expected this happy hour. The cross has been consecrated by the body of Christ hanging on it." He continued to preach to his tormentors for two days until he expired.[7]

Follow and Fish

Ministry is following Jesus *and* fishing for people. It is being a disciple *and* making disciples. It is growing *and* going. It is learning *and* evangelizing. It is being saved and leading others to do the same.

What Now?

Ministry is enrolling in the Jesus Discipleship Academy. It is following Jesus, the Rabbi into a life of discipleship and disciple making. Ministry is motivated by following Jesus and reproducing His life in others. Have you obeyed the call to "follow Jesus and fish for men"? Are you memorizing His words? Are you replicating His lifestyle? Are you telling others about Him? Are you making disciples? Have you fully replaced all of the aspects of your old life with a complete manifestation of the life of following Jesus? Are you willing to follow Him unto death?

Ministry Is . . .

1. Following Jesus as your Rabbi.
2. Joining the Jesus Academy.
3. Following Jesus *and* fishing for people.
4. A total commitment to leave everyone and everything else in order to follow Jesus.
5. Obeying the call into discipleship *and* disciple making.
6. A desire to reproduce Christ's life in others so that they will also follow Him as their Rabbi.

⤙ Quotes ⤚

Since it takes a disciple to build other disciples, the chain of multiplication begins with you.

—WAYLON MOORE[8]

Did you know that the term "evangelize," the Greek term is used no less than 53 times in the New Testament, and it is all summarized, as it were, in the great commission in Matthew 28

*when the Lord said, "Go into all the world winning people to
Christ and baptizing them, teaching them to observe all things
whatsoever I have commanded you."*

—JOHN MACARTHUR[9]

*If you are saved yourself, the work is but half done until you
are employed to bring others to Christ.*

—CHARLES SPURGEON[10]

*A fisher is a person who is very dependent, and needs to be
trustful. He cannot see the fish. One who fishes in the sea
must go and cast in the net, as it were, at a peradventure.
Fishing is an act of faith.*

—CHARLES SPURGEON[11]

*The purpose of discipleship is mission. . . . Discipleship requires
the recruitment and formation of believers who will continue
the work of Jesus wherever they may be and wherever
they are led. . . . The fruits of authentic discipleship will be
manifest in the continuing commitment of those who have
first encountered Jesus and then been sent by him on mission.*

—ANTHONY GITTINS[12]

Notes

1. O. Guinness, *The Call: Finding and Fulfilling the Central Purpose of Your Life* (Nashville, TN: Thomas Nelson, 2003), ix.

2. B. Witherington, *The Jesus Quest* (Downers Grove, IL: InterVarsity, 1995), 48.

3. "Is the Bible the Word of God? A Rational Defense of the Judeo-Christian Scriptures," chapter 2, www.biblestudy.org/maturart/is-bible-the-word-of-god/chapter2.html.

4. R. Vander Law, "Rabbi and Talmidim," Follow the Rabbi, http://www.followtherabbi.com/Brix?pageID=2753.

5. S. Harbin, "Welcome," Calvary Baptist Theological Seminary Web site, http://www.cbs.edu/about/welcome.html.

6. Vander Law, "Rabbi and Talmidim," www.followtherabbi.com/Brix?pageID=2799.

7. The details of the martyrdoms of the disciples and apostles are found in traditional early church sources as recounted in the writings of the church fathers and the first official church history written by the historian Eusebius in AD 325. See Grant Jeffrey, *The Signature of God* (Mississauga, ON: Frontier Research Publications, 1996), 254–57.

8. W. Moore, *Multiplying Disciples* (Colorado Springs, CO: NavPress, 1980), 112.

9. J. MacArthur, "Fishing for Men," sermon on Grace to You, http://www.gty.org/Resources/Sermons/2195.

10. C. Spurgeon, "How to Become Fishers of Men," sermon no 1906, delivered at the Metropolitan Tabernacle, Newington, England.

11. Ibid.

12. A. Gittins, *Called to Be Sent* (Liguori, MO: Liguori Press, 2008), 1, 15.

Part 2

The Motives of Ministry

6 Loving the Bride of Christ

Dave Earley

I love Jesus, but I don't like the Church.
—COMMENT BY AN OHIO STATE UNIVERSITY STUDENT

I (Dave) have hung out with enough postmoderns and people under the age of 30 that I've heard that same comment many times. Apparently I am not alone. Pastor Dan Kimball has even written a book titled *They Like Jesus but Not the Church*.[1]

In his book Kimball describes how many people today, especially among emerging generations, don't resonate with the Church and organized Christianity. Some are leaving the Church, and others were never part of the Church in the first place.

Michael Craven, in an article titled "They Love Jesus; They Don't Like the Church," notes that there is a growing sentiment among many younger Christians in America that they love Jesus but want little to do with His Church.[2] Why is this so?

It's no secret that Christianity's influence on American culture has waned in recent generations. A recent study offers the following proof: half of all Americans now believe Christianity isn't the country's default religion but is instead *one of many options* of faith. Americans—by a whopping three-to-one margin—are more likely to develop their own personal set of beliefs than accept those taught by a church or denomination. Even among born-again Christians polled, 61 percent adopt an a la carte approach to their faith. Not surprisingly, the group most likely to customize their faith consists of those under age 25 (82 percent).[3]

Dr. Aubrey Malphurs, professor of pastoral ministries at Dallas Theological Seminary, has made a wise observation on this culture shift. "Essentially," he says, "what was a churched, supposedly Christian culture has become an unchurched, post-Christian culture. People in our culture are not antichurch; they simply view the church as irrelevant to their lives."[4] Is the Church no longer relevant? Can you minister for Jesus without being involved in a local church? Is it possible to be a minister for Jesus and not love the Church?

How Does Jesus Feel About the Church?

How does Jesus feel about the Church? He loves the Church. In his letter to the Ephesians, the apostle Paul likens the union of husband and wife in marriage with the union of Christ and the Church. He writes:

> Husbands, love your wives, just as also Christ loved the church and gave Himself for her, to make her holy, cleansing her in the washing of water by the word. He did this to present the church to Himself in splendor, without spot or wrinkle or any such thing, but holy and blameless. In the same way, husbands should love their wives as their own bodies. He who loves his wife loves himself. For no one ever hates his own flesh, but provides and cares for it, just as Christ does for the church, since we are members of His body. For this reason a man will leave his father and mother and be joined to his wife, and the two will become one flesh. This mystery is profound, but I am talking about Christ and the church. (Eph 5:25–32)

In this passage we learn several important truths about Jesus and the church:

1. Jesus loved the Church.
2. Jesus sacrificed Himself for the Church.
3. Jesus sanctifies and cleanses the Church through His Word.
4. Jesus will be wed to the Church, with the Church being like a holy, blameless, glorious bride.
5. Jesus loves, nourishes, and cherishes the Church.
6. The Church is not only His bride but is also His body.
7. There is a mystic union between Christ and the Church.

As we understand eschatology, Jesus is currently betrothed to the Church. At a time in the future, Jesus will be wed to the Church as a husband to His bride. This event is called the Marriage Supper of the Lamb (see Rev 19:7–9; 21:9). Jesus may not always like the way His bride is behaving. He may not always be happy with the way she is responding. But one thing is very clear—Jesus loves His bride, the Church. He is deeply committed to her and invested in her well-being.

Lovers of Jesus Will Love His Church

I (Dave) love my wife, Cathy. Oh, I may not always love every little thing she is thinking, saying, or doing. But I am deeply committed to her. I am highly invested in her, and I passionately love her. We are one and getting closer each year we are married. If you love me, you will love my Cathy. She may not be someone you interact with frequently. She may not have your favorite type of personality or favorite style of hair. But, if you love me, you will love my wife. If you don't love my wife, don't tell me that you love me.

In a similar way, lovers of Jesus will love His bride the Church. As a lover of Jesus, you may not have pleasant, warm feelings about everything His bride does, but you will have a deep, bottom-line, core love for her.

What Is the Church?

The Church should be understood as existing simultaneously in two spheres: universal and local. In the universal sense the Church consists of all those during this age who have been born of God's Spirit and have therefore been baptized into the body of Christ. The Church was born seven days after Jesus ascended into heaven. On the Day of Pentecost, Peter and others preached the gospel in Jerusalem and 3,000 believed and were baptized. Since then every person on the planet who has been saved has been baptized into the body of Christ and is a member of the universal Church. The universal Church is nearly 2,000 years old and has billions of members from the apostles such as Peter, James, and John, to believers currently in Africa and Asia, to you and me.

In the local sense a church is a called-out, living assembly of baptized believers, associated by a covenant of faith, organized by New Testament principles, assembling regularly together, led by qualified pastors/elders who are supported by qualified deacons, under the discipline of God's Word and the headship of Christ. A local church observes the ordinances of baptism and the

Lord's table. It exists for the purpose of expressing praise and glory to God by evangelizing the lost and equipping the saved. Local churches usually have physical addresses where they meet. Most local churches in America have Web sites.

When people say they love Jesus but hate His Church, it's usually not that they don't like the their local church or even other Christians; it's that they don't like how Christianity in America is frequently represented by many professing Christians, which in their minds is often unloving, judgmental, arrogant, and hypocritical.

Portraits of the Church

In addition to the Bride and the Groom, the Bible paints several other insightful portraits of the relationship of Jesus and the Church. Understanding these portraits enables us to become more effective in ministry.

1. The Body of Christ

Jesus is the head; the Church is His body. The Church is to submit to Him as the ultimate authority (Eph 1:22–23; 4:22–24; Col 1:18), seek Him as the source of life and growth (Eph 4:11–16; Col 2:18–19), and be grateful for His loving care (Eph 5:29–30). As members of His body, we are united in Christ and should therefore strive for unity in the Church (Rom 12:4–5; Eph 4:3–5, 25). Since each member is different from the others we should therefore value diversity in the Church (1 Cor 12:12–20) and recognize our mutual dependency on one another in the Church (1 Cor 12:21–27).

Life flows from the head through the body. No member can function properly apart from the rest of the body. Just as it is foolish and ineffective for one member of my body to try to go it alone, so it is foolish and ineffective for one person in ministry to try to do ministry alone. We need one another. Together everyone accomplishes more.

2. The Vine and the Branches

The Father is the gardener, Christ is the vine, and we are the branches (John 15:1,5). As Gardener, the Father prunes us through His Word (John 15:2–3). As branches, our responsibility is to remain closely connected to the vine—Christ (John 15:4). By remaining connected to Christ, we will bear fruit (John 15:4–7). Our fruitfulness is to the Father's glory (John 15:8).

Life flows from the vine through the branches. No branch can function properly apart from a close connection to the vine. It is foolish and ineffective for a branch to try to go it alone. It is also foolish and ineffective for one person to try to do ministry unless closely connected to Jesus.

3. The Building and the Cornerstone

We are the stones of a spiritual house through faith in Jesus, who is the cornerstone (1 Pet 2:5–7). We are to be founded on the Word of God through the apostles and prophets and to be guided by the Chief Cornerstone, Christ. (Eph 2:19–22).

No building consists of a single stone. A beautiful building is the combination of many stones placed together by the wise and capable hands of the master builder. The beauty of the building brings glory to the architect and the builder. In a similar way no one Christian can bring the greatest glory to God. But together, with others in the church, we point people to the glory of our wise Architect and Builder.

4. The Shepherd and the Sheep

Jesus is the Good Shepherd of the Church. Jesus had a shepherd's heart for people (Matt. 9:36). He called His followers the "little flock" (Luke 12:32). He called Himself the "good shepherd" (John 10:11,14). The author of Hebrews called Jesus the great Shepherd (Heb 13:20). Peter called Jesus the chief Shepherd (1 Pet 2:25; 5:4). We were sheep going astray (Isa 53:6; 1 Pet 2:25). Jesus, the good Shepherd, gave His life for His sheep (John 10:11,17–18). He knows His sheep by name (John 10:14–15). He calls leaders to shepherd His sheep (John 21:15–17). Church leaders are to oversee sheep willingly without greed, as servants, stewards, and examples (1 Pet 5:2–4). The most dangerous place for sheep to be is on their own, away from the flock. Wolves never attack sheep in the flock. Wolves always go after the ones straggling on the edges. In a similar way, Christians are not safe from the attacks of the enemy on their own. Safety comes from being closely connected to other Christians in a healthy church.

Local Churches Fulfill the Great Commission

After Jesus rose from the dead, He shared the expectations He had for His followers. Repeatedly, Jesus gave a command that has become known as the Great Commission. The writers of the Gospels record that Jesus gave

His Great Commission five times (see Matt 28:18–20; Mark 16:15–16; Luke 24:46–48; John 20:21; Acts 1:8). The fullest statement of the Great Commission is found in Matthew.

> "Go, therefore, and make disciples of all nations, baptizing them in the name of the Father and of the Son and of the Holy Spirit, teaching them to observe everything I have commanded you. And remember, I am with you always, to the end of the age." (Matt 28:19–20)

When the Great Commission is analyzed more closely, it reveals several important practices essential to fulfilling the mandate. Each must be taken very seriously if a healthy new church is to be born.

Go. The first practice needed to fulfill the Great Commission is the intentional pursuit of the lost. Just as He was sent by His Father, Jesus has sent us out in a deliberate quest to win nonbelievers to faith in Christ (John 20:21,31). This command makes an obvious assumption that you want to go. Jesus isn't giving this command as a way to make us want to go. Rather, Jesus is assuming that we want to go, and He is saying that now is the time to go.

Teaching. It is not enough to go; we must also teach. The simplest giving of the Great Commission is found in Mark 16:15: "Go into all the world and preach the gospel to the whole creation." The second practice needed to fulfill the Great Commission is the proclamation of Christ's word. Christians have not only to show the gospel; they must also *tell* nonbelievers the message of Jesus' death, burial, and resurrection for their sins. The Commission states that "repentance for forgiveness of sins would be proclaimed in His name to all the nations, beginning at Jerusalem" (Luke 24:47). Believers are to preach the good news to nonbelievers with the goal of leading them to believe in Christ as their Savior.

Baptize. The third action that must be taken in fulfilling the Great Commission is "baptizing them in the name of the Father and of the Son and of the Holy Spirit" (Matt 28:19). This involves incorporating them into the group of people who identify themselves by the name of the Father, Son, and Holy Spirit, which is the church. Since baptism is an ordinance of the local church, it is obvious that the Great Commission cannot be fulfilled without the creation of local churches.

Make disciples. It is not enough to pursue the lost, win them to Christ, and baptize them. To fulfill the Great Commission means that we invest our lives into others in such a way that they learn to obey everything Jesus has taught us (Matt 28:20). The process does not stop at baptism. In order to fulfill the commission, the new believer must be taught to live the teachings of Jesus. The best place for a young believer to be taught is in the local church. There they not only hear the Word but also have abundant opportunity to put it into practice.

After examining the Great Commission, the obvious question that begs to be answered is, How does God expect His followers to implement it? The obvious answer is, "By planting *churches*." After the disciples heard the Great Commission, what did they do to obey it? The book of Acts reveals that they started new churches.

Ed Stetzer has planted churches in New York, Pennsylvania, and Georgia and transitioned declining churches in Indiana and Georgia. He writes, "New Testament Christians acted out these commands as any spiritually healthy, obedient believers would; they planted more New Testament churches."[5] He concludes, "The Great Commission is church planting."[6]

The way the first followers of Jesus carried out the Great Commission directly resulted in the planting of churches. Peter (and others) preached the gospel (Acts 2:14–36), the people were baptized (Acts 2:37–41), and the baptized believers were immediately incorporated into the life of obeying what Jesus had taught (Acts 2:42–47).

Youth camps, concerts, coffeehouses, and other ministries are all good. They can be helpful in the process of fulfilling the Great Commission. But the ultimate fulfillment of the Great Commission is church planting! There is really no way to fulfill the Great Commission apart from the local church.

What Now? Don't Complain About the Church; Be the Church

As we said at the beginning of this chapter, a growing group of people say they love Jesus but want little to do with His Church. It's often not a problem they are having with their local church or even other Christians. Instead they don't like how Christianity in America is frequently represented. Too often evangelicals are seen as shallow, anti-intellectual, unloving, judgmental, self-righteous, and hypocritical.

This assertion finds support in the data revealed in recent research by the Barna organization. David Kinnamon and Gabe Lyons, in their book *unChristian: What a New Generation Really Thinks About Christianity . . . and Why It Matters*, state:

Four out of five young churchgoers say that Christianity is anti-homosexual; half describe it as judgmental, too involved in politics, hypocritical, and confusing; one-third believe their faith is old-fashioned and out of touch with reality; and one-quarter of young Christians believe it is boring and insensitive to others.[7]

And those are the Christians!

Kinnamon and Lyons found that those outside the Church hold increasingly negative views of Christians as well. Among young people (aged 16–29), roughly 49 percent hold an "extraordinarily negative" view of evangelical Christians, and only 3 percent have a "good" impression![8]

As a result, many young Christians believe that being outwardly Christian will undermine their ability to connect with people and maintain credibility with them. As a result, they distance themselves from a North American church they view as in a pathetic state of decadence and decay.

But it does not take faith to drop out, stand back, and complain. What I say to young idealists is this, "If you don't like the way the church is, start one the way you think it should be. If you don't like what the church has become, change it."

We need to stop complaining about the church and roll up our sleeves and be the church. We must live radical Christian lives, love the unlovely, be authentic, live in simplicity and holiness, stay true to the Bible, put away childish and petty disputes, live in community, and refuse to be shallow and superficial.

Ministry Is . . .

1. Being the church.
2. Loving the church as Jesus loved the church and gave Himself for it.

⮐ Quote ⮑

Christian labors, disconnected from the church, are like
sowing and reaping without having any barn in which to
stow the fruits of the harvest—useful, but incomplete.

—C. H. SPURGEON[9]

Notes

1. D. Kimball, *They Like Jesus but Not the Church: Insights from Emerging Generations* (Grand Rapids, MI: Zondervan, 2007).

2. M. Craven, "They Love Jesus; They Don't Like the Church," Crosswalk.com 2008, www.crosswalk.com/pastors/11568526, accessed December 15, 2009.

3. "Default No More," *Ministry News, Ministry Today,* quote from Barna Research, January 12, 2009, www.ministrytodaymag.com/index.php/ministry-news/65-news-main/18224-default-no-more.

4. A. Malphurs, *Planting Growing Churches for the Twenty-First Century* (Grand Rapids, MI: Baker, 1992), 27.

5. E. Stetzer, *Planting Missional Churches* (Nashville, TN: B&H Publishing Group, 2006), 37.

6. Ibid., 35.

7. D. Kinnamon and G. Lyons, *unChristian: What a New Generation Really Thinks About Christianity . . . and Why It Matters* (Grand Rapids, MI: Baker Books, 2007), 33–34.

8. Ibid.

9. C. H. Spurgeon, quoted by D. and W. Wiersbe, *Making Sense of the Ministry* (Chicago, IL: Moody Press, 1983), 116.

7

Shouting the Worthiness of Jesus

Dave Earley

Last summer I (Dave) was having coffee with a missionary in a Turkish street café. This longtime missionary to the Muslims of Turkey was severely shaken because two of his colleagues had given their lives as martyrs just a few months earlier. He and his family had been rudely booted from the country during the escalated oppression of Christians, and it hurt my friend to see his wife and children suffer. Although he knew the answer, he was still troubled by one gnawing question:

"Is it worth it?"

If you are an honest and thoughtful person, you will run headlong into several questions as you go through life: *Is there a God? Who is God? Who am I? Why am I here? What is life really about? What makes me happy? What will make me fulfilled? What brings real meaning to life?*

I submit to you that there is another question that you better address somewhere along the way. In many ways it is deeper and more important than all of the others. In many ways it is the one question on which all the other ones hinge. The question is this: Who is worthy? That is . . .

Who is worth living for?

Who is worthy of my trust and allegiance?

Who is worth suffering for?

Who is worth dying for?

"Is it worth it?" Whether you are serving in a paid position or as a volunteer, ministry is hard. It carries a cost. Doing it right takes great expenditures of time, money, energy, and effort. Working with people can be frustrating. The enemy will creatively and relentlessly attack. You may face opposition and persecution. You won't make it if you haven't come to grips with the true motives for ministry. The highest motive for ministry is the worthiness of Jesus.

Who Is Worthy? Part 1

In an early period of world history, a man ran face-to-face into this question. His name was Abraham. His story is found in Genesis 22.

> After these things God tested Abraham and said to him, "Abraham!"
> "Here I am," he answered.
> "Take your son," He said, "your only [son] Isaac, whom you love, go to the land of Moriah, and offer him there as a burnt offering on one of the mountains I will tell you about." (Gen 22:1 2)

God told Abraham to take his son Isaac and offer him up as a sacrifice to the worthiness of God. This is huge. It is tough enough to consider putting the Lord ahead of our children, but this was extreme. Isaac was Abraham's only son. Isaac was a miracle baby given to Abraham and Sarah when he was 99 years old and Sarah was 90. He is the person through whom the Lord promised to make Abraham a nation. For Abraham to sacrifice Isaac would mean the death of Abraham's dreams, hopes, future, and legacy. It was much more than asking Abraham to sacrifice himself. This would be asking Abraham to answer the question: Is God worth it?

> So early in the morning Abraham got up, saddled his donkey, and took with him two of his young men and his son Isaac. He split wood for a burnt offering and set out to go to the place God had told him about. On the third day Abraham looked up and saw the place in the distance. Then Abraham said to his young men, "Stay here with the donkey. The boy and I will go over there to worship; then we'll come back to you." (Gen 22:3–5)

"The boy and I will go over there to worship; then we'll come back to you." When brought face-to-face with the issue, Abraham answered loud and clear—God is worth it!

All of us have been given an impressive stewardship; we have been given minutes, hours, days, weeks, months, years, and decades of time. We have various talents, gifts, and abilities at our disposal. We think countless thoughts and have countless feelings. We also have a heart and soul to which we will give our allegiance, our attention, and our devotion. I believe that most people give their hearts to objects that are unworthy of them. Some pour out their souls chasing frivolous pursuits. Others give themselves to hobbies, careers, and relationships looking for some sense of satisfaction and fulfillment.

Who is worthy? This is an issue you must seriously consider. Also, for those of us in ministry, it is a question that has only one answer.

Who Is Worthy? Part 2

You probably know the story. Job was an incredibly wealthy and a wonderfully good man. He had a successful commercial business in the world at that time and also had a large family with 10 children. He was a faithful follower of God. For him life was good.

Then one day, somewhere in the heavens, Satan and God had a discussion. The crux of the issue is this: Satan contented that the only reason Job served God so faithfully was because God had blessed him so abundantly. Satan's point was this: God is not worthy of worship if He is the only reward. The only reason people worship God is for what they can get out of it.

So they set up a test. God allowed Satan to take away everything Job had. Then they would see if Job believed God was worthy of worship because of the blessings He gave or just because He is God.

So in one horrendously horrific day Job lost it all—sheep, cattle, oxen, donkeys, camels were all killed. Plus, all but a handful of his servants were killed. But worst of all, Job's 10 children, every single one of them, were killed.

It happened. The blessed man has lost all the blessings. Now it would become evident. Did Job worship God because of the blessings God gave or because God was worth it? So what did Job do when he received the horribly bad news?

> Then Job stood up, tore his robe and shaved his head. He fell to the
> ground and **worshiped**. (Job 1:20, bold added for emphasis)

Job *worshipped*. The word *worship* comes from an old English word that meant, "worthiness." When crushed by the total loss of all the blessings he enjoyed on this earth, Job still declared that God is worthy of worship. Job's response made a statement that echoed through the universe up to the heavens:

God is worthy of worship because He is God, not merely because He is the giver of blessings. God is worth it!

Who Is Worthy? Part 3

In the early chapters of the book of Revelation, we have the story of an aged pastor named John. In his earlier days John's zeal and red-hot passion had been easily recognized, and he was given roles of leadership in the church. Eventually he became an influential minister serving as a pastor and author of a Gospel and several epistles.

Late in his life the country where he lived was going through extreme political turmoil and spiritual unrest. He was persecuted for his faith. Yanked from home and church, he found himself facing his twilight years mostly alone and forgotten.

But God does not forget His servants.

One Sunday John was enjoying his special time with the Lord when everything changed. The old man was stunned when an angel appeared in his room and took John on an amazing journey. In an eternal second John stepped out of the ordinary into the extraordinary. He left earth and was in heaven. He left the here and now, and was transported into the future. The whole experience might have taken days or maybe only hours, or even seconds. He couldn't tell. It didn't matter. What he saw and heard was beyond what any mortal had ever witnessed. John was privileged to witness the throne of the sovereign God of the universe.

Interestingly, the sight was more than he could describe. So rather than try to describe the Lord who sat on the throne, John merely described the throne itself and all that was happening around it.

He described an enormous white throne. It stretched upward at such a height John shrunk before it. Encircling the throne was the most amazing array of color any human had ever seen. It was like a rainbow on steroids, a color wheel in high definition. John's mouth must have hung open as he stared at the deep hues and rich colors. A series of seven fires danced in ascending, then descending steps before the throne, the smoke of their flames rising rhythmically to an unknown beat.

If the sights were not enough to leave him openmouthed and gasping in awe, the sounds were. Immense rumblings exploded as lightning ripped through the sky and thunder roared, shaking the poor old man's bones.

Anchoring the four corners of the throne were giant angelic beings. Unlike anything John had ever seen, each was a glorious symphony of wings, eyes, color, light, and beautiful eerie antiphonal praise as they chanted, "Holy, holy, holy, Lord God Almighty, Who was and is and is to come!" (Rev 4:8 NKJV).

John noticed others around the throne—wise men, elders, church leaders, saints. All were wearing pure white robes. Each wore a golden crown. Each was stretched out on his face. Smashed down, crushed, suffocated, and intoxicated by the mountainous, majestic, magnificent glory of the amazing One who sat on the throne. On their faces, in the place of worship, they cast their crowns at the feet of the worthy one.

> The 24 elders fall down before the One seated on the throne, worship the One who lives forever and ever, cast their crowns before the throne, and say: Our Lord and God, **You are worthy** to receive glory and honor and power, because You have created all things, and because of Your will they exist and were created. (Rev 4:10–11, bold added for emphasis)

I imagine that John also spread out on his face before God. I can picture him slowly and carefully opening his eyes and peaking through his fingers. He saw the One on the throne lifting a huge scroll. As a result, that one stunningly significant question:

> Then I saw in the right hand of the One seated on the throne a scroll with writing on the inside and on the back, sealed with seven seals. I also saw a mighty angel proclaiming in a loud voice, "**Who is worthy** to open the scroll and break its seals?" (Rev 5:1–2, bold added for emphasis)

No human could rightfully step forward and take the scroll. No angel would dare touch it. No demon would be allowed.

> But no one in heaven or on earth or under the earth was able to open the scroll or even to look in it. And I cried and cried because **no one was found worthy** to open the scroll or even to look in it. (Rev 5:3–4, bold added for emphasis)

Overcome by the overwhelming sights and sounds and broken by the complete unworthiness of all who are above the earth, on the earth, or under the earth, John told us that he wept. He must have been undone by the harsh reality that *"no one was found worthy."* The story does not end there.

The Lion King

> Then one of the elders said to me, "Stop crying. Look! **The Lion from
> the tribe of Judah,** the Root of David, has been victorious so that
> He may open the scroll and its seven seals." (Rev 5:5, bold added for
> emphasis)

I imagine John lifting his eyes from his hands and scanning the horizon.
Eagerly he would have looked for a massive Lion King, regal, royal, majestic
and magnificent, a lionlike Lord wearing a golden crown carrying a giant scep-
ter. He must have expected to see a proud chest, adored with medals of honor,
courage, and bravery. He would have sought for an all-powerful, savage, brutal,
violent, mighty, fearsome, holy, righteous warrior King. But what John did see
next stunned him. Center stage, in the midst of the throne, surrounded by the
angels and the elders, was not a giant lion.

> Then I saw **one like a slaughtered lamb** standing between the throne
> and the four living creatures and among the elders. He had seven horns
> and seven eyes, which are the seven spirits of God sent into all the earth.
> (Rev 5:6, bold added for emphasis)

He saw a Lamb that no doubt had at one time been wonderfully white,
pure, innocent, and holy. But now he saw its white coat covered in dried blood.
Beaten and bruised, a crown of thorns hung from its head. The Lamb John
saw, and the one we will one day stand before, was *the* Lamb of God who
takes away the sin of the world. He is the One wounded for our transgressions,
bruised for our iniquities, sacrificed for our sins.

Slowly, joyfully, mightily, triumphantly we too will see the Lamb hoist the
weighty scroll over His head. As He does, I imagine that He will transform into
the Lion King that John had expected.

> When He took the scroll, the four living creatures and the 24 elders fell
> down before the Lamb. Each one had a harp and gold bowls filled with
> incense, which are the prayers of the saints. And they sang a new song:
> **You are worthy** to take the scroll and to open its seals; because You were
> slaughtered, and You redeemed [people] for God by Your blood from
> every tribe and language and people and nation. (Rev 5:8–9, bold added
> for emphasis)

I imagine the crowd will spontaneously drop, as if cut down at the knees
by a giant sword. There will be rows of men and women from every age, from

every nation, and from every tribe. Joining them on their faces will be rows after rows of big, bright, strong, proud angels. Ear-piercing, thunderous silence will rumble through the crowd as all will gasp in a holy hush of acknowledgment. Not merely bowing gracefully, they will dive on their faces. They will spread out their arms, open their hands, empty their pockets, and lay bare their hearts. Tears will pour from their eyes, sobs piercing the cloud of awful silence.

Then slowly, sweetly, like incense, a chantlike song will rise from the crowd.

> And they sang a new song: **You are worthy** to take the scroll and to open its seals, because You were slaughtered, and You redeemed [people] for God by Your blood from every tribe and language and people and nation. You made them a kingdom and priests to our God, and they will reign on the earth. (Rev 5:9–10, bold added for emphasis)

Even though the crowd will contain the combined peoples from all over the globe from all of history, even though they will speak different languages, somehow it will all blend, as a symphony, a choir with billions of tongues and multitudes of voices.

So begins the climax of human history. God's Word predicted that all who have ever lived would eventually find their way to the throne of the Lamb. This is the moment when Jesus Christ will inherit all things, and He will truly have the last word (see 2 Cor 5:10; Eph 1:9–10; Heb 1:1–2). The Lamb was destined for this moment (1 Pet 1:18–20), and God has given us this preview to reassure us that Jesus is indeed worth it.

The apostle John lived a long, fruitful life of powerful ministry because he understood and experienced the worthiness of Jesus. The heart of ministry is shouting the worthiness of Jesus.

Who Is Worthy?

All John saw and wrote in the book we call the Revelation points to one dangerous question. It may be the most important question ever asked. It may be the most life- and destiny-defining question ever asked.

It is the question that was asked by the angel before the throne. It is the question that has been asked in one way or form by every thinking person through the ages.

That question is this:

Who is worthy?

I challenge you to ask yourself,
Who is worth my allegiance? Who is worth my affection?
Who is worth my devotion? Who is worthy of my faith?
Who is worth my time, my money, my possessions?
Who is worthy of my dreams, my hopes, and my future?
Who deserves my mind, mouth, hands, feet, and heart?

Who is worthy?
Who is worth staying pure for? Who is worth taking time to pray to?
Who is worth sharing with friends and strangers?
Who is worth giving a tenth of your money to?
Who is worth trusting completely? Who is worth giving your Sunday mornings to? Who is worth living a life of integrity for?

Who is worthy?
Who is worthy of going into full-time ministry for?
Who is worthy of going to a big city and starting a new church for?
Who is worthy of crossing cultures for?

Who is worthy?
Who is worth going to jail for?
Who is worth living for?
Who else is worth dying for?
Who is worth standing and singing to?

One day every precinct will report. All the votes will be counted. It will be unanimous.

They said with a loud voice: **The Lamb who was slaughtered is worthy** to receive power and riches and wisdom and strength and honor and glory and blessing! (Rev. 5:12, bold added for emphasis)

Casting Your Crowns

John's vision of our future gives us insight into what we will do when we come into the presence of the Worthy One. John saw the 24 elders falling down to worship and casting their crowns before the throne of God (Rev 4:9–11).

In the first century many major Greek cities held athletic games including Athens (the Olympic Games) and Corinth (the Isthmian Games). The winner of each event would stand before the judge's platform and receive a garland victor's crown.

Paul reminded the Corinthians that one day every believer will stand before Jesus to be evaluated and rewarded based on how we lived our lives and carried out our ministries (1 Cor 3:11–15; 2 Cor 5:10; Rev 22:12). We will be given crowns, commendations, and commissions as awards.

The crowns are primarily reserved for those who give their lives in ministry. They include: (1) *the crown of boasting*—given to us as recognition of the people we have led to Christ and discipled (1 Thess 2:18–19); (2) *the crown that will never fade*—given to those who evangelize, endure, and remain blameless (1 Cor 9:19–26); (3) *the crown of righteousness* for those who give their lives to others as they anticipate the Lord's return (2 Tim 4:8); and (4); *the crown of glory* for those who shepherd God's flock (1 Pet 5:4).

The purpose of winning crowns is not selfish. In fact it is the exact opposite. The purpose of gaining crowns is to have as many as possible to cast at Jesus' feet. This will be our way of telling Him "You are worthy" for all He has done for us.

Now What?

Where does a life of serving God with passion and confidence begin? What is ministry really all about? Ministry is living your life in such a way that it shouts out that Jesus is worth it! It is leading people into a relationship with the God who is worth it. It is working to have crowns to cast at the feet of the Worthy One.

If you were to stand before the throne of God today, what crowns could you cast at Jesus' feet? What changes do you need to be making in your life so your life and ministry will better proclaim that Jesus is worthy?

In this book we are examining what ministry means. We will present several essentials for being effective. Then we will give you many of the nuts and bolts of how to make an impact. But most importantly we want to challenge you to go into ministry with your eyes wide open and your motives clear. The highest motivation for doing ministry is so that your life will show forth the unprecedented worthiness of Jesus to a world that desperately needs to see and know Him.

Ministry Is . . .

1. Living your life in such a way that it shouts out that Jesus is worth it!
2. Leading people into a relationship with the God who is worth it.
3. Working to have crowns to cast at the feet of the Worthy One.

⤔ Quote ⤕

*But when His life has been created in me by His Redemption
I instantly recognize His right to absolute authority over me.
It is a moral domination— "Thou art worthy. . . ." It is only
the unworthy in me that refuses to bow down to the worthy.*
— OSWALD CHAMBERS[1]

Notes

1. O. Chambers, *My Utmost for His Highest* (Westwood, NJ: Barbour and Company, July 19, 1963 entry), 201.

The Overflow of Your Relationship with Jesus

Dave Earley

O uch! Peter, Jesus' top disciple, had completely fallen on his face just a few weeks earlier. After boasting that he would never deny Jesus (Matt 26:31–38), Peter had denied Jesus three times (John 18:15–18,25–27)! So even though all of the disciples were excited about the resurrection of Jesus from the dead, perhaps Peter was not so much. He had spent three years at the side of Jesus learning to be a rabbi and disciple maker, only to choke at crunch time.

So in order to restore some dignity, Peter decided that he had better go back to doing something that he knew he was good at—fishing. Being a leader, he recruited several of the other disciples to go along with him.

Yet, God is a God of the second chance. Jesus, the resurrected Christ, surprised His disciples as they were fishing on the Sea of Galilee. In their encounter, Jesus asked Peter one of the most significant, penetrating, dangerous questions that any potential minister can be asked.

"Do You Love Me?"

When they had eaten breakfast, Jesus asked Simon Peter, "Simon, son of John, **do you love Me more than these**?" "Yes, Lord," he said to Him, "You know that I love You." "Feed My lambs," He told him. A second time He asked him, "Simon, son of John, **do you love Me?**" "Yes, Lord," he said to Him, "You know that I love You." "Shepherd My sheep," He told him. He asked him the third time, "Simon, son of John, **do you love Me?**" Peter was grieved that He asked him the third time, "**Do you love Me?**" He said, "Lord, You know everything! You know that I love You." "Feed My sheep," Jesus said. "I assure you: When you were young, you would tie your belt and walk wherever you wanted. But when you grow old, you will stretch out your hands and someone else will tie you and carry you where you don't want to go." (John 21:15–18, bold added for emphasis)

Three times Jesus asked Peter, "Do you love Me?"

Three times Peter answered, "You know I love You."

Three times Jesus responded by giving Peter a responsibility. "Feed My lambs, shepherd My sheep, feed My sheep."

This scenario, summarized by John in four little verses shows us that the essence of effective ministry will always be an overflow of our love relationship with Jesus. If Peter hoped not to fail again in the future, it would only be because of the depth of his love for Jesus.

Initially Peter was painfully pierced by this pointed question. But his life was wonderfully changed as a result of Jesus' asking him, "Do you love me?" Oswald Chambers writes:

The Lord's questions always reveal the true me to myself. . . . Rarely, but probably once in each of our lives, He will back us into a corner where He will hurt us with His piercing questions. Then we will realize that we do love Him far more deeply than our words can ever say.[1]

"Do You Love Me?"

Jesus might have asked Peter all kinds of questions that day. If I had been in Jesus' position, I might have asked, "Why did you deny Me?" or "What were you thinking?" or "What do you have to say for yourself?" But those were not the questions Jesus asked. He asked, "Do you love Me?"

By asking this question, Jesus was not implying that Peter didn't love Him. Instead, He penetrated the core of what a life of dynamic discipleship is all about. The greatest command is, "He said to him, 'Love the Lord your God with all your heart, with all your soul, and with all your mind.' This is the greatest and most important commandment" (Matt 22:37–38). Christianity is a relationship, not a religion.

Jesus did not ask Peter if he was a gifted speaker, a talented leader, or even a person of sound character. Jesus also did not inquire about Peter's seminary training or Bible knowledge. While each can be important when we talk about ministry, none of them is *the* issue.

The issue is simple. The one basic qualification for lasting ministry is found in an overflowing love relationship with Jesus. Love for Jesus is the only motive for ministry that will endure the test.

Jesus also did not ask Peter, "Do you love people?" Loving people is important for ministering to people. But loving Jesus is more important. Pastor Richard Tow writes:

> Ministry does not begin with a love for people. It begins with a love
> for God and that love overflows to people. If we minister only out of a
> humanistic love for people we will be people-pleasers rather than God-
> pleasers. We ultimately will not help them nor serve the purposes of
> God. But if everything begins with a holy love toward the Lord we will
> love people and we will serve their best interest—not always their whims
> and desires but always their best interest. Nothing will keep ministry on
> course like a deep love for the Lord. Nothing will carry us through the
> hard times like a sincere devotion to Christ.[2]

Nothing Is More Important than
Our Relationship with Jesus

Three times Jesus asked Peter, "Do you love Me?" Notice that He asked this question *before* giving Peter the commission to shepherd His sheep. Why?

Jesus wanted Peter, and us for that matter, never to forget that the chief criteria of enduring, effective ministry is loving Him above all else. It is central; all else is peripheral.

Too often we assume that the prime prerequisite for serving Jesus well is great giftedness, immense talent, or impressive academic credentials. Yet Peter and most of the other disciples were ordinary fishermen from a backward part of the country. They were nobodies until Jesus called them.

The major requirement for making a difference *for* Jesus is being in love *with* Jesus. Jesus repeated the question three times because He wanted it to be crystal clear. Nothing is more important than a passionate, deep, growing, overflowing relationship with Jesus.

The first thing which makes a true Christian minister or missionary or evangelist or preacher or Sunday School teacher, or leader or Christian worker of any kind, is not learning, not eloquence, not wisdom, not organizing ability, not pleasing personality, not even a "passion for souls," but a love-passion for Jesus Himself. Nothing, nothing, NOTHING, can take the place of that. All else without that is like withered flowers.[3]

A Most Dangerous Disciple

When Peter realized the gravity of this question, and when he was able to respond positively, his life changed significantly. He became a most dangerous disciple. Just a few weeks later the former cowardly denier of Jesus stood in front of thousands of people and boldly preached Jesus. Amazingly, 3,000 gave their lives to Christ, and the church was born (Acts 2:1–41). Beyond that, this dynamic man was used of God to open the door of salvation to non-Jews (Acts 10:34–48).

What made Peter so positively dangerous? He rediscovered His passion for Jesus and continued to build their relationship. Before Peter and the others launched their ministry, they held an intense, weeklong prayer meeting (Acts 1:12–14). He was careful to maintain a regular hour of prayer (Acts 3:1). He along with the other disciples made a conscious decision to give their attention to prayer and the ministry of the Word (Acts 6:4).

Real Ministry for Jesus Flows Out of Our Relationship with Jesus

Getting sidetracked is so easy. As you begin a lifetime of ministry, we want you to understand that what you do *for* God is only a reflection of the relationship you have *with* God. If you want to do great things, you need to have a great relationship. If you want to have a ministry for Jesus that is strong, your relationship with Jesus must be strong.

Oswald Chambers was a man others recognized as being abandoned to God. He was a Scottish itinerant preacher and Bible college founder. In his early forties he died far from home in Egypt of a ruptured appendix while ministering to the troops during WWI. His meditations on the Christian life collected in the daily devotional classic *My Utmost for His Highest* have enriched millions. He deeply understood the essential nature of our relationship with Jesus.

> Service is the overflow of super-abounding devotion to Jesus. . . . The main thing about Christianity is not the work we do, but the relationship we maintain, and the atmosphere produced by that relationship. That is all God asks us to look after, and it is the one thing that is being continually assailed. . . . The central thing about the kingdom of Jesus Christ is a personal relationship to Himself, not public usefulness to others.[4]

Real ministry *for* Jesus flows out of our relationship *with* Jesus. Notice that the "with Jesus" is the basis of the "for Jesus." Often we get so caught up in what we are trying to do for Jesus that we totally overlook the source of anything we can do *for* Jesus comes out of who we have become *with* Jesus.

The Challenge

The challenge of building up our relationship with Jesus *and* doing service for Jesus is not an "either/or" matter. Rather it is to be a "both/and" matter. Jesus said to Peter both, "Do you love Me?" and, "Feed My lambs" (John 21:15). Jesus gave *both* the Great Commandment—love God (Matt 22:37–38) *and* the Great Commission—make disciples (Matt 28:19–20). The challenge is to so develop our hearts that we have a *passion* for Jesus and *compassion* for others.

The Kind of Lover Who Sets Others on Fire

Amy Carmichael spent 55 years of her life as a missionary in India. The majority of her ministry was focused on helping orphans and liberating young girls from their slavery as temple prostitutes. She was a gifted author whose pen was aflame with love for her Savior. Passionately she wrote:

> God wants lovers. Oh, how tepid is the love of so many who call themselves by His name. How tepid is our own—my own—in comparison with the lava fires of his eternal love. I pray that you may be an ardent lover, the kind of lover who sets others on fire.[5]

I find Amy's prayer to be a daily challenge. Ministry is becoming the kind of lover who sets others on fire!

The Disciple Jesus Loved

When Jesus was asking Peter the probing question, "Do you love Me?" the young apostle John was eavesdropping. He watched, he listened, and he learned. Later he wrote of the event in his Gospel. But he also wrote it into his life. In fact, he had already begun.

Of the 12 disciples the only one who followed Jesus all the way to the foot of the cross was John. Later John served as copastor of the thriving church of Jerusalem. He wrote one outstanding Gospel, three epistles, and the book of the Revelation! In spite of persistent heartache and persecution, he kept going strong up through his nineties!

What was his secret for effective, enduring ministry? Rather than identifying himself as "John, the pastor of First Church in Jerusalem," or "John, the author of the Revelation," or "John, the apostle," he identified himself by one name, "the one whom Jesus loved."

> One of His disciples, **the one Jesus loved**, was reclining close beside Jesus. (John 13:23, bold added for emphasis)

> So she ran to Simon Peter and to the other disciple, **the one Jesus loved**, and said to them, "They have taken the Lord out of the tomb, and we don't know where they have put Him!" (John 20:2, bold added for emphasis)

> So Peter turned around and saw **the disciple Jesus loved** following them. That disciple was the one who had leaned back against Jesus at the supper and asked, "Lord, who is the one that's going to betray You?" (John 21:20, bold added for emphasis)

Obviously Jesus loved all the disciples, but John was the most aware and appreciative. John lived the principle that first we must receive God's love for us, then out will flow our love for God and others. In order to maintain a red-hot passion *for* God, we must never get over the fact that we are loved *by* God.

One pastor keenly observed, "We will never have more affection or passion for God than we understand he has for us."[6] The source of ministry effectiveness is passionate love for Jesus. The key to loving Jesus is being consumed by how much Jesus loves us.

The apostle John wrote to remind us how much God loves us.

Look at **how great a love the Father has given us,** that we should be
called God's children. And we are! The reason the world does not know
us is that it didn't know Him. (1 John 3:1, bold added for emphasis)

Later in chapter 3 of John's first epistle, he tells his readers that as Christians
we should love one another. In 1 John 4:7 he says again, "Let us love one
another." But this time John provides a new perspective for his readers as a way
of explaining why we are to love one another:

Dear friends, let us love one another, because love is from God, and
everyone who loves has been born of God and knows God. The one who
does not love does not know God, because God is love. (1 John 4:7–8)

In John's Gospel and in this epistle, he made clear that we are to love one
another because Jesus commanded us to do so (see John 13:34–35; 15:12,17;
1 John 3:11,23). We might think that this is all we need to know. If Jesus commands it, that should be enough for us. What other motivation do we need? Yet
John feels compelled here to give us two more fundamental reasons why we
must love one another. First, he says that "love is from God" and second that
"God is love." I would like to suggest several implications of these statements.

1. All love originates with God. We do not understand love apart from
   God. That includes love for our family, love for our friends, love for
   our spouses, and certainly love for God.
2. We cannot love anyone if we are not in a close relationship with God.
3. We must know God before we can know how to love. And we must
   keep knowing God so we can keep loving others.
4. The only reason we love God is because He first loved us (see 1 John
   4:19).
5. When we are not loving others, we are not loving God.

John became an expert on love because he was passionate about his Lord.
Some may wonder why John would be so bold as to describe himself as the
disciple "whom Jesus loved." It was not arrogance that motivated him to say
that. It was love. John had given his life to his Lord, and in return John received
the love of his Lord.

The apostle Paul also understood the incredible power of the love of
God. He prayed that the Ephesians would be empowered to comprehend the
immense love God had for them.

I pray that He may grant you, according to the riches of His glory, to
be strengthened with power through His Spirit in the inner man, and

that the Messiah may dwell in your hearts through faith. I pray that you, being rooted and firmly established in love, may be able to comprehend with all the saints what is the length and width, height and depth of God's love, and to know the Messiah's love that surpasses knowledge, so you may be filled with all the fullness of God. (Eph 3:16–19)

Paul, in fact, told us that the one overruling, overmastering, irresistible influence in his own ministry was the love of Christ: "For Christ's love compels us" (2 Cor 5:14). Receiving the love of Jesus and returning it back to Jesus drove Paul to tell others about Jesus. His total abandonment to the lordship of Christ pushed him into the ministry of reconciliation and that of serving as an ambassador of Christ (2 Cor 5:17–20).

Cultivating Your Relationship with Jesus Every Day

Recently Cathy and I celebrated our twenty-fifth year of marriage. I can honestly say that I love her more today than I did the day we were married. Our love relationship has grown and deepened. But that did not happen by accident.

A good relationship with Jesus also does not happen by accident. It will take some intentional effort and discipline. It also requires a few key ingredients that are true of any good relationship.

Time

Relationships grow as we spend time together. Cathy and I talk on the phone several times a day. I always call her on my way home. We eat dinner together each day and share about our day. One day a week (usually Friday or Saturday) we spend all day together. Usually we take a bike ride or we walk and talk. We go away for a few days for a mini-vacation for our anniversary each year. Even when I have been traveling out of the country, there have only been a few days when we have not been able to talk together.

In a similar fashion, I try to spend the first 45 minutes of my day with God. I call this my Prime Time. I read a few chapters of the Word, write in my journal, and pray using my prayer journal. Then I spend about 15 minutes with the Lord listening to the Bible on CD and praying as I drive to work. I like to have a few short prayer times throughout the day. I find the more time I spend with the Lord the more I love Him.

Communication

Time alone does not make a good relationship. We have all spent time with certain people, and our relationship seemed to get worse rather than better. Good relationships require open and honest communication. Relationships grow when we feel the liberty to share what we really think and how we really feel. We are honest and share things about the other person we don't understand. We also are comfortable enough to share with them our deepest hopes and dreams.

Trust

There will be no open, honest communication if there is no trust. We have to feel confident that the other person won't laugh at us, or get angry, or use what we share to hurt us later.

Let me assure you, God is the only One in the universe you can always trust. He made you and already knows everything about you. He loves you. You can trust Him. Even when you don't understand what He is doing, it will ultimately work out for good (Rom 8:28).

Now What?

How would you feel if Jesus sat down next to you, looked you straight in the eye, and asked, "Do you really love me?" In a sense He is doing that right now as you finish reading this chapter.

Why are you interested in serving Jesus? Is it to relieve guilt or to feel significant? Real ministry is best when it flows out of our love relationship with Jesus.

Are you building that relationship each day?

What does the time you have spent with Him in the last 24 hours say about the depth and passion of your love for Jesus?

How have you thought about Him?

How have you spoken of Him?

What do you need to say to Him right now?

Ministry Is . . .

1. Loving Jesus more than you love anything or anyone else.
2. The overflow of your relationship with Jesus.
3. The result of realizing how much you are loved by God.

⪜ Quotes ⪛

*If you could begin to spend one hour a day with God, there is
no telling what God will do with you.*

—RONNIE FLOYD[7]

*Your walk with God determines everything about your
life. . . . As you deepen your walk with God, He will
broaden your influence. . . . You cannot expect God
to do something through you if you are not allowing
Him to work in you every day of your life.*

—RONNIE FLOYD[8]

*We actually slander and dishonor God by our very eagerness
to serve Him without knowing Him.*

—OSWALD CHAMBERS[9]

Notes

1. O. Chambers, *My Utmost for His Highest, Updated Edition* (Grand Rapids, MI: Discovery House Publishers, 1992), March 2 entry, 62.

2. R. Tow, "Ministry Essentials," John 21:15–25 on Sermon Central, http://www.sermoncentral.com/sermon.asp?SermonID=83277&ContributorID=10438 (March 8, 2006).

3. J. S. Baxter quoted by Dr. Stephen Seamands in doctoral ministry course at Asbury Theological Seminary, Asbury, Kentucky, July 2004.

4. Chambers, *My Utmost for His Highest*, 17, 217, 293.

5. A. Carmichael quoted in *Call to Prayer* for TEXAS HOPE 2010, 36, http://www.fbcplano.org/Websites/fbcplano/Files/Content/528426/2010PrayerBook.pdf, accessed March 20, 2007.

6. M. Bickle, *Passion for Jesus: Perfecting Extravagant Love for God* (Lake Mary, FL: Charisma House, 2007), 98.

7. R. Floyd, *10 Things Every Minister Should Know* (Green Forest, AR: New Life Press, 2006), 21.

8. Ibid., 24—26.

9. Chambers, *My Utmost for His Highest*, October 3 entry, 277.

9

Living Forever Grateful for His Appointment

Ben Gutierrez

Charlie Changed My Life

A good pastor friend of mine shared a story with me some time ago that I've never forgotten. I want to share it with you now.

I remember growing up in a church that celebrated in grandiose fashion any young man's decision to enter "full-time ministry." And the celebrations were grandiose indeed! That is, if an all-you-can-eat Sunday night potluck where each family brought two covered dishes and a dessert—one of which had to be fried chicken. Now that is my idea of a "grandiose" feast! It was a frequent experience at our church, and we were proud (and rightly so) that we hosted many of these celebrations.

The notice of such a celebration would be delivered in routine fashion. We would be informed of a young man's calling into ministry by a brief yet exciting announcement at the end of a Sunday morning service after the invitation. Immediately you would hear a low rumbling among the congregation as everyone turned to one another and inquired as to what their neighbor will be bringing to the potluck that night. These types of announcements seemed to lift the spirits of the regular Sunday night crowd who faithfully attended the evening services. Hearing the testimonies of the young men was considered a special opportunity. For me it definitely made attending the Sunday night service easy knowing that we would feast on pasta salad, fried chicken, and homemade desserts as far as the eye could see!

On that Sunday evening after the church service, we all made our way to the fellowship hall of the church. We enjoyed one another's fellowship and ate until we bordered on gluttony. When the pastor sensed we were winding down our meal, he called on the young man to share with the congregation his call to ministry.

I had attended so many of these celebrations at my church that I could pretty much predict what this new pastor in training would share with us. They all would start off by thanking their church congregation for coming tonight. Then they would thank their parents for always instilling a love for God's Word by taking them to church their entire life. Next they would talk about how they had accepted Jesus Christ as a small child and knew early on that they would be a pastor in the ministry. Admittedly, I grew a little insensitive to this stage of the process as every testimony by each young man seemed routine and predictable. But my attitude was about to change eternally because I heard what a man named Charlie had to say.

After we had enjoyed our smorgasbord of homemade delectables, we all pivoted our chairs toward a small stage in the fellowship hall that elevated slightly above the crowd the pastor and the newly called preacher boy. Then the pastor rose sporting an unusually large grin, almost as if he knew the profound impact the young man's testimony would have on us but choosing not to let the cat out of the bag.

"Ladies and gentlemen, this is Charlie. I have asked him to share his testimony of how God has called him into full-time ministry."

Immediately I could hear whispers and rumblings across the fellowship hall as if all were attempting to hide their opinions of the young man for fear that they would not be considered acceptable if spoken publicly. It seemed obvious to me that Charlie was not receiving a warm reception, and he hadn't even had a chance to open his mouth. And to be honest, I was not initially impressed by him either.

Charlie was an unkempt man in his early twenties. His hair looked like he had just walked through the church parking lot during a strong windstorm, and he either didn't have the time to return it to its rightful place or was unaware it was disheveled. He slouched slightly upon the gray, metal folding chair, and his suit-tie combo seemed to have been inspired by an old Blues Brothers movie.

Having set my opinion of him, I began to predict that his future scope of ministry and sphere of influence would be small and insignificant. I remember looking at him both sympathetically and pathetically. I thought to myself, *I am certain he won't be received as a senior pastor in any church that I know! At least, no church of any considerable size.* It is amazing how quickly we all came to a hasty and carnal decision of him. For me, I had my opinion of him locked in within the brief 20 seconds of the pastor's introduction.

As I sat there, I anticipated hearing broken grammar, run-on thoughts and ramblings, and a simple man's attempt to sound pastoral. After all, we deserve to send out impressive ambassadors of our church in lieu of what we have done to support a pastoral candidate, don't we? I mean, just take a look at the spread of food we all prepared for this evening, right? We ought to get a good return on our investment.

Then it was as if God shocked me with a million volts to get my attention. As Charlie spoke his first word, God pierced my heart and convicted me never again to question His choice for who should be called into ministry.

God had a lesson about ministry He wanted me to learn that night.

"Wretched!" Charlie shouted.

What did he just say? "Wretch?" "Witch?" "Widget?" What did he say?

Did he just say, "Wretched"? I must have heard it wrong, so I sat up, leaned forward, and carefully honed my eyes on him as if I were looking at him through a telescope in order to make sure I was hearing this right. And sure enough, I was right. He had said, "Wretched." But he didn't stop there.

"Wretched!"

"Dirty!"

"Angry!"

"Dark!"

". . . and sinful!" Charlie exclaimed.

"*I was all of this and more,*" he continued. "I guess 'unworthy' describes best how I view God's calling me into ministry."

I was mesmerized by his transparency, honesty, and sincerity as no young man had ever begun his testimony in this fashion. I was beginning to feel a deep sense of embarrassment as if God had publicly exposed my sinful, prideful comments to everyone in the room. But God wasn't finished making His point to me.

Charlie continued to share about how he lacked any positive spiritual influences while growing up. "I was not brought up in the church. I had zero biblical training from anyone," he continued. "My life was a total absence of godly, Christian examples. "

"I have never preached before," he said. "Truth is, I don't yet own a good-looking Bible.

"But one thing I do know I have received—God's grace!" Charlie said. "God has forgiven me and saved my soul. And if God can save me and call me into ministry, He can save and call anyone!" Then Charlie concluded his testimony by suggesting that he had no business being allowed to be used by God in His ministry work.

Then after saying all this, he bowed his head and concluded his testimony extremely softly after a long pause. No one moved. We weren't going anywhere. We were perched on the edge of our seats to hear his conclusion. You could have heard a pin drop in the room by this time. And then he concluded his testimony. And what he said so softly that Sunday night has unforgettably reverberated in my heart.

Charlie said, "But the more unworthy I feel, the more grateful I become."

Charlie probably preached his best sermon that day. The Holy Spirit worked through the sharing of his testimony in a powerful way that evening as we were gripped with a profound truth about ministry. The most influential ministers are grateful ministers. If we aspire to be ministers, we best be forever grateful for God's appointment into ministry!

God Uses Grateful Ministers

When my friend finished the story, I was speechless. He and I had just taken a break from a session at a Christian leaders retreat where we were receiving additional training to be effective ministers, but I was convinced that I had already gotten my money's worth during that break time.

Eventually I managed to utter a few deeply felt wows, and then I found myself repeating the phrase, "Praise the Lord!" I found my mind swirling with many portions of Scripture about gratitude, humility, and calling. I found myself gravitating to one particular biblical testimony in 1 Tim 1:12–16 that I believe every minister should read, memorize, and meditate upon until the truth of the Scripture resonates deep into his heart: "Be forever grateful for God's appointment into ministry!" It expresses the sentiment Charlie shared in his testimony.

Charlie wasn't the first to share such a profound testimony of gratitude. There was one who penned Holy Scripture who felt the same way about himself—wretched, sinful, unworthy—but experienced God's grace and mercy in order to be used in His ministry. His name was Paul.

Gratitude: A Common Characteristic Among God-Appointed Ministers

Paul's testimony of how God called him into ministry starts off the same routine and seemingly predictable way that many testimonies do. But just like Charlie's testimony, the words Paul shared are far from routine as he passionately testifies of God's grace, mercy, and power to change a life.

> "I give **thanks to Christ Jesus** our Lord, who has strengthened me, because He considered me faithful, appointing me to the ministry."
> (1 Tim 1:12, bold added for emphasis)

Seem routine? Just read the next word in the succeeding verse (v. 13), and you will be touched by a shocking testimony of wretchedness, sin, and unworthiness as . . .

> one who was formerly a blasphemer, a persecutor, and an arrogant man. Since it was out of ignorance that I had acted in unbelief, I received mercy, and the grace of our Lord overflowed, along with the faith and love that are in Christ Jesus. This saying is trustworthy and deserving of full acceptance: "Christ Jesus came into the world to save sinners"—and I am the worst of them. (1 Tim 1:13–15)

Paul assessed his own life and he concluded that he was utterly unworthy of God's grace and calling. In fact, he declared that he is the "worst" sinner of all. Paul was not being overly denigrating; he definitely knew where he stood prior to receiving God's gracious gift of salvation. When he was appointed by God to serve as a minister in His wonderful kingdom, his gratitude was endless.

Needed: A Generation of Grateful Ministers

It is hard to believe that the one biblical character we in church often hold up as one of the most dedicated, stalwart Christ followers of all time actually felt this way about himself. Yet it is true. The reason Paul shared these self-exposing words in his testimony with us is so that future ministers would actually shun the temptation to look upon him in such an exalted way. By doing so, Paul provides a profound lesson on gratitude to all of us in ministry. One of the most deeply respected ministers of all time was a wretched, angry, grotesquely sinful man who was unworthy of God's calling. But as a good minister, he mentors all future ministers by sharing his personal thoughts of how every minister should forever be grateful to God for His appointment into ministry.

Be Grateful to the God Who Appoints

Notice that Paul was quick to acknowledge who did all the work to place him into ministry in the first place. God who performed all that was necessary to prepare him to be a minister.

1. God equipped you: "Christ Jesus our Lord, who has strengthened me" (1 Tim 1:12).
2. God called you: "He considered me faithful" (v. 12.)
3. God appointed you: "appointing me to the ministry" (v. 12).
4. God cleansed you: "I received mercy" (v. 13).

We too ought to express our gratitude to our great God who has equipped, called, appointed, and cleansed us for ministry! The fact that you are reading a book about ministry or even considering becoming a minister is because of God's gracious work!

Be Grateful to the God Who Sustains

Paul continued his testimony by expressing his conviction that he knew God saved him and made him a minister so that Paul would proclaim his profound gratitude from the rooftops! And having expressed his gratitude to everyone he came in contact with, he believed they too would receive Christ and become ministers themselves.

"But I received mercy because of this, so that in me, the worst of them, Christ Jesus might demonstrate the utmost patience as an example to those who would believe in Him for eternal life." (1 Tim 1:16)

Paul reminds every minister that the same level of dependence on God that He used to grant us entrance into a saving relationship with Him is also required of us as we serve as ministers.

Gratitude Begets Gratitude

As ministers, the more we express our gratitude for what God has done in our lives, the more those around us will be drawn to this contagious practice by praising God for all He has done for each of them. People passionately desire to praise God for what He has done in their lives. But often they feel apprehensive to express their appreciation openly because either they do not know what to say or no one has led the way in showing them how to express their gratitude to God. As a minister you should lead the way.

Worshippers will learn how to express their gratitude to God by observing our constant spirit of gratitude as ministers. Notice how Paul set the example by sharing his passionate and personal expression of praise and gratitude. It was as if he could not contain himself after contemplating the work of God in his life: "Now to the King eternal, immortal, invisible, the only God, be honor and glory forever and ever. Amen" (1 Tim 1:17).

If we are truly grateful ministers, then gratitude will be a common anthem in our sermons, writings, publications, e-mails, and conversations. Like Paul, we should lead the way in testifying of God's great work in our lives. Grateful ministers beget grateful worshippers!

What Now? (Check Your Gratitude Gauge Every Three Months or 3,000 Miles)

I make it a habit to pause regularly during my busy ministry season to make sure my heart is running full steam with regard to expressing gratitude to God for all He has done in my life. At the beginning of every calendar year, I go through my calendar and partition off an entire day approximately every three months to devote to prayer, thanksgiving, and expressions of gratitude for all that God has done in my life in calling me into ministry. Leading up to these encounters with God, I sometimes find that seasons of ministry call for a more immediate appointment with God—especially if I am running on all cylinders around Easter, Christmas, churchwide events, or after preaching/teaching for a long stretch of time. My time with God in expressing gratitude and praise allows me to let the dust settle on the activities of ministry and to remember how blessed I am to be called into ministry.

How often do you pause to reflect on how blessed you are as a God-appointed minister? Have you gotten so busy in the activity of ministry that you view this intentional pausing as an inconvenient agenda item to be added to your calendar rather than a necessary spiritual exercise as a minister?

Is anything keeping you right now from securing a time in your schedule this week that will afford you an uninterrupted time of communion with God? Nail it down.

Begin immediately to list the many reasons you are grateful to Him for calling you to be a minister. Begin penciling thoughts in the margin of this page in this book. Do not put it off! While God is bringing thoughts to your mind, write them down right away.

A life of overflowing gratitude in a minister's life is one of God's most powerful encouragers to all Christ followers! Ministry is living forever grateful for God's work in your life.

Ministry Is . . .

1. Living forever grateful for God's appointment.
2. Allowing your expressions of gratitude to lead the way in your congregation.
3. Making time to express your gratitude to God in private so you will be able to serve in public.

◈ Quotes ◈

Ministering in the church constitutes the highest privilege. Nothing could be more honorable or have greater eternal significance than serving our Christ in His church.
—JOHN MACARTHUR[1]

Jesus Christ is not valued at all until He is valued above all.
—AUGUSTINE[2]

Gratitude . . . goes beyond the "mine" and "thine" and claims the truth that all of life is a pure gift. In the past I always thought of gratitude as a spontaneous response to the awareness of gifts received, but now I realize that gratitude

can also be lived as a discipline. The discipline of gratitude is
the explicit effort to acknowledge that all I am and have is
given to me as a gift of love, a gift to be celebrated with joy.

—Henri J. M. Nouwen[3]

We prevent God from giving us the great spiritual gifts
He has in store for us, because we do not give thanks for
daily gifts. We think we dare not be satisfied with the small
measure of spiritual knowledge, experience, and love that
has been given to us, and that we must constantly be looking
forward eagerly for the highest good. Then we deplore the
fact that we lack the deep certainty, the strong faith, and the
rich experience that God has given to others, and we consider
this lament to be pious. We pray for the big things and forget
to give thanks for the ordinary, small (and yet really not
small) gifts. How can God entrust great things to one who
will not thankfully receive from Him the little things?

—Dietrich Bonhoeffer[4]

Notes

1. J. MacArthur, *Pastoral Leadership* (Nashville, TN: Thomas Nelson, 2005), xi.

2. Augustine.

3. H. J. M. Nouwen, Nouwen Centre, ww.nouwen.org.

4. D. Bonhoeffer, *Life Together* (New York, NY: Harper One, 1978), 13.

10

Taking Your Turn

Ben Gutierrez

One generation plants a tree, and another gets the shade.

—Author unknown

There is no *I* in *Team*. Ministry is a team sport. Ministry is not about individual achievement. Ministry is not a job that begins with the first full-time position we hold and ends when we take down our name plate in retirement. Rather, ministry is all about what God is *doing* in the world, and He invites us to be a part of what He is doing!

Doing ministry is likened to walking up to the scrimmage line to execute the specific play that God has given you to execute. Unlike football where the star quarterback may play the entire game, God directs the game and allows us to join Him on the field. He simply requires that we play with all our might and support our teammates. Then, after our play is over, we must be willing to hand off to another player who continues the game and plays with everything he or she has.

Ministry is all about fulfilling our role on the team for as long as God wants us in the game. We appreciate the teammates who prepare us, and we value those who will succeed us in playing the game. As a result, we play with great care and spiritual excellence. We help prepare those who will play the game after we are done. Ministry is all about faithfully fulfilling our role in the long continuum of the game of ministry.

A an important verse speaks to the issue of ministry being a team effort:

> And what you have heard from me in the presence of many witnesses,
> commit to faithful men who will be able to teach others also. (2 Tim 2:2)

Many in the body of Christ who have the spiritual gift of teaching love this verse because it is a direct command to "commit" (i.e., teach or deposit) truth into the lives of other believers. But this verse is actually more focused on the results of your teaching. True, this would be a verse that emphasizes teaching alone if we only had the first half. For example, this verse would be emphasizing teaching if this is all it said:

> And what you have heard from me in the presence of many witnesses,
> commit to faithful men.

If this is all it said, you would make every professor in college very happy—a mandate simply to lecture and lecture and talk and talk! But it doesn't end there. The apostle Paul intentionally added the following words to make an important distinction, "who will be able to teach others also."

In this verse the apostle Paul emphasizes why we preach and teach truth to other believers. Namely because someday your turn will expire and it will be their turn to minister. It will be your responsibility to help those you teach embrace the same commitment you have to teach others.

When you decide to go into ministry, God asks you solemnly to vow that you will take the ball from those handing it off to you and run the race with precision, passion, and purity—understanding that while you are in ministry for the Lord you are also training others to "run the race" who will one day replace you.

It's a Good Fight

Paul gave us a good example of how this process of ministering and preparing others for ministry is accomplished. In 2 Timothy, Paul is handing off his mantle of leadership in Ephesus to a younger minister named Timothy. In Paul's final chapter of his final letter to his friend Timothy, and before Paul was martyred for his faith, he made this statement that served as Timothy's example on how he should now execute his duties as a minister:

> I have fought the good fight, I have finished the race, I have kept the
> faith. (2 Tim 4:7)

This verse is a favorite to many in the body of Christ. As a result, I have heard many treatments on this one sentence that focus on Paul's clear testimony that he served God all the way to the end of his life and never gave up. And indeed this is clearly stated in this verse. But don't miss Paul's implicit encouragement to Timothy that it is now his turn to carry the ball.

The phrase "I have fought the good fight" (v. 7a) is often taught that Paul was emphasizing here that he fought well (and there is no doubt that Paul fought well!). But notice in this particular statement, Paul was not emphasizing his own individual performance as a minister but rather on the fact that the "fight" (i.e., ministry) was an honorable "fight" to fight. And young Timothy should also conclude in his life that functioning as a minister is a good and honorable fight to choose.

Notice that the word *good* (which means "honorable" or "noble") is not qualifying the word *fought*. On the contrary, the word *good* is describing the word *fight*. Paul was testifying that the fight he fought all these years was a noble, honorable, or "good" fight to fight. In essence Paul was saying, "Since you are going to have to choose your battles in life, the ministry of Jesus Christ is your best choice." Paul testified that he jumped into the game, carried the ball, got bumped around a lot, but overall it was a good and noble run and now it is time for you to fight. It's your turn!

Appreciating Your Spiritual "Offensive Line"

A quarterback's best friend is a group of men called the "O line" or "offensive linemen." These men hike the ball to the quarterback then plow ahead to make the smoothest path toward the end zone. These men take the hits for the quarterback and receive the brunt of the abuse from the opposing team so that the quarterback only experiences minor brushes of opposition.

Likewise every minister today should never forget that we are marching down the field in the wake left by a virtual powerhouse of spiritual offensive linemen. They took some major hits for us when it was their turn in ministry. The testimony in God's Word of how they fought their battles gives us a playbook of sorts that helps us fight our battles.

Hebrews 12:1 reminds us never to forget the line of ministers that have braved the path for us today:

> Therefore since we also have such a large cloud of witnesses surrounding us, let us lay aside every weight and the sin that so easily ensnares us, and run with endurance the race that lies before us. (Heb 12:1)

Who are those "witnesses"? Look no further than the previous chapter. Hebrews 11 lists for us these witnesses who have run before us. Just look at the first few words of each of the following verses in Hebrews 11 and you'll recognize this.

- 11:4   By faith Abel . . .
- 11:5   By faith Enoch . . .
- 11:7   By faith Noah . . .
- 11:8   By faith Abraham . . .
- 11:11   By faith Sarah . . .
- 11:20   By faith Isaac . . .
- 11:21   By faith Jacob . . .
- 11:22   By faith Joseph . . .
- 11:23   By faith Moses . . .
- 11:31   By faith Rahab . . .
- 11:32   Through faith Gideon, Barak, Samson, Jephthah, David, Samuel, and the prophets . . .
- 11:36   Still others . . .

This amazing group of heavenly heroes has gone on before us. Now it is our turn!

When Taking Your Turn Turns into Taking the Praise

While it is true that there is no *I* in *team*, you are still able to find the word *me* within *team*. In fact, just using the letters TEAM you can actually construct the statements, "Me met team [and] me ate team!" This just goes to show that if there is a desire to get around the ideal, the flesh will certainly find a way. When we get the call to take the field and it is our turn to contribute to the long and honorable succession of ministers, our pride gets the best of us. We tend to enjoy the recognition, and too often we look to improve our own personal stats in ministry rather than thinking about how to sacrifice for the team. As a result, we tarnish the strong, reputable chain of testimony of those who have set the stage for us with our hearts deciding that we are going to draw all attention to ourselves as we minister.

Travis Whittaker is a dear friend and effective minister/musician.[1] He travels internationally and ministers to many people groups in a myriad of life situations that few are willing passionately to pursue. But what I (Ben) appreciate most about my friend's ministry is his *motive* for *why* he should pursue his music ministry prior to formulating his band and begin traveling across the world. He chose to settle any and all heart issues with regard to *why* he should pursue ministry. Because he has done this, the Lord has multiplied his impact for God's kingdom.

Pride cannot have any place or play any role in a minister's life whatsoever! I remember one night Travis and I were having a conversation while sitting in his large pickup truck on the edge of a college campus parking lot. We were talking about his prayerful attempt to begin this new adventure, and Travis shared an observation with me that I have never forgotten. He said, "I believe that every minister has to settle the 'pride issue' at some time in his/her life." To which I instantly replied, "And my prayer is that every minister would settle it *very early* in his/her life!"

In Romans, Paul describes the decision to say no to pride once and for all in your life as a necessary decision to make. We are in the middle of a war for our affections. On one side is the Holy Spirit showing us the way to humility and sacrifice; on the other side is our flesh showing us the way to pride and selfishness.

> So then, brothers, we are not obligated to the flesh to live according to the flesh, for if you live according to the flesh, you are going to die. But if by the Spirit you put to death the deeds of the body, you will live. All those led by God's Spirit are God's sons. (Rom 8:12–14)

Within us is a desire to steal the praise of our Creator and take credit for all of the accomplishments we experience in our lives. It is a result of the curse of sin and permeates the soul of every human being upon birth. What can help you "put to death the deeds of the body" in order to make sure you do not steal an ounce of God's well-deserved praise? It starts in your heart. Every day you have to give your affections to our Lord, and you make a decision that in every area of your ministry you commit to do whatever it takes to make sure people talk about how great God is and what He is doing in their lives much more than they talk about you and how great you are! This point cannot be emphasized enough!

Highly Exalted

The book of Philippians explains that all praise is reserved for Jesus Christ![2] It is a level of praise that acknowledges that He is awesome, unique, wonderful, and has the greatest impact on our lives.

For this reason God also highly exalted Him and gave Him the name
that is above every name, so that at the name of Jesus every knee should
bow—of those who are in heaven and on earth and under the earth—and
every tongue should confess that Jesus Christ is Lord, to the glory of
God the Father. (Phil 2:9–11)

The phrase "highly exalted" is taken from a unique word from Paul's day.
In fact, the word is seen only one time in the entire New Testament. Today we
translate it with two words because we aren't quite sure how to interpret it. We
know what each part of the word means, but we don't have a one-word equivalent in our language today. Let me explain.

The phrase "highly exalted" is taken from the Greek compound word
huperupsao (pronounced hoo-pear-oops-SAH-oh). We know how to translate
the second half of the word because Bible writers used that portion of the word
often—*upsao* (pronounced oops-SAH-oh). The Greek word *upsao* means "to
exalt," "to lift up," "to elevate," or "to prop up." But we rarely see the first
half of this compound word attached to the beginning of this word *huper*. The
Greek word *huper* is where we get our word *hyper*.

The Bible often says that if we obey God's commands and demonstrate
faithfulness to Him, then God will *upsao* (exalt/lift up) us! For example, the
word *upsao* is used in Jas 4:10: "Humble yourselves before the Lord, and He
will **exalt you**." The words "exalt you" are the translation from James' first-
century word *upsao*.

Another example is found in 1 Pet 5:6: "Therefore humble yourselves under
the mighty hand of God, that He may **exalt you** at the proper time" (NASB).
Once again the words "exalt you" are the translation from Peter's first-century
word *upsao*. God promises us that if we obey His commands and demonstrate
faithfulness to Him, He will then *upsao* (exalt/lift up) us!

But, as mentioned earlier, the apostle Paul writes a word in Phil 2:9 that we
are not used to seeing and translating. The apostle Paul takes the word "exalt"
and adds "hyper" to it. Literally Phil 2:9 teaches that Jesus Christ is and should
be "hyper-exalted!" This simply isn't a concept we are accustomed to in the
twenty-first century. That is also why many Bible translations add a couple
more English words to attempt to translate this word for which we do not have
an English equivalent.

What does it mean to be "hyper-exalted"? Let's think about what *hyper*
implies. This word implies that you "exceed the limits." For example, when
athletes hyperextend a joint it means they have exceeded the limit of normal use.
Another example is when you hyperventilate. When this occurs, you breathe

excessively, continually, and more than what is accepted as normal. It describes an action that exceeds all normal actions and responses.

Therefore, Phil 2:9 tells us that we should make sure that the Lord Jesus Christ receives more glory, more praise, and more honor than absolutely anything and everything that has ever existed and ever will exist! His name, His praise, His glory should be exalted above everything!

How should we translate this word in Phil 2:9? Well, believe it or not, you can provide a translation for it! Here's how: just figure out in your mind how you would describe something that should be praised and exalted higher and more passionately beyond anything else in the world, both now and in the future. Put that into the fewest words possible, and you have captured the nature of this somewhat untranslatable word! That is exactly what Bible translators have done! Consider some of these Bible translations that have grappled with this challenge:

Therefore God exalted him to the highest place and gave him the name that is above every name. (Phil 2:9 NIV)

For this reason also, God highly exalted Him, and bestowed on Him the name which is above every name. (Phil 2:9 NASB)

Therefore, God elevated him to the place of highest honor and gave him the name above all other names. (Phil 2:9 NLT)

Because of that obedience, God lifted him high and honored him far beyond anyone or anything. (Phil 2:9 *THE MESSAGE*)

Then God gave Christ the highest place and honored his name above all others. (Phil 2:9 CEV)

Never, at anytime, should we seek the level of attention and glory that our precious Lord should receive. In everything we do, we should draw all eyes to our great and majestic Savior Jesus Christ! Every note we sing, every sermon we preach, every word we speak should be employed to draw all attention to God! Jesus Christ deserves *more* attention, *more* honor, *more* glory, and *more* praise than what we should ever receive.

The highest level of praise is reserved only for Jesus. Whatever we do in life and ministry, we must commit to do whatever it takes to make sure people talk about how great God is and what He is doing in their lives much more than they talk about us.

A Principle to Live By

If, after we minister to the body of Christ, people talk more about how great we are and how impressed they are with *our* skill and talent rather than talking about how great our *God* is, something is seriously wrong with the way we are ministering to people! All ministers should rather be motivated by the desire to bring more praise to the One who placed us into ministry in the first place, Jesus Christ!

An Angel Said It Best

As a minister, I attempt to make sure the truths presented within this chapter remain on my mind constantly. One statement in the Bible helps me keep all of these truths in check. The statement came from the mouth of an angel.

The statement humbles me because this particular angel was so powerful and beautiful that he most certainly had many things he could have boasted about and shown off. Instead the angel was deeply committed to focusing all praise to his Creator who had appointed the angel into ministry.

If you recall, after all of the magnificent glories and horrors of the predictions of the end times were presented to the apostle John by this angel in the book of Revelation, the faithful apostle could not contain his desire to praise. And in a brief moment of euphoria, he mistakenly bowed down before the angel in order to express his great praise for all God had done and would do in the days to come.

What was the angel's response? Did the angel stand there and say, "Oh, I understand this is indeed a lot to take in. And I understand that you as a human can get so overwhelmed by all this knowledge. So it is understandable that you would want to express your thanks to me. After all, I did give you a guided tour through all this, and God Himself did appoint me to this post. So go ahead and express a few more statements of thanks and appreciation to me. Then you can get up and we'll move along." No way!

The angel immediately rebuked the great apostle.

> I, John, am the one who heard and saw these things. When I heard and saw them, I fell down to worship at the feet of the angel who had shown them to me. But he said to me, "Don't do that! I am a fellow slave with you, your brothers the prophets, and those who keep the words of this book. Worship God." (Rev 22:8–9)

Why was the angel so quick to react to the apostle's misstep? Because the angel dwells in the presence of God all of the time, communes with Him all of the time, and is able to see His mighty hand work all of the time. As a result, the angel has a deep conviction that God alone should receive all of the credit for all that He has and is doing.

My prayer is that we would all adopt this same perspective about ourselves as we play our part in God's continuum of faithful ministers: "I am a fellow slave with you, your brothers the prophets, and those who keep the words of this book" (Rev 22:9).

What Now? ("Tag! You're It!")

Remember the childhood game tag that we used to play? One child would chase down another and touch him or her, thus changing the role of the child who was once running from the leader to becoming the leader of the game.

In a similar fashion this chapter effectively tags you and calls for you immediately and consciously to change the way you have thought about your purpose for why you are a minister. Effective immediately you are part of a long tradition of ministers who will make an impact on both the current generation and future generations of ministers. The foundation you lay now will be what the next minister builds upon. You have effectively been tagged, and now you must lead according to the truths presented within this chapter. How will you lead?

Begin ushering all praise upward toward Him for any and all victories you experience within your season of ministry. Also be honest and transparent with God about any battle you may have with pride and the temptation to steal His glory.

Consider the words you say when receiving a compliment from others. Do these words cause others to thank God for what He has done in their lives, or does your response focus the attention on you? What can you do to make sure people are talking more about what God has done in their lives through your ministry rather than talking about how great you are? Be intentional about how you can redirect everyone's thinking about your ministry to praise and give thanks to God!

Ministry Is . . .

1. Fulfilling our part in God's continuum of faithful ministers.
2. Feeding the Holy Spirit in order to overcome the desire to live according to the flesh and its desires that tempt us to look out for our own interests in ministry.
3. Ushering all praise to God and not stealing any praise due God.

⌐ Quote ⌐

"Worship God!" In other words, don't worship angels, worship God! This is the last chapter of the Bible, and this is the last duty of man: worship God!

—JOHN PIPER[3]

Notes

1. For more on Travis Whittaker, go to http://www.station2music.com.

2. For more on Philippians 2 see Ben Gutierrez, *Living Out the Mind of Christ: Practical Keys to Discovering and Applying the Mind of Christ in Everyday Life* (Lynchburg, VA: InnovateChurch, 2008), 80–82.

3. J. Piper, sermon, "Worship God!" November 9, 1997, Desiring God, http://www.desiringgod.org/ResourceLibrary/Sermons/ByScripture/17/1016_Worship_God.

Part 3

The Essentials of Ministry

11

Saying, "Here Am I. Send Me"

Dave Earley

I believe that when God calls you, He always gives you an insatiable passion to make a difference with your life.

RONNIE FLOYD[1]

Nearly 3,000 years ago, Israel had become commercially and militarily strong yet was rotting spiritually. She was cancerously corrupt and riddled with the putrefying sores of sexual immorality, greedy idolatry, and religion without relationship. At the highest level godly leadership was being replaced by untested and ungodly leaders.

There was a young man who passionately loved God and had a longing to see his nation return to God. His heart was broken, and he was burdened to make a difference—just like many of you.

God gave him an amazing experience that changed his life and his nation forever. You can read Isaiah's story in the sixth chapter of the book that bears his name.

"I Saw the Lord"

> In the year that King Uzziah died, I saw the Lord seated on a high and
> lofty throne, and His robe filled the temple. (Isa 6:1)

Stop. Don't miss those four words: "I saw the Lord." This young man was
given a vision only a handful of humans have ever seen. He saw the Lord. He
was taken into the throne room of Almighty God. If I could give you any gift,
it would be a vision of God!

Notice that Isaiah did not really try to describe God. Why? God is indescribable. He truly is beyond words. God is infinite; therefore when we throw
out adjectives like *awesome, glorious, majestic, powerful, kind, wise, compassionate*, or *huge*, we are only giving a tiny glimpse of the real thing. He is
incomprehensible. We have no words in our language that can come close to
describing Him accurately.

We can only guess at what Isaiah saw. In those moments of seeing the
Lord, Isaiah's mind must have exploded with images of raging fires of holiness,
laser lights of purity, rivers of wisdom, oceans of love, and torrents of truth. He
saw the good Shepherd, the heavenly Father, the King of kings, and so much
more.

He saw the Lord *seated on a throne*. The throne must have been humon-
gous, hundreds of stories high. We know from elsewhere in Scripture that the
throne of God is covered in jewels, radiating rainbows of colors, surrounded
in glorious light.

> Seraphim were standing above Him; each one had six wings: with two he
> covered his face, with two he covered his feet, and with two he flew.
> (Isa 6:2)

Seraphim were standing above Him. The beings closest to God are a special
type of angels called "seraphim." The word *seraphim* is a Hebrew word meaning "burning ones." Why burning ones? God's holiness is a consuming fire
(Heb 12:29). These seraphim are asbestos angels, burning constantly throughout eternity in the presence of a holy God.

> And one called to another: Holy, holy, holy is the LORD of Hosts; His
> glory fills the whole earth. (Isa 6:3)

"Holy, holy, holy." Those magnificent, glorious angels not only burn con-
tinuously in the presence of God and fly perpetually in the presence of God,
but they also worship unceasingly in the presence of God. Their worship is in

the form of a declaration that they cannot help but make. The essence of the One before them is so intense that the words are irresistibly drawn from their lips. "Holy, holy, holy is the LORD of hosts; His glory fills the whole earth"!

Imagine. Minute after minute, hour after hour, day after day, year after year, decade after decade, century after century, millennium after millennium these glorious angels sing and shout their praise by repeating *"Holy, holy, holy."*

Holiness is a word that means "separation." God is absolutely separate from any and all sin. Through all eternity the only moment sin and God ever came together was on the cross when Jesus Christ took our sin on Himself as He died for us. God's holiness gives God's love form and strength.

> The foundations of the doorways shook at the sound of their voices, and
> the temple was filled with smoke. (Isa 6:4)

The holiness of God is so intense that the Seraphim do not quietly call out, "Holy, holy, holy." No, they bellow it out so loudly that heaven shakes under their thunderous song of worship.

Imagine seeing the holiness of the Lord! In seeing the Lord, Isaiah was confronted with an amazing, astounding awareness of the absolute holiness of God, and it crushed him.

"Woe Is Me"

> Then I said: Woe is me, for I am ruined, because I am a man of unclean
> lips and live among a people of unclean lips, and because my eyes have
> seen the King, the LORD of Hosts. (Isa 6:5)

If we were to see the Lord today, it would, at best, be through our shaking fingers as we'd dive facedown in His presence. We would literally be knocked off our feet by His glory, majesty, power, and blazing holiness. Like Isaiah we'd cry out, "Woe *is* me!"

When Isaiah cried, "Woe is me," he was acknowledging his sin. The Hebrew rendering of this term is intense. He is literally saying, "I am damned, guilty, and condemned to hell."

Then he cried, "I am *ruined*!" This means literally "I am melting." God, the holy fire, is such that when Isaiah saw the unabashed holiness of Almighty God, he knew that apart from forgiveness, he deserved to burn forever in hell, and it crushed him.

Then one of the seraphim flew to me, and in his hand was a glowing coal that he had taken from the altar with tongs. He touched my mouth with it and said: Now that this has touched your lips, your wickedness is removed, and your sin is atoned for. (Isa 6:6–7)

Fire can do two things. It can burn and consume, or it can cleanse and purify. The angel took a burning coal from off the altar and placed it up to Isaiah's trembling lips. Instead of burning and consuming him, it purified him. What a gracious, merciful, compassionate God who is willing to cleanse us of our sins!

Isaiah's cleansing occurred 739 years before the coming of Jesus, and as such it provided a *temporary* cleansing by fire. When you and I come to God with broken-hearted sorrow and repentance, we are cleansed with the *permanent* cleansing of blood, the blood of the Christ slain for our sins.

Now that Isaiah was clean before God, he was ready to hear from God. When we are ready to hear, God will speak.

"Whom Shall I Send, and Who Will Go for Us?"

Then I heard the voice of the Lord saying: Who should I send? Who will go for Us? I said: Here I am. Send me. (Isa 6:8)

In 739 BC the Lord saw the nation of Israel and He saw what Isaiah saw. He saw the sin, the spiritual charades, the cancerous corruption, the religion without relationship. Like Isaiah it broke His heart.

The Lord sees the needs of our world today, and it breaks His heart. When He looks at America, He sees the third largest unchurched nation in the world. He sees more than 300 million people, most of whom desperately need Jesus. He sees a nation addicted to pornography and gambling. He sees a nation that no longer takes the sanctity of marriage or the sanctity of human life seriously, and it breaks His heart. So He cries out, "Who should I send? Who will go for Us?"

Just as the angels are perpetually crying out, "Holy, holy, holy" because they cannot help it, God is constantly crying out, "Who will go?" because He cannot help it. God is everlastingly looking for people who will go to the ends of the earth until the end of the age telling all peoples the gospel.

We must never lose sight of the fact that our God is a sending God. Jesus was a cross-cultural missionary who was *sent* from heaven to earth. The last prayer Jesus prayed in the garden of Gethsemene was a *sending* prayer.

I am not praying that You take them out of the world but that You protect them from the evil one. They are not of the world, as I am not of the world. Sanctify them by the truth; Your word is truth. As You sent Me into the world, I also have **sent** them into the world. (John 17:15–18, bold added for emphasis)

"Here I Am. Send Me."

When you read Isaiah's story, you read about God, angels, and Isaiah. Apart from Isaiah, no other humans are mentioned as being in the room. As far as Isaiah was concerned, the only human in the throne room on that day in 739 BC was Isaiah. God looked around the room, and His eyes settled on Isaiah.

When God asked, "Who should I send? Who will go for Us?" Isaiah assumed that the Lord was speaking directly to him. Rather than argue, excuse, or rationalize, Isaiah responded immediately. "I said: Here I am. Send me" (Isa 6:8).

Isaiah already had a burden. He already had a passion. He was just waiting for his calling. When it came, he responded, "Here I am. Send me."

When Isaiah said the words, "Here I am," he was making a total commitment. He was literally saying, "Lord, here, take all of me. Here is my past, my present, and my future. I give you all of me—my dreams, my hopes, my aspirations. Here I am. Send me. I am available. Use me. Send me to turn Judah back to You. Send me to my people. Send me."

God did not hesitate.

"Go and Tell"

And He replied: **Go! Say** to these people: Keep listening, but do not understand; keep looking, but do not perceive. (Isa 6:9, bold added for emphasis)

Just as the angels are perpetually crying out "Holy, holy, holy" because they cannot help it, God is constantly searching for those of us who will "go" and tell others about Him because He wants everyone to know Him.

God pours out His favor and power on those who are willing to go. You cannot truly be a follower of Jesus until you are willing to go. You are not truly *following* Jesus until you are intentionally *going* for Jesus.

Isaiah is not the only one God told to "go." Seven hundred years later, Jesus encountered a creepy, demonized man who lived in the cemetery. Jesus delivered the man from the demons, and the fellow wanted to travel with Jesus and the disciples. But Jesus gave him a higher calling.

> But He would not let him; instead, He told him, "**Go** back home to your own people, and **report** to them how much the Lord has done for you and how He has had mercy on you." (Mark 5:19, bold added for emphasis)

The last words Jesus gave His disciples of that age and all ages were essentially the same words God had given Isaiah—go and tell.

> Then He said to them, "**Go** into all the world and preach the gospel to the whole creation." (Mark 16:15, bold added for emphasis)

> **Go**, therefore, and make disciples of all nations, baptizing them in the name of the Father and of the Son and of the Holy Spirit. (Matt 28:19, bold added for emphasis)

We need to hear the voice of God calling us to spend our lives going and telling people about Jesus. For some of you that will mean going across oceans to share the gospel with those who worship other gods such as the Hindus, Muslims, and Buddhists. Others will respond to the call to *go and tell* by going to a South American tribe and translating the gospel into their language. Others will plant a new church in the inner city or on a secular college campus. But all of us must be willing to spend our lives going and telling people about Jesus.

Going to the ends of the earth often begins by going across the street. It is getting up every morning praying, "Here I am. Send *me*." Yes we should send our money. Yes we should send our prayers. But most importantly we need to send *ourselves*. We must say, "Here I am. Send *me*."

"Send Me Today"

Imagine what could happen if you woke up every morning saying, "Here I am. Send me." You would be amazed at how the Lord will use you.

When I was finishing seminary, I was serving as the campus pastor of Liberty University. I woke up one day just like every other day. I read Isaiah 6 and briefly prayed about the day. The only thing out of the ordinary was that I did something I had done on only a few other occasions. I happened specifically to pray the "send me" prayer. I told God to send me to make a difference in someone's life for His sake. Then I forgot about it and went off to work.

All morning long I had a gnawing thought. "I need a haircut. I ought to go to the mall and get a haircut." But I argued with myself, "I am a thrifty (some might even say cheap) person. I have never gone to the salon in the mall for a haircut before. I usually save money by having some student do it for a few bucks." But over and over I kept getting the thought that I needed to go to the mall to get a haircut.

Just before lunch I remembered that I had prayed the "send me" prayer that morning. It hit me like a thunderbolt, "It must be God!" I realized. "But why is He sending me to the mall? What could He want me to do for Him by getting a haircut?"

Yet when the thought immediately returned, "Go to the mall for a haircut," I got up, grabbed my coat, and headed for my car. I must confess that I was grumbling as I drove the short distance to the mall. "I wonder how much this haircut is going to cost? How will I explain to Cathy my sudden urge for extravagance? Why would God want me to go to the mall? This was not a very glamorous assignment."

I walked into the hair salon and was given the only open chair. A wild-looking young lady put a sheet around my neck and asked me how I wanted my hair cut. Then we engaged in small talk. As we did, she asked me where I worked.

"I am the campus pastor of Liberty University."

"Oh my God!" she gasped. (I became worried at this point because she was holding scissors and I was unarmed).

"I don't believe this!" she said, as she started to cry. "This morning as I got ready for work, I told God I would give Him one last chance. If He did not send me a Christian to talk to today, I was going to end it all tonight." I guess this assignment was worth it after all!

What Now?

Get alone with God. Tell Him that you will go anywhere He wants you to go, do anything He asks you to do, and be anything He wants you to be.

Ministry Is . . .

1. Getting a fresh vision of God.
2. Coming clean before God so we can hear His voice.
3. Responding to His call.
4. Living a life of saying and praying, "Here am I. Send me."

⪎ Quotes ⪏

Here I am, Lord. Send me to the ends
of the earth, send me to the rough, the savage
pagans of the wilderness. Send me to all . . . from
all that is called comfort on earth. Send me even to death
itself if it but be in Thy service and in Thy Kingdom.

—HENRY MARTYN[2]

Spiritual Leadership is not an occupation. It is a calling.

—HENRY AND RICHARD BLACKABY[3]

Whether I hear God's call or not depends on the
condition of my ears, and exactly what I hear depends
upon my spiritual attitude. If we will allow the Holy
Spirit to bring us face to face with God, we too will hear
what Isaiah heard— "the voice of the Lord." In perfect
freedom we too will say, "Here am I! Send me."

—OSWALD CHAMBERS[4]

We take our own spiritual consecration and try to make
it into a call of God, but when we get right with Him He
brushes all this aside. Then He gives us a tremendous,
riveting pain to fasten our attention on something
that we never even dreamed could be His call for us.
And for one radiant, flashing moment we see His purpose,
and we say, "Here am I! Send me." (Isa 6:8)

—OSWALD CHAMBERS[5]

It is a good thing to be controlled by a holy ambition.
Are you controlled by a holy ambition? I am calling
it "holy" because its aim is holy—to see people from
all the nations who have never heard of Jesus believe
in him and become obedient to him and be saved
by him from their sin and from God's wrath.

—JOHN PIPER[6]

Notes

1. R. Floyd, *10 Things Every Minister Needs to Know* (Green Forest, AR: New Leaf Press, 2006), 19.

2. H. Martyn, missionary to India, quoted by John MacArthur in the sermon, "Celebrating a Consecrated Church, Part 1," Grace to You, http://www.gty.org/Resources/Sermons/2018.

3. H. and R. Blackaby, *Spiritual Leadership* (Nashville, TN: B&H Publishing Group, 2002), xi.

4. O. Chambers, *My Utmost for His Highest* (Burns, TN: Discovery House Publishers, 1963), January 4 entry, 4.

5. Ibid., September 30 entry, 274.

6. J. Piper "Holy Ambition: To Preach Where Christ Has Not Been Named," August 27, 2006, http://www.desiringgod.org/ResourceLibrary/Sermons/ByTopic/4/1790_Holy_Ambition_To_Preach_Where_Christ_Has_Not_Been_Named.

12

Responding to the Call of God

Dave Earley

Do not enter the ministry if you can help it.
— C. H. SPURGEON[1]

Have you ever experienced the clear, unmistakable call of God? It can change everything. Several times in my life I have heard the clear, undeniable call of God. Have you?

The Call to Salvation

The first time I heard the call of God, I did not know what it was. I was sitting in church as a seven-year-old. The pastor was preaching the gospel, and for the first time in my life, I came under conviction of my sin and sensed God speaking to me. But being unfamiliar with such things, I was terrified. In fact I was so shaken up that I jumped up in the middle of the sermon and ran out the back of the church into the parking lot, sat in the car, and waited for the service to let out.

Unfortunately no one followed up by asking me why I had left so suddenly. So the event was soon forgotten.

Fortunately, God extended the call to salvation to me a second time. I was almost 10 years old. I was again sitting in church, and the pastor was again preaching the gospel. He told of the sinless life, the horrible death, and the glorious resurrection of Jesus Christ for our sins. Again I came under the conviction of my sin and sensed God calling me to Himself. This time I anxiously waited until the end of the sermon. Then I ran up to the front of the church and gave my life to Christ.

The Call to Ministry as a Vocation

I spent most of my middle school years and early high school years running from God. I found myself doing all the wrong things with all the wrong people. On one occasion, in the fall of my sophomore year, my drinking had gotten me in an especially embarrassing situation. This was the last straw in my mind. I had gotten so low that I did not want to continue living. One night I sat on the edge of my bed with a bottle of homemade wine and a handful of pills. I was going to take my life. I wanted to fall asleep and never wake up again.

Then a thought ran through my head, *Don't do it.* That was it. But it was enough. So I didn't. Yet, I did continue to run from God.

Eventually the Lord caught up to me. Even though I was not really living for God, I was still expected to go to church. On Sunday morning I was heading into the balcony of our church so I could hide in the back and sleep during the sermon, as I always did. On this particular day an usher handed me a bulletin on the way in, and I happened to glance at it. On it were these words: "Christian commitment is giving all you know of yourself to all you know of God."

Immediately the thought hit me, *I can do that.* I knew that in my own strength I could not live for Christ. I had tried that a few times and had failed miserably. I knew that I did not have my act together and that I was not perfect. But I could give God all of me. If He wanted me, He could have me.

I was leery of making some sort of emotional decision I would never keep. So I waited until that night. In the same bedroom, sitting in the same place where I had wanted to take my life a year earlier, I gave my life completely to Jesus. For the first time in years, I had a good night's sleep.

The next week I was so full of joy that people asked me, "Dave, what are you high on?" I was high on Jesus and did not care what anyone thought. God began to use me as I worked with a couple of committed Christian guys from my church. By the beginning of my senior year, we had more than 100 students coming to Bible studies we held at our large public high school. We were leading many kids to Christ and many back into a real relationship with God. I found that I loved serving Jesus.

The summer between my senior year and college, I went with our youth group on a choir tour. We sang in a different church each night for a couple of weeks, and I gave my testimony. I also used the rest of the time to minister to the younger kids who were in the choir. Serving Jesus all day long was so fulfilling.

After the tour I was at home taking a bath and praying for some of the kids in my high school.

"I want you," a voice broke my concentration.

"What?" I asked startled. Looking around and seeing no one, I asked, "Who is that?"

"I want you," the voice repeated.

Then I knew immediately who it was and what He wanted. It was the voice of God calling me into full-time vocational ministry.

That night at a church league softball game, I spoke with my youth pastor. "I know this is really crazy, but do you think that maybe God might possibly, one day in the future, actually use me in the ministry like as a youth pastor or something like that?" I was afraid that he would laugh. He didn't.

"Dave, I have been praying for you regarding that very thing," he said solemnly. "I think God has His hand on you and wants you in the ministry."

The Call to a Specific Ministry

I attended a Christian college and took in everything like a sponge. I knew I was called to ministry, but I did not know what ministry I was called to do. I spent a summer as a missionary in England and enjoyed it, but that was not it. I started a man-to-man disciple-making ministry on campus, but I knew that was not exactly it either.

I was studying youth ministry in college, and that opened the door for me to spend the next summer traveling around the United States as a youth evangelist helping lead evening crusade meetings in a different church each evening. Many were new churches meeting in rented buildings and schools that were struggling to attract members.

We had started in New York and had preached our way to Idaho. One afternoon as I waited for the evening service, I was sitting on the steps of a church in Lewistown, Idaho. I had raided the pastor's bookshelves and was reading a book about Bible characters. One of the books referred to Elijah passing his ministry mantle to Elisha. In the book the author told the story of how God "called him to preach." As I read his story, it happened again.

"I want you." It was that voice again.

"Are you sure?" I asked.

"Yes, I want you," God quietly repeated.

I knew immediately who was speaking and what was expected of me. The voice of God was calling me to be a senior pastor and start a church.

"I humbly accept," I said. "But I need You to give me the right town, the right team, and the right time." I prayed over those three requests—town, team, and time—every day for the next six years. Little by little God answered, and six years after that day in Idaho, a new church was planted in Gahanna, a suburb of Columbus, Ohio, with a team of nine graduates from my school, Liberty University.

What Is the Call to Ministry?

It is helpful to think of a calling as "a compelling invitation." The call to salvation is the compelling invitation to trust Jesus Christ as your Savior. The call to ministry is a compelling invitation to cooperate with God in advancing His kingdom and building His church as a vocational pursuit. A specific ministry call is a compelling invitation to cooperate with God in ministering in a specific way (global missions, church planting, preaching, leading worship, writing), or in a specific place (a city, a region, a country, or a people group), or to a specific group of people (such as children, teens, college students, or Muslims).

On rare occasions a person may receive all three calls at once. But usually the calls are separate and spaced out somewhat in time.

A calling is different from a career choice. A career is what you're paid to do, but a calling is what you're *made* to do. Understanding the difference between the two can make all the difference between fulfillment and frustration.

The dictionary defines calling in this way: "a strong inner impulse toward a particular course of action especially when accompanied by conviction of divine influence."[2] James George is more detailed in his definition of the pastoral calling. He writes, "The call of God to vocational ministry is different from God's call to salvation and His call to service issued to all Christians. It is a call to select men to serve as leaders in the church."[3]

Professor James Bryant and Pastor Mac Brunson state, "As much as anything, answering God's call is a step of faith. It is like enlisting in the army, you put your life and future in someone else's hands."[4] Gordon MacDonald adds, "Once you are called, financial security, location, notoriety, applause, and power become increasingly less important. *Obedience* becomes the primary issue. Let others feel free to build fortunes and empires; the call binds you to surrender to the will of God."[5]

I define and describe the call to church ministry as an inner conviction from God confirmed by the church, verified by giftedness, supported by results. It is an unmistakable sense that I have been summoned by the Lord to lifelong vocational service in building His Church on planet Earth.

Professor Keith Drury writes, "While the call may come in a variety of ways, the results are always the same; I become inwardly convinced that God is calling *me*."[6] Drury reminds us that the initial use of the concept of calling was tied to vocational Christian work and that the word *vocation* was only used to describe church ministry. He states that it is for the rest of your life. He clarifies, "While it is true God calls everyone to minister to others, to do what they can to serve those around them, God does not call everyone into professional ministry as a lifetime vocation."[7]

How Does It Occur?

In the beginning of the chapter, I told of three times I have experienced a clear, undeniable call from God. Although no thunder or lightning were involved, each event was rather dramatic. This is not always the case with each of us and the way God calls us. For some the call is dramatic. But for many the call of God is more like a continual dripping. Longtime pastor and author Gordon MacDonald writes:

> For some of us, the call-story is dramatic. In one forceful moment, you gain a sense of conviction that God has spoken and directed. You are never the same again. For others, like myself, the call is like a continual dripping; it just beats on you until you capitulate.[8]

Glenn Wagner's call was more along the lines of a continual dripping. He writes:

> There was for me a constant awareness that God was after me. No matter what I did, I couldn't escape the thought that God said, "You're mine." Right before I turned 21, I surrendered to the Lord, I could not get away from the impression that I was to be a pastor. It was an "F.I.F.," Funny Interior Feeling. It was constantly there. I could not see myself being anything else."[9]

Among our students the calling is mostly a continual dripping. However, among older pastors the call is mostly specific and dramatic. According to research complied by *Christianity Today*, 62 percent of pastors surveyed indicated that calling was defined by specific events, and for 37 percent the call was a gradual process of slow realization.[10]

The Calling and Bible Characters

If we search through the various calls extended to the characters of the Bible, several characteristics become clear.

1. The calling originates from God. God approached them to fulfill a task before they approached Him.

2. The calling was often to a seemingly impossible task: build a giant boat —Noah (Genesis 6); deliver a nation from slavery—Moses (Exodus 3); fill the shoes of a legendary leader—Joshua (Deuteronomy 31; Joshua 1).

3. The calling involves leaving a comfort zone— Moses (Exodus 3); Jeremiah (Jeremiah 1)

4. The calling is accompanied with the promise of God's protection and provision (Exodus 3; Joshua 1; Judges 6).

5. The calling comes to those who are listening—Samuel (1 Sam 3:10); Isaiah (Isa 6).

6. Obeying the calling unleashes our personality –Gideon (Judges 6); Timothy (1 Tim 1:7).

7. A calling may take a long time to be fulfilled—Abraham was called to father nations, but his child did not come until he was 99 years old; Joseph was called to be a leader, but he was in slavery and prison the next 12 or more years; David was called to be king as a teen, but he lived as a fugitive until he was 37.

8. The calling may seem intimidating and hard to understand at first— Ezekiel (Ezekiel 1–2).

9. Running from your calling hurts you and others—Jonah (Jonah 1).

How Do I Know If It Is Legit?

No one should pursue a life of vocational church ministry unless he or she is certain it is what God wants them to do. Several indicators help authenticate such a calling.

Confirmation

When we have been called by God, He usually provides confirmation through the body of Christ, through others, and through circumstances. My youth pastor gave me confirmation as he said that he had seen God's hand on my life and that He thought I would be effective in the Lord's service.

Results

Often the confirmation God gives comes to us through the results He gives. Jerry Falwell was wrestling with the call of God to be a pastor. He had been successfully working in the youth ministry when his senior pastor asked him to preach. Falwell prayed that God would confirm or deny the call through the results of that Sunday's message.

After Jerry's sermon several people responded to his invitation to trust Christ as Savior. One of those coming to be saved was an elderly woman. She told Falwell that, while she had been a member of the church for many years, she had never been saved. That day it became clear to her that she was not saved and needed to be. What the Lord did in her life that day was the confirmation Jerry needed to know that he was indeed called into the pastoral ministry.

Although there have been exceptions, the person with the calling leaves a mark for God. People are touched by God. Lives are impacted. Christians are encouraged, instructed, or motivated. Lost people are drawn to Christ.

Giftedness

With a call comes giftedness. Called people are able to teach effectively. They are good at leading people to Christ. It is obvious that this person has received the God-given ability to serve Him with God-honoring impact and results.

Increased Intensity

If someone is called and is walking with the Lord, the desire to serve the Lord deepens and continually intensifies. Keith Drury writes:

> An authentic call gets stronger not weaker over time. But a call does not grow in clarity all by itself. A call grows clearer as we respond to what we've already sensed . . . Once we begin to respond to God's initial call, He often turns up the volume of His inner voice. . . . Most of us move through several years of this "dance" with God.[11]

The great preacher, pastor, and mentor Charles Spurgeon agrees. He said, "The first sign of a heavenly calling is an intense, all-absorbing desire for the work . . . . I have such a profound respect for this 'fire in the bones,' that if I did not feel it myself, I would leave the ministry at once."[12]

Sense of Completeness, Rightness, and Joy

People can know when they are fulfilling their calling because service in that area is accompanied by great energy and peace. They feel like "this is what God made me to do." It feels right and they feel complete. They can serve all day in that area and not be exhausted. Jeremiah said that obeying his calling and sharing the Word of God brought him great joy (Jer 15:16).

Consuming Conviction

Church ministry is not glamorous. It is not easy. Stepping up to give leadership in a church puts a larger target on our backs for the enemy to attack us. The financial compensation rarely matches the work given. Therefore the advice is often given that when it comes to church ministry, if you can do anything else, then do it.

But those with the calling can do nothing else. They will be inwardly miserable otherwise. They have a consuming conviction and compulsion; they have a driving passion. Those with the calling feel like they cannot do anything else. One church planter wrote, "This thing inside me was so strong, that I had to act on it. I felt if I didn't, I would be violating something . . . or somebody."[13]

What Do I Do Now?

- Let me ask you, have you responded to God's calling to be saved?
- Has God called you to church ministry as a vocation?
- Has He clarified the specifics regarding time, place, people?
- If you are unclear, let me offer some advice. Take extra time alone with God. Tell God, "I need to know if this calling really is from You." Ask Him, "If this calling is from You, please confirm it."
- Let me also recommend what I call a simple prayer to "mess up" your life . . .
  - Lord, I will go where You want me to go.
  - I will do what You want me to do.
  - I will be what You want me to be.
  - I am trusting You.

Ministry Is . . .

1. The only thing you want to do.
2. Responding to the call of God.
3. Saying yes to God's gracious invitation to join Him in advancing His kingdom and building His church.
4. A compulsion to serve God in a church as your full-time vocation.
5. Something inside of you that is so intense you have to act on it.

⮔ Quotes ⮔

The first and foremost of all the inward strengths of a pastor is the conviction, deep as life itself, that God has called him to ministry. If this persuasion is unshakeable, all other elements of the pastor's life will fall into beautiful order and place.

—W. A. CRISWELL[14]

We are not workers for God by our own choice. . . . Never choose to be a worker, but when once God has put His call on you, woe be to you if you turn to the right hand or to the left. God will do with you what He never did with you before the call came. . . . Let Him have His way.

—OSWALD CHAMBERS[15]

Ministry is a supernatural calling . . . not [a] preference. Your calling from God is the only thing that will keep you in it. From time to time, revisit your ministry calling. Revisit it from the day you were first called by God, and then revisit the time God called you to where you are presently serving. The minister who forgets his calling will become ensnared with performance.

—RONNIE FLOYD[16]

We are not professionals. We are fools for Christ's sake. . . .
Professionals are held in honor. We are in disrepute. We do
not try to secure a professional lifestyle, but we are ready to
hunger and thirst and be ill-clad and homeless. When reviled,
we bless; when persecuted, we endure; when slandered, we
try to conciliate; we have become the refuse of the world, the
off-scouring of all things. Or have we?

—JOHN PIPER[17]

Should it not be the office that seeks the man,
rather than the man the office?

—OSWALD SANDERS[18]

Notes

1. C. H. Spurgeon, *Lectures to My Students* (Grand Rapids, MI: Zondervan, 1954), 26.

2. *Webster's Ninth New Collegiate Dictionary* (Springfield, MA: Merriam-Webster, 1986), 198.

3. J. George, "The Call to Pastoral Ministry," in John MacArthur, *Pastoral Ministry* (Nashville, TN: Thomas Nelson, 2005), 81.

4. M. Brunson and J. Bryant, *The New Guidebook for Pastors* (Nashville, TN: B&H Publishing Group, 2007).

5. G. MacDonald, "God's Calling Plan: So What Exactly Is 'A Call to Ministry'?," *Leadership Journal*, Fall 2003, 37.

6. K. Drury, *The Call of a Lifetime* (Indianapolis, IN: Wesleyan Publishing House, 2003), 34.

7. Ibid., 38.

8. MacDonald, "God's Calling Plan," 37.

9. G. Wagner, "Called to What?," *Leadership Journal*, Fall 2003, 26.

10. Research Report on Pastoral Leadership, *Christianity Today*, quoted in *Leadership Journal*, Fall 2003, 26.

11. Drury, *The Call of a Lifetime*, 38.

12. Spurgeon, *Lectures to My Students*, 28.

13. R. Bell, "The Storage Room Meltdown," *Leadership Journal*, Fall 2004, 122.

14. W. A. Criswell, *Criswell's Guidebook for Pastors* (Nashville, TN: B&H Publishing Group, 1980), 345.

15. O. Chambers, *Approved unto God* (Grand Rapids, MI: Discovery House, 1946), 9.

16. R. Floyd, *10 Things Every Minister Should Know* (Green Forest, AR: New Leaf Press, 2006), 38–39.

17. J. Piper, *Brothers, We Are Not Professionals* (Nashville, TN: B&H Publishing Group, 2002), 1.

18. O. Sanders, *Spiritual Leadership* (Chicago, IL: Moody Press, 1967), 11.

13

Living a Life of Prayer

Dave Earley

In spiritual work everything depends upon prayer.

—ANDREW MURRAY[1]

Moses' Top Responsibility

Poor Moses. Imagine the enormous task of trying to lead a motley crew of a million slaves out of four centuries of slavery through a wilderness and into a promised land of their own. Consider the difficulty of establishing them as a nation with their own laws, leaders, and identity. Envision the challenge of bringing them into a relationship centered on God and His law.

Such heavy burdens could easily crush a man. In fact, they were beginning to overwhelm Moses when his father-in-law gave him some inspired advice.

> The next day Moses sat down to judge the people, and they stood around Moses from morning until evening. When Moses' father-in-law saw everything he was doing for them he asked, "What is this thing you're doing for the people? Why are you alone sitting as judge, while all the people stand around you from morning until evening?"
>
> Moses replied to his father-in-law, "Because the people come to me to inquire of God. Whenever they have a dispute, it comes to me, and

I make a decision between one man and another. I teach them God's
statutes and laws." (Exod 18:13–16)

At this point in his ministry, Moses was obviously missing the big picture
and was overly absorbed in the details of the day-to-day grind of ministry.
Fortunately his father-in-law Jethro, an experienced shepherd-rancher, was
there to help.

> "What you're doing is not good," Moses' father-in-law said to him.
> "You will certainly wear out both yourself and these people who are
> with you, because the task is too heavy for you. You can't do it alone."
> (Exod 18:17–18)

Pastoral burnout is a big problem. It not only hurts the pastor but also
disables their family and derails their flock. Too many good leaders burn out
or wear out under the immense weight of spiritual leadership. Research of
25 years ago showed clergy dealing with stress better than most professionals.
However, since 1980, studies in the U.S. show a sharp change. Recent studies
describe an alarming spread of burnout among pastors. One reported three out
of four parish ministers (out of a sample of 11,500) reported severe stress causing "anguish, worry, bewilderment, anger, depression, fear, and alienation."[2]

In a recent Assemblies of God survey, 17 percent of those who responded
said that often they were depressed to the extent it affected their ministry performance. Another 20 percent said they experienced this level of depression
every two or three months.[3]

In the September/October 2000 edition of *Physician* magazine, Dr. Walt
Larimore, vice president of medical outreach at Focus on the Family, along
with Rev. Bill Peel reported that 80 percent of pastors and 84 percent of their
spouses are discouraged or dealing with depression. Forty percent of pastors
and 47 percent of their spouses say they are suffering from burnout. The norm
among men in our country who are experiencing depression at any given time
is about 10 percent. The norm among pastors is 40 percent.[4]

Burnout was exactly where Moses was headed. Instead, God sent him a
much needed counselor, his father-in-law, Jethro. We all need people in our
lives who bring an outside perspective. We need people who will tell us what we
need to hear and not just what we want to hear. We need people like Jethro.

Jethro narrowed Moses responsibilities down to three. See if you can find
them in the verses given below.

"Now listen to me; I will give you some advice, and God be with you. You be the one to represent the people before God and bring their cases to Him. Instruct them about the statutes and laws, and teach them the way to live and what they must do. But you should select from all the people able men, God-fearing, trustworthy, and hating bribes. Place them over the people as officials of thousands, hundreds, fifties, and tens. They should judge the people at all times. Then they can bring you every important case but judge every minor case themselves. In this way you will lighten your load, and they will bear it with you. If you do this, and God so directs you, you will be able to endure, and also all these people will be able to go home satisfied."

Moses listened to his father-in-law and did everything he said. (Exod 18:19–24)

First, Moses was prayerfully to intercede for the people—"represent the people before God and bring their cases to Him" (Exod 18:19). Second, he was practically to teach the Word—"Instruct them about the statutes and laws, and teach them the way to live and what they must do" (Exod 18:20). Third, he was personally to select, train, and deploy layers of leaders to deal directly with the people:

But you should select from all the people able men, God-fearing, trustworthy, and hating bribes. Place them over the people as officials of thousands, hundreds, fifties, and tens. They should judge the people at all times. Then they can bring you every important case but judge every minor case themselves. (Exod 18:21–22)

Notice the results: Moses was able to endure the strain for the next 40 years and the people experienced peace (Exod 18:24). Note also that prayer was one of his top three responsibilities. Observe the fact that of Moses' three primary tasks, prayer was first.

The Apostles' Number-One Duty

In the first century, after the church was launched in Jerusalem, it grew at an incredible rate. Persecution only added fuel to the growing flame. Yet with growth came the inevitable growing pains.

In those days, as the number of the disciples was multiplying, there arose a complaint by the Hellenistic Jews against the Hebraic Jews that their widows were being overlooked in the daily distribution. (Acts 6:1)

The size of their growing congregation overwhelmed the apostles. Plus, the Greek widows were not getting cared for properly. So the apostles evaluated the situation, reevaluated their priorities, and came up with a plan to solve the problem.

> Then the Twelve summoned the whole company of the disciples and said, "It would not be right for us to give up preaching about God to wait on tables. Therefore, brothers, select from among you seven men of good reputation, full of the Spirit and wisdom, whom we can appoint to this duty. But we will devote ourselves to prayer and to the preaching ministry." (Acts 6:2–4)

Not unlike Jethro's advice to Moses, instead of trying to do it alone, the apostles delegated some of the work to responsible leaders. Then, just as Jethro had told Moses, they devoted themselves more fully to two priorities—prayer and teaching the Word of God. Note that of the two, prayer was listed first.

Observe that when they followed godly priorities, God blessed the outcome with even greater impact and evangelism. Prayer-first ministry is God-blessed ministry.

> The proposal pleased the whole company. So they chose Stephen, a man full of faith and the Holy Spirit, and Philip, Prochorus, Nicanor, Timon, Parmenas, and Nicolaus, a proselyte from Antioch. They had them stand before the apostles, who prayed and laid their hands on them. So the preaching about God flourished, the number of the disciples in Jerusalem multiplied greatly, and a large group of priests became obedient to the faith. (Acts 6:5–7)

Timothy's Prime Priority

Timothy was a young pastor leading the large and significant church of Ephesus. Ephesus was the strategic hub for church planting and evangelism throughout the region. Timothy had the heavy responsibility of following the legendary apostle, Paul, as pastor. In over his head, he needed help. So his mentor Paul wrote him two letters of advice. Like Jethro, Paul encouraged him to train and appoint godly leaders (1 Tim 3:1–13; 2 Tim 2:2). Paul also reminded him to value, study, and teach the Word (1 Tim 4:6; 2 Tim 3:15–16; 4:2).

Yet, Paul gave the young pastor one priority to honor above all the others.

First of all, then, I urge that petitions, prayers, intercessions, and thanksgivings be made for everyone, for kings and all those who are in authority, so that we may lead a tranquil and quiet life in all godliness and dignity. . . . Therefore I want the men in every place to pray, lifting up holy hands without anger or argument. (1 Tim 2:1–2,8)

Just as Jethro told Moses to pray first, just as the apostles decided to devote themselves to prayer first, Paul's advice to Timothy was to pray first—"First of all, then, I urge that petitions, prayers, intercessions, and thanksgivings be made for everyone" (1 Tim 2:1). When Paul said, "first of all," he used the term prōton, which means first in chronology *and* in priority, first in time *and* in rank. In other words, Paul told Timothy to pray first, pray most, pray above all else; and if you don't do anything else, pray. Pray every way you know how, for everyone you know. Prayer was to be priority number one!

Jesus, Son of God, Man of Prayer

Jesus Christ is the divine son of God. He is fully God, but He is also fully man. As a minister, Jesus was an amazing man of prayer. S. D. Gordon summarizes the prayer life of the leader, Jesus, well when he writes, "The *man* Christ Jesus *prayed*; prayed *much*; *needed* to pray; *loved* to pray."[5] He added, "Jesus prayed. He loved to pray. . . . He prayed so much and so often that it became a part of His life. It became to Him like breathing—involuntary."[6] E. M. Bounds concurs, "Prayer filled the life of our Lord while on earth. . . . Nothing is more conspicuous in the life of our Lord than prayer."[7]

Yes, I have heard the argument that we cannot pray like Jesus did because He was the Son of God. But that is the point. If Jesus Christ, the Son of God, needed to pray, *how much more* do you and I?

In the Gospels are 15 accounts of Jesus praying. Eleven are found in Luke's Gospel. Why? The answer is that of the four Gospel writers, Luke focused most on the *human* aspect of Jesus. Luke wanted us to see that as a *human* leader, Jesus lived a life of prayer. Jesus was fully God *and* fully man. If Jesus, the human, made time to pray, how much more should you and I?

Not Enough Prayer

I have trained pastors, missionaries, church staffs, and small-group leaders all over the nation and in many parts of the world. When we discuss prayer, all will nod their heads and agree that prayer is important. Yet too often North

American Christian leaders are guilty of doing nearly everything else but pray. One survey said the average pastor prays only seven minutes a day![8] Another said that 80 percent of pastors surveyed spend less than 15 minutes a day in prayer.[9]

The most generous survey said that pastors pray all of 37 minutes a day. But it also showed that only 16 percent of Protestant ministers across the country are satisfied with their personal prayer life. This survey stated that a disheartening 21 percent typically spend 15 minutes or less per day in prayer.[10]

I am not sure which survey is most accurate, but at any rate they all tell us the same thing. Most pastors pray too little. No wonder so many pastors are discouraged. No wonder so many will burn out. No wonder so many quit.

Church growth experts have stated that 85 percent of the churches in America are declining. Of the 15 percent that are growing, only 1 percent is growing through conversion growth.[11] Isn't it entirely possible that our ineffectiveness in prayer can be traced to our lack of prayer?

All other factors being equal, the difference between effective and ineffective spiritual leaders is prayer. As you evaluate your leadership quotient, be careful not to neglect prayer. If you want to maximize your impact, prioritize your prayer life. Effective spiritual leaders value the power of prayer.

Prayer: The Common Denominator

A few years ago I completed a study of 75 of the most influential Christian leaders in history.[12] It spanned from Abraham to Billy Graham. A study of the truly great spiritual leaders reveals that their gifts, talents, personalities, backgrounds, educational levels, and social status varied. But they all had one common denominator: they were people of prayer.

Prayer is certainly not the only act of leadership, but it is the indisputable common denominator of spiritual difference-makers in every generation and in any setting. Listen to the voices of renowned authorities in the realm of spiritual leadership.

Henry Blackaby states, "More than any other single thing leaders do, it is their prayer life that will determine their effectiveness."[13] Peter Wagner says, "Great leaders pray!"[14] Charles Swindoll, best-selling author, megachurch pastor, and former president of Dallas Theological Seminary writes, "Prayer, I repeat, is absolutely essential in the life of a leader."[15]

Nineteenth-century Christian leader Andrew Murray said that prayer in the life of the leader should be regarded "as the highest part of the work entrusted to us, the root and strength of all other work. . . . there is nothing we need to study and practice as the art of praying alright."[16]

J. C. Ryle, another well-known nineteenth-century Christian leader, writes:

> I have read the lives of many eminent Christians who have been on earth since Bible days. Some of them, I see, were rich, and some poor. Some were learned, some unlearned . . . some were Calvinists, and some were Arminians. . . . But one thing, I see, they all had in common. They all had been men of prayer."[17]

E. M. Bounds, who spent the last 17 years of his life locked away given to studying, writing, and practicing prayer writes, "Great praying is the sign of God's great leaders."[18] He was right.

Too Busy Not to Pray

Everyone is busy, especially leaders. There is always another meeting to attend, another person to see, another event to plan. We never seem to have enough time. To think we are too busy to pray shows a failure to understand that prayer actually saves time and effort.

Prayer allows God to do more in days, hours, minutes, or even seconds than we could accomplish without Him in months, or even years, of work. How often we have taught, encouraged, and counseled people with little or no result? How often have we shared our faith with seemingly little or no breakthrough in the other person's defenses? But, when God moves, He helps people make changes in seconds that we could not get them to do in years. Prayer is a powerful time-saver. Once we understand this principle, we will learn to say, "I am too busy not to pray."

Charles Spurgeon, the incredibly successful and busy English pastor, agreed. When preaching on the subject of prayer, he observed:

> Sometimes we think we are too busy to pray. That also is a great mistake, for praying is a saving of time. . . . God can multiply our ability to make use of time. If we give the Lord his due, we shall have enough for all necessary purposes. In this matter seek first the kingdom of God and his righteousness, and all these things shall be added to you. Your other engagements will run smoothly if you do not forget your engagement with God.[19]

"Praying is a saving of time." Do you view prayer in that fashion?

Martin Luther towers as a giant in church history. The highly active and influential pastor, professor, author, and father of the Protestant Reformation understood the power of prayer to save time and effort. When asked of his plans for the coming week, Martin Luther mentioned that he generally spent two hours a day in prayer, but his coming week was extra busy. Therefore, he said, "Work, work from early till late. In fact I have so much to do that I shall spend the first three hours in prayer."[20]

Three hours in prayer on a busy day!

The average pastor may spend three hours in prayer during a leisurely week!

Maybe Martin Luther understood something we need to grasp. Time spent praying can be the best time-saving device we have.

Now What?

If you hope to minister well, you must pray well. If you want to reach your maximum effectiveness as a Christian leader, you must spend more time in prayer. Let me give you several suggestions for enhancing your prayer life.

1. Remind yourself of the value and power of prayer.
2. Determine a *time* or *times* when you will pray each day.
3. Decide on the amount of time you plan to spend praying each day.
4. Choice a *place* or *places* to have your prayer times.
5. Do it!

Ministry Is . . .

1. Doing spiritual work by spiritual means.
2. Making prayer your number-one priority.
3. Refusing to think that you are too busy to pray.
4. Making and taking time to pray.

≈ Quotes ≈

In spiritual work everything depends upon prayer.
—ANDREW MURRAY[21]

Prayer is the key that unlocks all the storehouses of God's infinite grace and power. All that God is and all that God does is at the disposal of prayer. But we must use the key. Prayer can do anything God can do, and as God can do anything, prayer is omnipotent.
—R. A. TORREY[22]

God will do nothing on earth, except in answer to believing prayer.
—JOHN WESLEY[23]

Words fail to explain how necessary prayer is . . . while God never slumbers or sleeps He is inactive, as if forgetting us, when He sees us idle and mute.
—JOHN CALVIN[24]

Prayer is the most important thing a pastor has to do every day. . . . You can't succeed without it.
—STAN TOLER[25]

Notes

1. A. Murray, *The Prayer Life* (Springdale, PA: Whitaker House, 1981), 8.

2. Quoted in S. Daniel and M. Rogers, "Burn-out and the Pastorate," *Journal of Psychology and Theology* 9, no. 3 (Fall 1981): 232–49.

3. "Coming Out of the Dark: Two Pastors' Journey Out of Depression," W. I. Goodall and E. G. Wagner, *Enrichment Journal*, http://enrichmentjournal. ag.org/200603/200603_040_journey_pastors.cfm.

4. As quoted by Dustin Benge, "A Dirty Little Secret: Pastoral Depression," http://pastorandpeople.wordpress.com/2007/08/28/a-dirty-little-secret-%E2%80%93-pastoral-depression.

5. S. D. Gordon, *Quiet Talks on Prayer* (Grand Rapids, MI: Baker Book House, 1980), 209.

6. Ibid.

7. E. M. Bounds, *The Reality of Prayer* (Grand Rapids, MI: Baker Book House, 1978), 69, 73.

8. W. Brehm, "Why Should We Pray? Be Ready!" http://www.beready.org/whypray.html.

9. "Statistics About Pastors," Maranathalife.com, http://www.maranathalife.com/lifeline/stats.htm.

10. "Study shows only 16% of Protestant ministers are very satisfied with their personal prayer lives," Ellison Research, http://www.ellisonresearch.com/ERPS%20II/release_16_prayer.htm.

11. W. Arn, *The Pastor's Manual for Effective Ministry* (Monrovia, CA: Church Growth, 1988), 41.

12. For more on the subject of prayer in the lives of Christian leaders see D. Earley, *Prayer: The Timeless Secret of High-Impact Leaders* (Chattanooga, TN: AMG Publishers, 2008).

13. H. Blackaby and R. Blackaby, *Spiritual Leadership* (Nashville, TN: B&H Publishing Group, 2001), 151.

14. P. Wagner, in George Barna, gen. ed., *Leaders on Leadership* (Ventura, CA: Regal, 1997), 282, 295.

15. C. Swindoll, *Hand Me Another Brick* (Nashville, TN: Thomas Nelson, 1978), 37.

16. A. Murray, *With Christ in the School of Prayer* (Grand Rapids, MI: Zondervan, 1983), xii.

17. J. C. Ryle, *A Call to Prayer* (Grand Rapids, MI: Baker Book House, 1976), 14–15.

18. E. M. Bounds, *Prayer and Praying Men* (Grand Rapids, MI: Baker, 1997), 13.

19. C. Spurgeon, "Pray Without Ceasing," Metropolitan Tabernacle Pulpit, A Sermon Delivered on Lord's Day Morning, March 10, 1872, http://www.spurgeon.org/sermons/1039.htm.

20. M. Luther as quoted in J. O. Sanders, *Spiritual Leadership* (Chicago, IL: Moody, 1974), 76.

21. A. Murray, *With Christ in the School of Prayer,* 133.

22. R. A. Torrey, *The Power of Prayer* (Grand Rapids, MI: Zondervan, 1924), 17.

23. J. Wesley quoted by P. Wagner in *Prayer Shield* (Ventura, CA: Regal, 1992), 29.

24. J. Calvin, ibid., 29.

25. S. Toler, *Stan Toler's Practical Guide to Pastoral Ministry* (Indianapolis, IN: Wesleyan Publishing House, 2007), 34.

14

Maintaining an Eternal Perspective

Dave Earley

2,000 pastors quit the ministry every month,
never to return.
— GLOBAL PASTORS NETWORK, AUGUST 2004 NEWSLETTER

Too many of us start out in ministry highly motivated, full of optimism and energy. But within a few years, we get discouraged and lose heart. We find ourselves either giving in to merely going through the motions or giving up ministry all together.

Why Quit?

In some ways quitting is understandable. The moment we step up to serve and lead, we place a large target on our back. We attract a greater level of enemy attention than ever before. Enemy-induced temptation, accusation, oppression, and frustration will increase when we choose to give our lives to serving Jesus.

Beyond that, we quickly discover that church work is never finished. There seems to be a never-ending line of people to serve, witness to, pray for, disciple, and counsel. Ministry does not fit into a nice nine-to-five, Monday-through-

Friday-box. People need ministry late at night, on weekends, and especially when we try to take a day off.

Authentic ministry has a way of attracting needy, messy, broken people. People are hurting, and when we step up to minister, they flock to us with their needs. If they had it all together, they wouldn't need us. Dealing with problem people and people problems is exhausting.

Many of us in ministry get frustrated because churches are often guilty of giving unclear expectations. We think we are doing a good job of serving effectively, but some are mad at us because we are not doing what they expected us to do.

Some of us are called to be change agents in churches that have struggled to keep up with the culture. Serving as a catalyst for change takes a clear focus, great amounts of energy, a sense of humor, a good support system, and strong inner resolve.

Serving Jesus with passion in the twenty-first century is a continual upstream battle. Culture is flowing strong and fast away from God. Our job is to swim upstream against the flood and bring as many people as possible with us. While initially exhilarating, it quickly wears us down.

Calling people to a life of discipleship can be disappointing. Some of the people we pour our lives into will tube out on serving, church, and even God. Even Jesus had dropouts and disappointments. No wonder people quit.

How Not to Lose Heart

Few of us who are trying to please Jesus by serving in the church will ever face the level of temptation to quit with which the apostle Paul dealt. He endured intense frustration, deprivation, and persecution. Yet he did not quit. He never lost heart.

How did he keep from losing heart in the ministry despite intense difficulties? He lived with an eternal perspective. In 2 Corinthians 4, Paul pulled back the veil to give us a look into his view of ministry. He showed us that ministry is maintaining perspective. He revealed several essentials for maintaining the right perspective.

Be Grateful

Therefore, since we have this ministry, as we have received mercy, we do not give up. (2 Cor 4:1)

"We do not give up." The word translated "give up" is the Greek term for *discouragement*. Ministry has a way of stealing our courage. We become discouraged and want to quit when we feel that we are entitled to more or better. Don't forget that being allowed to minister to others is a gift to be appreciated, not a right to be demanded. We only minister because God is merciful. He allows messed-up, ex-sinners like you and me to have the privilege and honor of serving Him by ministering to His people.

"I quit!"—Several years ago I was on the verge of quitting. I experienced a perfect storm of circumstances that totally devastated me.

Cathy and I had moved 10 other people with us to start a church in a town where none of us knew another living soul. By the grace of God, we had seen God grow the church to more than 400 people in four years. We had run out of places large enough for our church to meet. So the school where we were meeting doubled the price we paid every couple of months. Then they told us we had to be out in a few months. By the grace of God, we had to buy land, finance it ourselves, and build a building. In order to pay for it, I was the general contractor, and we did the lion's share of the work ourselves. Leading a church all day and working on constructing a building every night and all day Saturday wore me down. I was exhausted.

The good news was our new building was overflowing the first Sunday we moved in. The bad news was our new building was full, so soon I was preaching four services every Sunday.

Believing that God would provide, we had added four of the guys who moved with us to the full-time staff at the church. Then seven out of our ten largest givers were transferred, moved, or got mad at me and left. So our giving did not increase, and our attendance began to flatline.

Four of our deacons were transferred hundreds of miles away. Our head deacon, who had pledged his loyalty to me for the rest of our lives, got mad at me and left. I went by his house to take him some books he had lent me and tried to talk to him, but he would not even see me. His wife came to the door and told me to leave the books on the porch. I had to drive by his house everyday on my way to work. His son was my son's best friend. Try explaining to a four-year-old why his best friend would not be at church and would not be coming over to play anymore.

On top of that, one of the original members of our church planting team had an undiagnosed and bizarre bipolar episode. We did not know what was wrong with her or how to help her. She had no family; our church was her family. I was only 31 years old and was already overwhelmed with all that was happening at the church.

Then some of our pastoral team pushed for a change in worship style in order to help people engage in worship more effectively. In one Sunday they switched from piano-led worship with a song leader to a full band and worship team. As the senior pastor it was important that I invest additional energy in helping navigate the church through the challenging waters it faced. Yet I did not have any extra energy.

In the middle of all this, I got a severe case of the flu. I lost 18 pounds in three weeks, which at that time was a huge percentage of my body weight. I began to feel a terrible, steady pain in my joints and muscles. The slightest bit of cold air made it all the worse. I carried around a giant headache that would not go away. Suddenly I was allergic to all sorts of things. My cognitive capacities would sometimes short-circuit as I could see words in my head but had great difficulty getting them to come out of my mouth. (This is not a good thing if you are a pastor.) I could not sleep for more than a few hours at a time. Strangely, about five o'clock every night I would get a terrible sore throat.

Yet none of that could compare with the crushing fatigue. I felt like I was wearing cement and trying to run underwater. I woke up exhausted and stayed exhausted all day long. I had been a varsity athlete in college, yet at one point I was so weak the only thing I could do all day was crawl down the hall to the bathroom. It was so frustrating.

On top of that, my three boys were all under the age of five. They just could not understand why I could not play with them like I used to.

But worse than that was the awful guilt I felt. With three little boys my wife really needed me to help out around the house and with the children. Yet it was all I could do to take care of myself and try to keep working. I hated to see that my exhaustion was wearing her out.

Eventually I was diagnosed with chronic fatigue immune deficiency syndrome—CFIDS for short. (My male ego was hurt when I found out that it is an illness contracted most frequently by overachieving females.) CFIDS at that time was an illness few people understood and doctors were at a loss to treat.

I was frustrated from being the slave of my pain and fatigue. I was frustrated because I was a goal-oriented person who was now unable to pursue any goal other than survival. I was frustrated because when I was home I did not have the strength to get off the couch to play with my boys. I was frustrated because my fatigue was exhausting my wife.

I was not only on the verge of quitting the ministry; I was on the verge of quitting life itself. Every night about nine o'clock, I felt like a wall of depression fell on me like a ton of bricks. Cathy would ask, "Can I get you anything?" I found myself saying, "Yes, bring me a gun. I want to put everyone out of their misery." This morbid scene played itself out night after night.

Get thankful and get going. One day I got a card from my mom. She is in heaven now, but at 4 feet 11 inches she had become a gigantic woman of God late in life. For most of her life, she battled a plethora of physical ailments. In the card she basically said, "Feeling sorry for yourself will do you no good. Get thankful and get going." God smote me.

I put myself on a one-month fast from any type of prayer other than thanksgiving. After about 10 days the cloud of depression began to lift, and by three weeks it was gone. Interestingly, as I began to be grateful, I began to feel better.

Being in ministry is a privilege. Actually, just being alive is a privilege. Paul endured in ministry because he had no sense of entitlement. He was grateful for the privilege of serving Jesus in ministry. He maintained his perspective and was grateful for the opportunity to be in ministry. Enduring ministry is the result of maintaining a perspective of gratitude.

Keep It Real

> Instead, we have renounced shameful secret things, not walking in deceit or distorting God's message, but in God's sight we commend ourselves to every person's conscience by an open display of the truth. (2 Cor 4:2)

Paul maintained his perspective and endured in ministry because he refused to play games. He kept it open and authentic. He was transparent and real. I like the way Eugene Petersen renders this passage in his translation.

> We refuse to wear masks and play games. We don't maneuver and manipulate behind the scenes. And we don't twist God's Word to suit ourselves. Rather, we keep everything we do and say out in the open, the whole truth on display, so that those who want to can see and judge for themselves in the presence of God. (2 Cor 4:2 *The Message*)

Some people put on a ministry mask. It is easy to do. When we get hurt or disappointed, we put on the mask to cover our true inner feelings when we relate to others. Unfortunately, it takes a great deal of energy to keep the persona polished and clean. Wearing one makes you appear artificial or fake.

In order to endure in ministry, we must maintain authenticity. We should invest our time and effort into being our best selves as opposed to trying to be someone we are not. Enduring ministry is the result of maintaining a perspective of authenticity.

Reflect Christ, Not Self

> For we are not proclaiming ourselves but Jesus Christ as Lord, and ourselves as your slaves because of Jesus. For God, who said, "Light shall shine out of darkness"—He has shone in our hearts to give the light of the knowledge of God's glory in the face of Jesus Christ. Now we have this treasure in clay jars, so that this extraordinary power may be from God and not from us. (2 Cor 4:5–7)

Paul was a gifted scholar, a great leader, and an incredible author. He had amazing abilities, powerful gifts, and a strong personality. If anyone could build a ministry on himself, it would be Paul. But people who build ministry on themselves always eventually see their ministries crumble.

Paul wisely focused in ministry on Christ, not himself. He astutely noted that the power was in the message, not the messenger. He said that he carried the light of Jesus in the unadorned clay jar of his ordinary life. He wanted no one to confuse God's incomparable power with his.

Paul, of course, is right. I find the most energy in ministry comes when I take God seriously and don't take myself too seriously. You will last in ministry when you learn to accept your shortcomings, admit your mistakes, and laugh at yourself as you place the focus on Christ.

Stay Positive

Paul was battered, confused, spiritually terrorized, knocked down, tried, tortured, mocked, and mutilated in ministry. If most of us endured a fraction of what Paul went through, we would have whined, complained, and given up. But Paul did not lose heart. Why? Check out his perspective on his suffering.

> We are pressured in every way but not crushed; we are perplexed but not in despair; we are persecuted but not abandoned; we are struck down but not destroyed. We always carry the death of Jesus in our body, so that the life of Jesus may also be revealed in our body. For we who live are always given over to death because of Jesus, so that Jesus' life may also be revealed in our mortal flesh. So death works in us, but life in you. And since we have the same spirit of faith in keeping with what is written, I

believed, therefore I spoke, we also believe, and therefore speak, knowing that the One who raised the Lord Jesus will raise us also with Jesus and present us with you. For all this is because of you, so that grace, extended through more and more people, may cause thanksgiving to overflow to God's glory. (2 Cor 4:8–15)

Paul was gifted at seeing the spiritual, the eternal, and the positive in every circumstance. He honestly believed that every detail of his ministry worked to others' advantage and the glory of God. He was convinced that every apparent setback actually produced more and more grace, more and more people, more and more praise! His suffering actually brought him joy because he was able to see how God was using it to multiply his ministry. Therefore, he did not let any setback leave him discouraged.

Paul understood that every time we go through suffering, God gives us a key to unlock another set of hearts. Over the years we can accumulate a priceless ministry key chain.

Through my trials and going through even more pain with people I love, I now have a key to the heart of people with chronic illness, people who have lost loved ones, people bound by addictions, people with mental illness, people with deep depression, people who have been abused, people with prodigal kids, and people who have been betrayed by those they trust. Every one of those keys was painful to earn but is priceless today.

Focus on the Invisible Glory of Eternity

Therefore we do not give up; even though our outer person is being destroyed, our inner person is being renewed day by day. For our momentary light affliction is producing for us an absolutely incomparable eternal weight of glory. So we do not focus on what is seen, but on what is unseen; for what is seen is temporary, but what is unseen is eternal. (2 Cor 4:16–18)

Because he had the right perspective, giving up was not an option or even a consideration for Paul. He saw all of life through the lens of eternity. He looked beyond the outward, the momentary, and the temporary. He was convinced that even though on the outside it often looked like things were falling apart, on the inside God was actively at work. He believed that all the hard times were small potatoes compared to the coming good times. He looked forward to a lavish celebration to come. He looked for and lived for eternity.

What Now? (Eternity Is a *Long* Time)

John Ankerberg illustrates eternity by comparing it to the efforts of a parakeet to move sand. Let's say you commanded a parakeet to pick up a single grain of sand in its beak, fly to the moon, and drop it off. Let's say it takes one million years for the parakeet to get to the moon. He puts the grain of sand down and flies back to earth. It takes a million years for him to get back.

Let's say that the little bird systematically transferred one grain at a time all the sand from the beaches and deserts of all the earth until there was not even one grain of sand left on the earth. If you could add up all of the millions of years it had taken to remove all of the sand from all of those places, eternity would just be beginning.[1]

Eternity is a long time. Live for God. As you serve the Lord, you are making investments that will last forever. Therefore, don't give up! If you could only see it from God's point of view, you would know that ministry will be worth it all.

Ministry Is . . .

1. Maintaining an eternal perspective.
2. Being grateful for the opportunity to serve.
3. Keeping the focus on Christ.
4. Staying positive.

⮞ Quotes ⮜

No other reward could possibly equal the joy that comes from knowing almighty God is pleased with you and what you have done with your life. To sense God's affirmation and pleasure in the present life and to know that he has eternal rewards waiting in the next life is to experience a prize of immeasurable value. No earthly treasure can compare with it.

—HENRY AND RICHARD BLACKABY[2]

One word of encouragement: the Lord rarely lets a pastor
see how much good he is doing. When you feel the most
discouraged, God is probably using you in the greatest way.
Be faithful. God will take care of the rest (1 Cor. 4:2).

—HOWARD SUGDEN AND WARREN WIERSBE[3]

Notes

1. J. Ankerberg, "How Long Is Eternity?" Ankerberg Theological Research Institute, http://www.ankerberg.org/Articles/practical-christianity/PC0101W1.htm (May 15, 2006).

2. H. Blackaby and R. Blackaby, *Spiritual Leadership* (Nashville, TN: B&H Publishing Group, 2001), 266.

3. H. Sugden and W. Wiersbe, *Confident Pastoral Leadership* (Chicago, IL: Moody, 1973), 159–60.

15

Refusing to Coast

Dave Earley

The secret of our success is found in our daily agenda.
—Tag Short[1]

No Coasting!

Cathy and I used to live in central Virginia on the edge of the Blue Ridge Mountains. The first winter we were married, we had an early December storm with extra snow and ice. That evening we were trying to visit some people from my church, and it began to snow again. I was still a fairly inexperienced driver and had to drive up a steep hill to get to their house. Even though it had a custom hatchback and a red racing stripe, the tires on my classic '79 Ford Pinto were nearly bald.

I did not have much momentum when I got to the hill, so I began to spin and stopped about a third of the way up. Then a frightening thing happened. Instead of staying still, we began to slide back down all the way to the bottom. The second time I got a little more speed before I hit the hill. But this time we stopped about two-thirds of the way up. Again we did not stay still. We slid all the way back down to the bottom.

The third time I backed up as far as I could. I floored it. Snow was flying everywhere; and Cathy, with her eyes covered, was praying fervently in the front seat. I determined we would keep moving forward no matter what. Spinning, sliding, twisting, and turning, we slowly made progress. Eventually we made it to the top. There we hit a dry patch and shot past the home of the people we were planning to visit.

That night on the icy hill, I learned two valuable lessons. First, if you are on a slippery slope, don't stop your forward progress. Coasting doesn't cut it. Second, if you live near the mountains, buy snow tires or at least have tires with tread.

Coasting does not cut it. If you try to coast physically, you wake up one day to find yourself overweight and out of shape. Coasting relationally leaves you either dealing with a lot of conflict or all alone. If you try to coast as a parent or spouse, you end up with an empty or broken heart. If you coast on your job, you soon find yourself missing out on receiving promotions and discover that you are no longer getting raises. Eventually they find someone else to do your job. Coasting does not work in any area of life. This is especially true of our spiritual lives. You cannot coast spiritually. You are either going forward or going backward. You are either getting closer to God or getting farther from God.

Effective ministers need to declare themselves to be "No Coasting" people. Instead of simply trying harder, we must learn to train better so we can become all God wants us to be. Instead of spiritual coasting, we must learn to be spiritual climbers who scale new heights with God.

Discipline Yourself

Timothy was a young pastor of the strategic church at Ephesus. His mentor, the apostle Paul, wrote him two letters of encouragement and instruction. Paul wanted Timothy to remember that one key to being a good minister was living a life of disciplined spiritual growth (1 Tim 4:6–15).

Paul told Timothy that if he was to be "a good servant of Christ Jesus" his progress would continue to be made "evident to all." The word *progress* means "pioneer advance into new territory." This requires maximum effort as he would have to give himself entirely to the process. What process?

Notice the phrase "train yourself in godliness." Paul told Timothy that godliness was ultimately the result of disciplined exercise and intentional pursuits. Godliness would not just happen. It is not a sudden magical, mystical experience for the spiritually elite. Rather godliness is the fruit of a spiritually disciplined life.

The word for train is *gymnazo*. From it we get our word *gymnasium*. At its core it means "go into the gym and sweat." It has been translated as "to exercise vigorously, to train diligently, to discipline." It was used for Olympic athletes who spent their lives training for the competition of the games. So Paul told Timothy that in order to be a good minister, he needed to live the dedicated, disciplined life of a spiritual athlete.

The Greek student will tell you that this phrase, "Train yourself toward godliness," is a present imperative. An imperative is a command. Therefore, to fail to discipline yourself in the direction of godliness is to disobey a command of Scripture. As a present-tense verb, it speaks of an ongoing activity. In other words, *keep* on disciplining yourself; *continue* to train. Training is not a one-time event. It is not a once-a-month activity. It is not a once-a-week event. It is a daily discipline.

The DNA of a Champion

Peter tells his readers that God has already given us everything we need to please God and live godly lives. Beyond that, because we are born again by the Spirit of God, we are partakers of the nature of God. In other words, in Christ we have divine DNA. God has given us the DNA of a champion. But we must make efforts to bring it out.

> His divine power has given us everything required for life and godliness, through the knowledge of Him who called us by His own glory and goodness. By these He has given us very great and precious promises, so that through them you may share in the divine nature, escaping the corruption that is in the world because of evil desires. For this very reason, make every effort to supplement your faith with goodness, goodness with knowledge. (2 Pet 1:3–5)

It is great to have the DNA of a champion. But such an astounding DNA will do us no good unless we add diligence, determination, and discipline to bring it out. Great talent only yields great achievement when it is linked with great discipline and persistent practice effort.

Imagine having the USA Olympic committee show up at your door. Excitedly they say to you: "Congratulations! We have been looking for someone to run the 26-mile marathon in the next Olympics. We have statistics on every person in the entire nation on computer. We have checked everyone's body type, bone structure, and DNA. We have determined that out of 200 million people, you are the one person in America with a chance to bring home the gold medal in the marathon. So you are on the squad. You will run the race. This is the chance of a lifetime."

While you initially are surprised by this information, you start to get excited. You see yourself in the Olympic stadium bursting across the finish line in world-record time. You imagine your mom in the stands with tears running down her proud face. You picture your face being shown on the television sets of every home in America.

Then it dawns on you. You have never even run 26 miles before, let alone at world-record pace. How can you expect to run a marathon when you get out of breath walking from the couch to the refrigerator? John Ortberg writes:

> If you are serious about seizing this chance of a lifetime, you will
> have to enter into a life of training. You must arrange your life around
> certain practices that will enable you to do what you cannot do now
> by willpower alone. . . . Training is necessary for anyone who wants to
> change deeply and do things exceptionally well. Whether its running
> a marathon, or hitting a golf ball, or playing a musical instrument or
> learning a new language or running a successful business, training is
> required. Trying harder won't get it done. Training is necessary.[2]

Training is necessary. The only way to experience fully the potential of your amazing DNA is to live a life of diligence and disciplehsip. Maybe you are thinking, *I'm not so sure about this. Discipline is so hard.* Yes, discipline is hard, but ultimately living without discipline is harder. Ortberg writes:

> People sometimes think that learning how to play Bach at the keyboard
> by spending years practicing scales and chord progressions is the "hard"
> way. The truth is the other way around. Spending years practicing scales
> is the easy way to learn to play Bach. But imagine sitting down at a grand
> piano in front of a packed concert hall and having never practiced a
> moment in your life. That's the hard way.[3]

Sharpen Your Axe

If I had eight hours to chop down a tree, I'd spend six sharpening my axe. —Abraham Lincoln

The story is told of a young man who was hired to cut down trees as a lumberjack. The more trees he cut down, the more he was paid. Although he had never done it before, he was confident because he was big, strong, in great shape, and willing to work hard.

The first day he got right to work and cut down 10 trees. The next day he went right to work and cut down eight. The third day he was only able to fell six trees. The fourth day his total was four. The fifth day he cut down only three trees. His total for the week was 31. He was discouraged. He had worked just as long and hard each day, yet his total kept declining.

He noticed that during the same week an older, skinnier, yet more experienced lumberjack had dropped nine trees each day for a week-ending total of 45 trees. The new lumberjack approached the experienced one and said, "Let me ask you two questions: First, why were you able to cut down the same number of trees each day and my total kept declining? Second, I got right to work each morning and you didn't. What were you doing?"

The lumberjack smiled and said, "I can answer both questions with one answer. Each morning, I take time to sharpen my axe."

In some ways effective ministry is like cutting down trees. Highly effective leaders know the value of "sharpening their axes." They take time each morning to meet with God in the Word and in prayer. They build times for exercise and reading into their schedules. They don't neglect their families. They watch less TV than other people, play fewer video games, and don't waste time surfing on the Internet because they are joyfully finding fulfillment in their personal growth and development.

Personal Growth Is One Thing You Can Control

Most things are out of our control. About the only thing you can directly improve is yourself. However, when you do improve yourself, everything else within your sphere of influence begins to get better. When you grow yourself as the leader, you allow God to grow your ministry and your people through you. You could say that the key to changing the ministry is changing the minister, the key to improving the ministry is improving the minister, and the key to growing the ministry is growing the minister.

Paul told Timothy, "Train *yourself* in godliness" (1 Tim 4:7). No one else could do it for him. As Christians, we understand that we are not the victims of our environment. What we are is more the product of our decisions than our conditions. God says that we will have to give an account *of ourselves* when we stand before Him (Rom 14:12). No one else is responsible for our personal growth. No one else can grow for us, learn for us, and improve for us. We have to grow, learn, and develop for ourselves.

Highly effective ministry leaders know the value of investing in their personal growth. They intentionally plan to maintain and grow their spiritual lives. They build time into their schedules to help them grow as a leader and as a person.

Intentional Growth Prevents Unintentional Decline

I learned from the icy hill that if you stop going forward, you quickly go back. The same is true of our character, knowledge, and especially our skills. When we stop learning, growing, and developing, we will not remain the same. We will quickly begin to lose ground. Note the attitude of the apostle Paul.

> Not that I have already reached the goal or am already fully mature, but I make every effort to take hold of it because I also have been taken hold of by Christ Jesus. Brothers, I do not consider myself to have taken hold of it. But one thing I do: forgetting what is behind and reaching forward to what is ahead, I pursue as my goal the prize promised by God's heavenly call in Christ Jesus. (Phil 3:12–14)

Think about it. If the apostle Paul, who was probably in his sixties, felt the need to continue to grow, how much more do you and I?

John Maxwell noted that "developing as a leader is a lot like investing successfully in the stock market. If you hope to make a fortune in a day, you are not going to be very successful."[4] He also said, "The learning process is ongoing, a result of self-discipline and perseverance. The goal each day must be to get a little better, to build on the previous day's progress."[5]

The Secret Is in Your Daily Habits and Weekly Plan

Several years ago I began to feel the need to increase all of my levels of personal effectiveness. This included leadership effectiveness, physical health, spiritual capacity, and the quality of my relationship with my wife and sons. I made the choice aggressively to invest time in a more disciplined and challenging personal growth plan that addressed the areas in which I needed to grow.

I made goals to build several daily disciplines into my schedule. Daily I would set aside time either to serve or really listen to my wife. I set a goal to have at least one 30-minute personal prayer time daily and to fast one day a week. I read my Bible daily. I attempted to exercise at least five days a week. I severely limited the time I spent watching TV. We tried to have family devotions four nights a week. I tried to listen to two teaching podcasts a week and read one book a week. Later I added the goal of writing an hour a day.

Sometimes I did not reach all my goals, but by the end of a few months, I could tell the difference. I was making progress in all the key areas of my life. When one area seemed to need to be addressed, I hit it harder the next month.

Over the next few years of being aggressive with my growth plan, I had slowly made big strides in all the key areas of my life. I had read hundreds of books. I had listened to hundreds of hours of Bible teaching or leadership training. I had written 12 books. I had read through the Bible several times. I saw answers to prayer almost every day.

When I got intentional about my personal growth, every part of my life became better, including my ministry. My church doubled in attendance. God multiplied my small group numerous times. I enjoyed life more than ever.

The secret of growth and long-term effectiveness is found in your daily habits and weekly plans. Effective ministry leaders build necessary disciplines in their lives and live those disciplines daily. Personal, spiritual, and professional fitness are like physical fitness. They come from learning the right exercises and doing them regularly until they become habits.

By Failing to Prepare, You Are Preparing to Fail

Benjamin Franklin, one of the founding fathers of the United States, was a leading printer, satirist, political theorist, politician, scientist, inventor, civic activist, statesmen, and diplomat. He also published *Poor Richard's Almanack*. In between each dated calendar page, he sprinkled various bits of wisdom including: "There are no gains, without pains." "One today is worth two tomorrows." "Have you somewhat to do tomorrow, do it today." "Early to bed, and early to rise, makes a man healthy, wealthy, and wise." But most importantly for this discussion, he also noted, "By failing to prepare, you are preparing to fail." If you are serious about reaching your ministry potential you need to have an aggressive growth plan.

1. Set a few growth goals. Start with a few goals that you can work on every day or every week. Make them as simple, yet measurable, as possible. For example, "Read Bible 15 minutes a day," or "Read two chapters a day." Pick goals that address the areas in which you need to grow.

2. Gather necessary tools. You may need some tools to get the maximum benefit from your growth plan. For me the key tool is my notebook/journal with my growth plan chart written into the back pages. I check things off every morning as I read my Bible, pray, and journal. Then I check off yesterday's reading, exercise, and family relationship investments from the previous day. Other tools may be a good Bible, a prayer notebook, exercise clothes or equipment, and books. I have the Bible on CD and now listen to three chapters a day when I drive to work every morning.

3. *Develop a plan that fits you.* Those who are effective in personal growth do not adopt someone else's plan. They prayerfully develop a plan that fits them. Then they adjust their plan each month with new goals and disciplines. As you grow, your goals may grow. As your schedule changes, so must your plan.

4. *Schedule time to grow.* Henry Ford said, "It is my observation that most successful people get ahead in the time other people waste." Growth takes time. Make appointments with yourself to work on your growth plan. Earl Nightingale stated, "If anyone will spend one hour a day on the same subject that person will be an expert on that subject." Try to find an hour or so a day to work on personal growth. This time can include Bible reading, prayer, book reading, and exercise. It can be broken into increments of 10–30 minutes. You may do some of it in the morning and some in the evening.

5. *Get started.* The best time to get started is now. You have to sow in order to reap. If no seed is sown, no harvest will be reaped. You have to sow before you reap. You cannot cram for harvest. You need to plant in the spring, or you will never reap in the fall. Cutting corners and waiting till that last minute just won't work. Start working hard now in order to enjoy the positive results later. Look at the time you spend on personal growth as seeds sown that will one day begin to yield a great multiplying harvest.

SAMPLE GROWTH GOALS

Grow mentally by:

- Reading a _____ a _____.
- Listening to _____ podcast(s) _____.

Developing spiritual fitness by:

- Reading the Bible _____ minutes daily or _____chapters daily.
- Praying _____ minutes daily.
- Journaling _____ minutes daily.

- Leading family devotions _____ minutes a day, _____ days a week.
- Fasting _____ days a month.

Increasing physical fitness by:

- Exercising _____ minutes _____ days a week.
- Sleeping _____ hours a night.
- Eating healthy by: eating less _____ and more _____

Investing in relationships with:

- Disciples _____ minutes a day / hours a week.
- Mentor _____ minutes a day / hours a week.
- Spouse _____ minutes a day / hours a week.
- Children _____ minutes a day / hours a week.
- Other _____ minutes a day / hours a week.

SAMPLE PERSONAL GROWTH PLAN

GOAL	Mon	Tues	Wed	Thurs	Fri	Sat
Bible	2 chapters	2 chapters	1 chapter	0	2 chapters	0
Prayer	30 minutes	30 minutes	20 minutes	30 minutes	10 minutes	0
Journal	X	X	0	X	X	0
Exercise	30 minutes	30 minutes	0	30 minutes	0	20 minutes
Meet w/ Disciple	Josh	Jason		Chad		
Fasting	yes					
Reading	2 chapters	2 chapters	1 chapter	0	2 chapters	0

Ministry Is . . .

1. Refusing to coast.
2. Disciplining yourself for continual growth.
3. Planning to continue to grow and improve.
4. Training better, not merely trying harder.

❧ Quotes ❧

Effective leadership results from hard work and a continuing effort to learn. . . . Leaders grow. They learn. They continue to change until they have the character and walk with God that is required to lead their organization effectively. Leaders who are willing to make the effort will experience the joy and satisfaction of being used by the Lord to make significant difference in their world.

—HENRY AND RICHARD BLACKABY[6]

Leadership develops daily, not in a day.

—JOHN C. MAXWELL[7]

Complacency is a deadly foe of all spiritual growth.

—A. W. TOZER[8]

Notes

1. T. Short, quoted by John C. Maxwell, *The 21 Irrefutable Laws of Leadership* (Nashville, TN: Thomas Nelson, 1998), 2.3.

2. J. Ortberg, *The Life You Have Always Wanted* (Grand Rapids, MI: Zondervan, 2002), 55.

3. Ibid., 56.

4. Maxwell, *The 21 Irrefutable Laws of Leadership*, 23.

5. Ibid., 24.

6. H. Blackaby and R. Blackaby, *Spiritual Leadership* (Nashville, TN: B&H Publishing Group, 2002), 285–86.

7. Maxwell, *The 21 Irrefutable Laws of Leadership*, 21.

8. A. W. Tozer quoted by S. Toler in *Stan Toler's Practical Guide to Pastoral Ministry* (Indianapolis, IN: Wesleyan Publishing House, 2007), 13.

16

Loving People

Dave Earley

"How He Loved Him!"

Jesus is the model minister and master leader. One of the foundational stones and distinguishing marks of His ministry was His obvious love for people. A quick read through the Gospels makes clear that Jesus loved people.

Jesus loved the hurting and hopeless. When He saw the crowds, it broke His heart.

> When He saw the crowds, He felt compassion for them, because they were weary and worn out, like sheep without a shepherd. (Matt 9:36)

Jesus loved spiritual seekers. When Mark described Jesus' dealings with the rich young ruler, Mark noted Jesus' love for the young man. Mark wrote, "Then, looking at him, Jesus loved him" (Mark 10:21).

Jesus also loved His friends. In order to escape the crowds and persecution of Jerusalem, Jesus often retired to the home of Lazarus, Mary, and Martha, located in Bethany on the outskirts of Jerusalem. Lodged in the story of Jesus raising Lazarus from the dead is this observation by the apostle John. Jesus loved His friends.

> Jesus loved Martha, her sister, and Lazarus. . . . When Jesus saw her crying, and the Jews who had come with her crying, He was angry in His spirit and deeply moved. . . . Jesus wept. So the Jews said, "See how He loved him!" (John 11:5,33,35–36)

Jesus loved deeply and it was evident. He was deeply moved. He was angry. He wept or literally burst into tears. Those observing the scene had only one response: "How He loved him!" What a statement. If we hope to be powerful in ministry, we need to be like Jesus. We must be people of evident love.

Jesus' disciples knew that He loved them. For example, even though John was an influential leader among the apostles, in his Gospel he chose never to refer to himself by the name "John." Instead he continually called himself "the disciple Jesus loved" (John 13:23; 19:26; 20:2; 21:7,20).

Jesus repeatedly told His followers that He loved them. His love for them became the basis of His expectations. He was able to command His disciples to be people of love based on the fact that He obviously loved them (see John 15:9–17).

Ministry in its purest sense is loving people. It is taking the love that Jesus has given to us and passing it on to others.

Ministry Runs on the Tracks of Relationships

I thrive on projects. Assign me a project that I like, and I am in heaven. But God called me to ministry. I learned quickly that real ministry runs on the tracks of relationships. If I hope to deeply impact people for Jesus, I must have a good relationship with them. I need continually to grow in my ability to connect with people.

Ronnie Floyd is an effective Christian worker and leader. In his 20 years of ministry in Springdale, Arkansas, Pastor Floyd's church's membership grew from 3,700 to over 16,000 members. The church baptized more than 11,700 persons in those 20 years.

In his book, *10 Things Every Minister Should Know*, he devotes an entire chapter on relationships. He states, "Ministry leadership is all about relationships. . . . Ministry is about people, people, and more people. . . . Influencing people in our generation will come because you have a relationship with them."[1] He warns, "You limit your influence when you do not relate well to people. . . . You limit your influence when you have no interest in people."[2]

John Maxwell has been a successful pastor, speaker, and author. Many of his books on leadership deal with relationships. He says, "Good relationships are more than the icing on the cake in life. They are the cake—the very substance we need to live a successful and fulfilling life."[3]

Understanding how valuable relationships are for a person in ministry cannot be emphasized too strongly. Relationships will make or break you. Learn to be good at relationships, and your life will be blessed and your ministry multiplied.

Ministry Is People

Someone said that ministry would be great if it were not for the people. People can be stubborn, selfish, and lazy. The Bible repeatedly calls the people we minister to "sheep" because sheep are notoriously distracted, stubborn, and helpless. But if we hope to be effective in ministry, we must lovingly shepherd people.

If you are in ministry, you are in the people business. Effective ministry is more than Greek words and theological phrases. It is loving people. Church ministry is not primarily about buildings, budgets, or boards. Effective ministry is about much more than committees and constitutions. Ministry is all about people. Church ministry is not merely a matter of programs and planning. It is people. There is no way to be effective in ministry without loving people.

Without people, a minister has no one to lead. Ministry effectiveness is indelibly linked with our ability to get along with people and to influence them. As the Chinese proverb states, "He who thinks he is leading and no one is following is only taking a walk."

Simply put, if people don't like you, they won't let you lead them or minister to them very long. If you don't effectively love people, you won't be able to influence them positively. If you aren't influencing people, you aren't ministering to them.

"Love One Another"

Jesus wanted His followers to be like Him in their love for people. He listed as the second greatest of all the commands to "love your neighbor as yourself" (Matt 22:38–40). Jesus commanded His followers to love one another:

> "I give you a new commandment: love one another. Just as I have loved you, you must also **love one another**. By this all people will know that you are My disciples, if you have love for one another." (John 13:34–35, bold added for emphasis)

The challenge and the encouragement of this command is that He tells us to love one another *as* Jesus has loved us. This is challenging because He has loved us with an amazingly unconditional, undeniable, unrelenting, unstoppable love.

His love for us is sacrificial and selfless. It always seeks to do what is best for us. It is also the key to leading people effectively.

His command to love one another as Jesus loves us is also encouraging because the bottom line is that we don't have that type of love and never really will on our own. We need to allow the Holy Spirit to produce the fruit of love in our hearts for others as we yield control of our lives to Him.

The command to "love one another" is one that every Christian is to obey. It is repeated throughout the New Testament. John refers to it over half a dozen times (John 15:12,17; 1 John 3,23; 4:7,11–12; 2 John 1:5). Peter and Paul also remind us of this important command (Rom 13:8; 1 Pet 1:22; 4:8).

If every Christian is to love others, how much must we who hope to be ministers love others? Ministry is loving people. But what does it look like to love people?

Love Is an Action

Jesus was a man of love. He personified love in action. At His last meal with the disciples before the crucifixion, Jesus washed their feet because He loved them.

> Before the Passover Festival, Jesus knew that His hour had come to depart from this world to the Father. **Having loved His own** who were in the world, He loved them to the end.
> Now by the time of supper, the Devil had already put it into the heart of Judas, Simon Iscariot's son, to betray Him. Jesus knew that the Father had given everything into His hands, that He had come from God, and that He was going back to God. So He got up from supper, laid aside His robe, took a towel, and tied it around Himself. Next, He poured water into a basin and began to wash His disciples' feet and to dry them with the towel tied around Him. (John 13:1–5, bold added for emphasis)

Notice the active nature of Jesus' love. It is displayed by what He did; He set aside His robe and put on an apron. Then He poured water into a basin and began to wash the disciples' feet, drying them with His apron. Ministry is more than words. It is active love.

Love Is a Choice

In ministry you will encounter many unlovely people. Some will even act like your enemies. No excuse. We still must love them. Jesus commanded His disciples not to only love one another but to love even their enemies.

"But I say to you who listen: **Love your enemies,** do what is good to those who hate you, bless those who curse you, pray for those who mistreat you. If anyone hits you on the cheek, offer the other also. And if anyone takes away your coat, don't hold back your shirt either. Give to everyone who asks from you, and from one who takes away your things, don't ask for them back. (Luke 6:27–30, bold added for emphasis)

Jesus commanded His followers to love their *enemies.* Obviously no one *feels* like loving their enemies. So how can we love them?

We can love our enemies because love is a choice and an action, not a feeling or an emotion. Over and over again in the Bible, God commands us to love one another. You can't command an emotion. If I told you to "be sad!" right now, you couldn't be sad on cue. I guess you could fake it, but you're not wired for your emotions to change on command.

If love were just an emotion, God couldn't command it. But love is a choice. It is something you do. It can produce emotion, but love is an action. Ministry is choosing to love people even if they are unlovely.

Love Is a Skill

Paul was obviously a wise and effective minister. He loved people and prayed for them that they would in turn grow in their love for others.

And may the Lord cause you to increase and **overflow with love** for one another and for everyone, just as we also do for you. (1 Thess 3:12, bold added for emphasis)

Paul prayed for the Thessalonians that their love would "increase and overflow." This is because love is a skill that can be learned. In other words, you can get good at love. You get better at love by *practicing* love. You can become an expert at relationships.

Wouldn't you like to become known as a person of extraordinary love? When people speak of you, they might say: "He doesn't care who you are or what you look like," or, "She doesn't care where you've been or what you've done or where you're from," or, "He is so good at relationships."

The only way you get skilled at something is to practice. You do it over and over. The first time you do it, it feels awkward. But the more you do it, the better you become. The only way to get better at people skills is to practice.

When I was 30 years old, my church staff gave me a hard time because I was such a project person that I often came across as uncaring for people. It hurt my pride, but I determined to work hard on developing my people skills.

The last several years I have been pleased to have people comment that I was "so good with people" and such a "strong relational person."

Love Is a Deposit

> For where your treasure is, there your heart will be also. (Matt 6:21)

Jesus taught us that love is an investment. We invest in what we love and love what we invest in. If our challenge is to love people, the key to loving is investing.

Over the years I have learned the valuable art of relational banking. Relationships can be understood as bank accounts. Realize it or not, you have a relational account with every person within your sphere of influence. Every positive interaction makes a deposit in that account. Every negative dealing with a person creates a withdrawal in your relational account with them.

Billy Hornsby is a highly effective ministry coach for church planters. He says, "The value of a relationship is in proportion to the amount of time you invest in it."[4] Every time we obey God and act in love, we make a deposit into the relationship.

We influence people most easily when there is a positive balance in the relational account. We struggle to influence people when there is little or no equity in the relationship account.

Leaders who practice active love continually place deposits in the relational accounts of others. As a result, they earn the ability to influence them for Christ. Then, when they need to call out a member to make a change or go to a new level of commitment, the member is willing to follow because the leader's continual investments have created a large balance in the relational bank account.

Effective ministers actively love people. They determine to master relational banking. They constantly think of ways to make deposits in the lives of the people around them. They are not only well liked, but they are also easily followed. They understand that effective ministry runs on the train track of healthy relationships and thrives in the atmosphere of positive relational bank accounts.

Love Is Costly

> No one has greater love than this, that someone would lay down his life for his friends. (John 15:13)

Jesus *spoke* of His love for His followers. He actively *served* them. But His love went beyond that. He *gave* His life for them. Effective ministers must love their people with a sacrificial, often costly love.

Moses also was willing to die for his people (Exod 32:30–35). So was the apostle Paul. He was willing to be accursed for his Jewish brethren (Rom 9:1–3).

Paul was a stubborn, fearless, spiritual warrior. He was tough enough to endure extreme deprivation and severe persecution. Paul had incredible natural abilities, spiritual gifts, and spiritual experiences. He had a brilliant mind and a cunning intellect. He worked hard taking the gospel to the least reached people in his world.

There was another reason for his deep and profound impact in the lives of people. Paul impacted people deeply because he loved them profoundly. For example, in corresponding with the Thessalonians, he reminded them of his ministry approach. He told them he was gentle like a nursing mother, diligent like a laborer, and encouraging like a good father—all because he loved them.

> Although we could have been a burden as Christ's apostles, instead we were gentle among you, as a nursing mother nurtures her own children. We cared so much for you that we were pleased to share with you not only the gospel of God but also our own lives, because you had become dear to us. For you remember our labor and hardship, brothers. Working night and day so that we would not burden any of you, we preached God's gospel to you. You are witnesses, and so is God, of how devoutly, righteously, and blamelessly we conducted ourselves with you believers. As you know, like a father with his own children. (1 Thess 2:7–11)

Notice the tender words and phrases that describe his love for them— "gentle," "nurtures," "cared," "dear to us." Notice the words in verse 8: "We were pleased to share with you not only the gospel of God but also our own lives, because you had become dear to us." He tells them he shared more than words with the Thessalonians; he poured out his own life.

This was his approach to everyone he was called to serve. The Corinthians were certainly not easy sheep to shepherd. They repeatedly questioned his authority and rebelled against his leadership. Yet, just as he had with the Thessalonians, Paul had gladly sacrificed on their behalf. He knew that love is costly.

> Look! I am ready to come to you this third time. I will not burden you, for I am not seeking what is yours, but you. For children are not

obligated to save up for their parents, but parents for their children. I will most gladly **spend and be spent** for you. If I love you more, am I to be loved less? (2 Cor 12:14–15, bold added for emphasis)

Paul was a master of relational banking. He was willing to "spend" or invest in the Corinthians. Paul's attitude was that he was willing to do whatever it took. He would empty his pockets or even mortgage his life on their behalf. Even if they gave no love back, he would not stop loving them.

John Henry Jowett noted that "ministry that costs nothing accomplishes nothing."[5] If we hope to have a high-impact ministry, it will take a costly love.

Now What?

List the names of the people in your sphere of ministry. Prayerfully think of ways you can actively invest in your relationships with them this week.

⟡ Quotes ⟡

People. That's what ministry is all about. Serving people. Teaching people. Caring for people the way Jesus did.
—CHARLES SWINDOLL AND GARY MATLACK[6]

All things being equal people will work with people they like: all things not being equal, they still will.
—JOHN C. MAXWELL[7]

Individuals with excellent people skills connect with us easily, make us feel good about ourselves, and lift us to a higher level. Our interaction with them creates a positive experience that makes us want to spend time with them.
—JOHN C. MAXWELL[8]

Love of the brethren is a basic essential in the life of every Christian worker.
—WATCHMAN NEE[9]

Notes

1. R. Floyd, *10 Things Every Minister Needs to Know* (Green Forest, AR: New Leaf Press, 2006), 95–96.

2. Ibid., 97.

3. J. C. Maxwell, *25 Ways to Win with People* (Nashville, TN: Thomas Nelson, 2004), xvii.

4. B. Hornsby, *101 Relationship Rules* (Mt. Pleasant, SC: Billy Hornsby Ministries, 2002), 15.

5. Henry Jowett quoted by D. Wiersbe and W. Wiersbe, *Making Sense of the Ministry* (Chicago, IL: Moody Press, 1983).

6. C. Swindoll and G. Matlack, *Excellence in Ministry* (Fullerton, CA: Insight for Living, 1996), quote taken from back cover.

7. Maxwell, *25 Ways to Win with People*, 239.

8. Ibid., xiii.

9. W. Nee, *The Normal Christian Worker* (Hong Kong: The Church Book Room, 1965), 33.

17 A Life without Compromise

Ben Gutierrez

What is your definition of a "spiritual giant"?—someone who has loads of theological education; a person who has memorized a lot of Scripture verses, a person who prays six hours a day, a pastor with a big church, a woman who has written amazing books?

How would you describe a "man of God" or a "woman of God"? Is it a person who leads many people to Christ regularly or one who lovingly serves the unlovely or is a missionary to the least reached?

One thing is certain, the answers could cover the gamut from education, to years of experience, to describing someone who has earned a specific title and has been ordained as a minister. These are all good characteristics to have said about us, but I don't believe they would parallel God's definition of a spiritual giant or of a man or woman of God.

The Scriptures highlight some fantastic spiritual heroes who performed some miraculous feats of faith. But, according to the Word of God, we can see that spiritual giants are anyone who has developed an *uncompromising* commitment to live according to the truths of the Word of God . . . no matter what. The ones that God said possessed a commendable testimony are a group of unnamed people mentioned at the end of Hebrews 11. They are commended for their uncompromising faith:

> And others experienced mockings and scourgings, as well as bonds and imprisonment. They were stoned, they were sawed in two, they died by the sword, they wandered about in sheepskins, in goatskins, destitute,

afflicted, and mistreated. The world was not worthy of them. They
wandered in deserts, mountains, caves, and holes in the ground.

All these were approved through their faith, but they did not
receive what was promised. (Heb 11:36–39, bold added for emphasis)

Spiritual giants are not necessarily those who involve themselves in magnificent physical battles and glorious miracles. Rather, a spiritual giant is one
who in their own life situation has never wavered from the truth. They have
remained faithful to the call of God no matter how difficult the hardships.

Strong integrity and godly character are essential for long-term effectiveness in ministry. Ministry is the result of living an uncompromising life of
unwavering faith.

I remember asking a Christian leader of a large global ministry his definition of a true man of God. His response reveals how difficult it is to remain
faithful to the Lord in today's culture. He replied, "Any minister who can
remain in the ministry for more than 15 years without falling morally is a true
man of God." Sobering. To him a man of God was determined by the level of
compromise in his life. Even though far more theologically acute definitions
can probably be formed as to what a man of God and spiritual giant is, I have
recognized that when you are in the trenches in the ministry—in the churches,
schools, colleges, ministries—people attribute honor and spirituality to a person who exhibits one major characteristic: an uncompromising life.

The Making of an Uncompromising Minister

Of all the characters displayed in the Bible, none portrays an uncompromising life any more clearly than the prophet Daniel. He lived in a pagan kingdom and served closely under pagan kings. Yet not once did he fudge on any
of God's principles.

His life reveals basic spiritual disciplines that produced in him the stalwart
faith we talk about today. You and I can put these practical commitments into
our lives in order to create uncompromising character.

But first let's look at the final product that most illustrates Daniel's
uncompromising life, the final days of Daniel's life. Then we'll go backward
toward the early days of his life and see how he reached the status of "spiritual
giant."

Daniel in the Lion's Den

First look at one of the most popular Bible stories in the Bible. You likely remember this one from Sunday school—Daniel in the lion's den. Daniel was confronted with the news that a deadly decree had been made. For a period of 30 days, no one was permitted to offer up prayers and worship to any other person other than to the ruler Darius. Daniel's response reveals the uncompromising faith he had in God not to compromise his lifestyle of prayer.

> When Daniel learned that the document had been signed, he went into his house. The windows in its upper room opened toward Jerusalem, and three times a day he got down on his knees, prayed, and gave thanks to his God, just as he had done before. (Dan 6:10)

Notice the words "Daniel learned that the document had been signed." It is not as if Daniel was surprised by being taken into custody by maintaining his faithful prayer life. Rather, he knew what the consequences would be and filtered his actions through his uncompromising faith and determined that his prayers to God should not cease in light of this decree.

As a result Daniel was thrown into a den of ferocious (and hungry) lions.

Fortunately we see how God honored Daniel's great faith and spiritual discipline:

> At the first light of dawn the king got up and hurried to the lions' den. When he reached the den, he cried out in anguish to Daniel. "Daniel, servant of the living God," the king said, "has your God whom you serve continually been able to rescue you from the lions?"
>
> Then Daniel spoke with the king: "May the king live forever. My God sent His angel and shut the lions' mouths. They haven't hurt me, for I was found innocent before Him. Also, I have not committed a crime against you my king."
>
> The king was overjoyed and gave orders to take Daniel out of the den. So Daniel was taken out of the den, uninjured, for he trusted in his God. (Dan 6:19–23)

The final few words capture the essence of an uncompromising minister, "For he trusted in his God." He simply believed that if he did not compromise then God would take care of him. Just like that.

How could a man have such amazing, uncompromising faith? Because by this time in Daniel's life, it had become his *default reaction* to obey God! This level of spirituality didn't just happen. It didn't just become an immediate characteristic of Daniel's life. Daniel took time to reach this level of spirituality. You see, at this point in his life, Daniel is approximately 90 years old!

Remember that it took Daniel a lifetime to reach this "spiritual giant" status. You will experience anxiety and feel that this level of spiritually is unattainable if you begin by comparing yourself to the minister in Daniel 6. To compare yourself to the man in Daniel 6 is likened to being a newlywed and coveting the possessions, status, and accomplishments of your parents who have been married for over 30 years! It is unfair and unrealistic to assume that it could be the norm in every minister's life. Rather, you should focus on what he did in his life in order to develop him to this level in his life.

Two Spiritual Commitments

Daniel had spent his life adhering to two spiritual commitments made early on in his life that produced in him an uncompromising character. If you make the same commitments in your life and ministry, you will develop an uncompromising character that the Lord will commend you for.

1. Begin Now to Create the Pattern of Obedience

Decide *now* and begin cultivating a pattern of obedience so that you will exercise spiritually *before* any temptation comes! Start stringing together acts of obedience now while the temptation to sin is not raging. The sooner the better!

That is exactly what Daniel did in his life. Remember when Daniel was 90 years old and demonstrated an uncompromising life in the face of certain death in the lions' den? Did you notice the final words in Dan 6:10 that telegraphed to us how Daniel became a spiritual giant? Let's read it again:

> When Daniel learned that the document had been signed, he went into his house. The windows in its upper room opened toward Jerusalem, and **three times a day** he got down on his knees, prayed, and gave thanks to his God, just as he had done before. (Dan 6:10, bold added for emphasis)

Daniel had made a commitment to begin a life devoid of compromise at a young age, even as a teenager. When the book bearing his name opens, Daniel was probably about 14 to 16 years old. At this young age Daniel was placed in his first of many major situations in his life where he was tempted to compromise his commitment to our Lord.

Daniel had been captured by the Babylonians along with his friends and family. In custody the pagan rulers attempted to convert the young men to their belief system and culture. They wanted these Hebrew boys to serve later as leaders over their countrymen and cabinet members in the pagan kingdom in which they now lived.

In attempting to break the commitment to their faith in the one true God of Israel, the Babylonians educated them in their customs, language, and literature in hopes it would produce indoctrination in the young men (Dan 1:3–4). Daniel's reply was essentially, "Teach me what you wish, but it will not change what I believe in my heart to be true."

Next they attempted to persuade young Daniel and the others to ignore the teachings and disregard the teachers of their spiritual roots by changing their names (Dan 1:6–7). In their culture names were a meaningful description of their spiritual roots. Yet again it did not negatively affect Daniel. In essence, Daniel replied, "Call me what you wish, but it will not change what I believe in my heart!"

Then they attempted to force Daniel to practice their pagan lifestyle by causing him to identify intimately with the Babylonian culture by fellowshipping and eating the king's choice food (Dan 1:5). By doing this Daniel was called to make a statement of fellowship and agreement with all the king stood for.

Daniel's reply was stronger than the first two attempts. In essence Daniel said, "Now that's going too far, and I will not comply even if it means death for me!" At this young age we see Daniel stood uncompromisingly. As a result he was able to witness how God will honor an uncompromising life!

Daniel, the "spiritual giant" and epitome of an uncompromising minister, began early in his life. He began stringing together a few acts of obedience while he was young. These allowed him uncompromisingly to say no to strong temptation when he became older. He then surrounded himself with good friends who committed not to compromise in their own lives and to sharpen the life of their friend, Daniel. That is how he was able to stand strong at the age of 90 and defy an unbreakable decree of a king and continue to obey our living God.

2. Surround Yourself with Uncompromising Friends

Early in his life Daniel understood the value of having godly friends (see Daniel 1). Daniel's friends were Shadrach, Meshach, and Abednego. Together they refused to compromise by eating the king's meat. Together God blessed them.

A few years later Daniel was away, traveling on appointed business. The king had decreed that all in the kingdom would worship him. (What is up with these egotistical kings?). He brought together all of the citizens of his country and called for them to bow down to an idol honoring himself.

Daniel's friend knew what the consequences would be. Yet they filtered their actions through their uncompromising faith and determined that they should not bow down to the idol.

When the king and his cronies saw three young men standing tall in the midst of this massive sea of compromisers, he summoned the young men to him and fiercely threatened them to obey his decree. Yet they were men of uncompromising commitment.

> Shadrach, Meshach, and Abednego replied to the king,
> "Nebuchadnezzar, we don't need to give you an answer to this question.
> If the God we serve exists, then He can rescue us from the furnace of
> blazing fire, and He can rescue us from the power of you, the king. But
> even if He does not rescue us, we want you as king to know that we
> will not serve your gods or worship the gold statue you set up." (Dan
> 3:16–18)

As promised, they were thrown into the fiery furnace. But God was with them, and they did not perish. Sometime later they were pulled out, and the nation acknowledged the power of the God of Shadrach, Meshach, and Abednego.

I can only imagine Daniel's reaction when he heard what his closest friends had gone through? "Way to go! Praise God!" I guess the reunion of Daniel with his three friends was a joyous time of celebration and faith-building.

Being good friends with this type of men certainly contributed to Daniel's uncompromising faith. Friends determine to a great degree the kind of people we will be. The world's wisest man promised that our friends can sharpen our faith in God. "Iron sharpens iron, and one man sharpens another" (Prov. 27:17).

The question is this: Are your closest friends sharpening your faith? Has anyone in your life walked through the fire of life's trials and temptations and demonstrated an uncompromising life? Better yet, are you serving as such a friend for someone in your life and ministry?

Characteristics of a True Friend

A good friend is one who . . .
    Has made the same commitment to live an uncompromising life.

Will commit to pray for/with you every day of your life.

Will commit to viewing life through spiritual eyes with you.

Will not allow you to insert sin into your daily decision-making.

Won't judge insensitively when you make mistakes but will walk life's journey with you.

And realizes that he/she needs you to do all of the above for him/her.

Friends are important and certainly provide an environment more conducive to practice spirituality, but when it comes down to it, even if you have great friends, no one else can really make you an uncompromising minister. The issue of becoming an obedient servant is always an issue of your own heart. You must be making the uncompromising choices today in order to be a person of unwavering character tomorrow.

The Character of Daniel Can Be Yours!

Strong integrity and godly character are essential for long-term effectiveness in ministry. Ministry is the result of living an uncompromising life of unwavering faith.

The testimony of the uncompromising faith of Daniel can be your story! No matter what your past mistakes have been, or whatever the evil one desires to throw your way in the future, you can be an uncompromising minister for the glory of God. Just remember this equation to produce a life absent of compromise and a heart full of devotion to God:

Personal Commitment + Spiritual Companionship = No Compromise

What Now?

As a fellow minister and colaborer in the kingdom, I feel a deep compulsion to pause here and speak to where you are in your own life. Are you one of the many people who has gotten to the end of this chapter and said, "Boy, I was with you until the very end when you 'start at a young age.'" Have you made some regrettable and unfortunate mistakes in your life? Did your commitment to creating an uncompromising life start a little later in your life than what you had hoped? Or have you been serious about your commitment to live an uncompromising life but are haunted by the memory of the moments you demonstrated weakness and compromised your commitment to Christ?

Maybe you recently accepted Christ as your Savior and now regret not having accepted His grace much sooner than you did?

Of course, there is a place for dealing with your sin and grappling with the repercussions of sin. But I have a feeling that if you resonate with one of the questions I posed in the previous paragraph, you have probably already done your fair share of sincere confession of sin, passionate apologies to your merciful Lord, and now desire holiness throughout the remainder of your life. So, believing this, let me offer you some encouragement that I pray goes straight to the aching part of your heart that leaves you discouraged.

Spirituality is not based on the amount of academic degrees you possess; it is based on your uncompromising commitment to obey God moment by moment of your life!

Spirituality is not contingent on where you grew up, who your parents are, or if you were exposed to Christianity at a young age; it is based on your uncompromising commitment to obey God moment by moment of your life!

Spirituality is not reserved solely for those who have followed the example of Daniel from the earliest years of their life; it is based on your uncompromising commitment to obey God moment by moment of your life!

Spirituality is not withheld from those who really desire righteousness but have made several severe mistakes in their past; it is based on your uncompromising commitment to obey God moment by moment of your life!

Therefore, by the authority of Almighty God and His Word, be encouraged that you can start today—*right now*—building an uncompromising life! You are still eligible to be a spiritual giant for the Lord. You can yet become a man or woman of God. Nothing you have done can prohibit you from growing in your faith and becoming a Daniel within the body of Christ. Nothing!

Yes, the memories will be there, and the regrets will remain, but use those thoughts and feelings to fuel your commitment to stay on your uncompromising path! Change the meaning of those memories!

So end this chapter by offering up a prayer of thanksgiving to our gracious and merciful God for allowing you a second chance to live a life that honors Him. Then go out and begin surrounding yourself with uncompromising friends and minister in the body of Christ together!

Ministry Is . . .

1. Remaining faithful to God no matter what.
2. Living a life of uncompromised faith.
3. The result of personal commitment and spiritual companionship.

⮞ Quotes ⮜

There is never a reason to compromise God's standards in order to maintain God's blessings.

—ANDY STANLEY[1]

Great achievement plus weak character equals disaster. Keep your character strong and your influence will be irresistible.

—STAN TOLER[2]

An unmistakable sense of authority accompanies leaders with integrity.

—HENRY AND RICHARD BLACKABY[3]

Notes

1. A. Stanley, *Next Generation Leader* (Sisters, OR: Multnomah, 2006), 145.
2. S. Toler, *Stan Toler's Practical Guide for Pastoral Ministry* (Indianapolis, IN: Wesleyan Publishing House, 2007), 28.
3. H. Blackaby and R. Blackaby, *Spiritual Leadership* (Nashville, TN: B&H Publishing Group, 2002), 107.

18

Loyalty to the Truth

Ben Gutierrez

*It's your time to go to battle. It's your time now to go out and
face the enemy and to make a difference as soldiers of light
and salt. . . . You're to win multitudes to Christ and mold the
culture again in the image of Christ. You can be God's change
agents to save America and to enable us to change the world
in our generation.*

—Dr. Jerry Falwell[1]

Don't Blink!

The world is constantly changing around us. Take technology for example. Music was recently delivered to us on a plastic record. These 12-inch
records were engraved carefully and could only be played on one device, a
record player, in order to produce music. Cars, therefore, did not install anything but AM-FM radios as records could obviously not be played inside the
car. The records had to be stored at room temperature for fear of warping that
would render the entire record unusable. In fact, during the era of the record,
it was a common site to walk into a community library and see a display of a
warped, wrinkled record with a warning that the borrower would have to pay

a whopping 52 cents to replace any record returned distorted and not cared for properly.

Soon thereafter the world experienced an invention that would permit people to listen to their favorite tunes while driving in their cars. The eight-track tape was an amazing invention that gave an option to the AM-FM radio. People loved the invention so much that no one complained that they had to listen to the entire tape in order to return to a song they wanted to hear again (no rewind function!). The eight-track tape fit perfectly within a normal size shoebox, so it wasn't long until at least one passenger's seat was reserved for the storage of a driver's collection of these wonderful eight-track tapes.

Not long after the eight-track tape, inventors improved it by making it smaller and constructing it in such a way to allow for forwarding and rewinding the tape. The biggest complaint of both the eight-track tape and the cassette tape still remained; that is, the music was delivered on a very thin, fragile strip of magnetic tape that was easily torn, snagged, and/or severed.

If you lived during the era of the cassette tape, you will never forget the introduction of the device that allowed you to walk around town with a large square device that was powered by a bunch of batteries that hooked onto your belt. With this device you could go mobile and listen to your cassette tape through headphones. This life-altering invention continued with the invention of the compact disc.

A compact disc (CD) resembled a small record but was coated with a protective coating that in no way distorted the ability to play the music. The CD was produced in such a way as to allow 10 times as much music as could be produced on a record, as the CD was the first digital mode of delivery of music.

Currently music is delivered in digital formats via the computer and handheld devices that are no larger than a credit card. These devices can hold up to 150,000 songs and fit comfortably in your pocket. Don't worry if you forget how to use these small, technologically advanced inventions because your seven+ years little brother is already familiar with the technology and would be more than willing to give you a quick tutorial.

Talk about changing swiftly—just look at your child or grandchild, and you'll realize that they tend to change even more swiftly than technology. One night you are holding them in your arms whispering in their soft, newborn ear that you can't wait to take them to the playground or wrestle them to the ground and tickle them profusely. Then you wake up the next morning, and you notice that your precious little one has grown six feet, learned how to drive, and is double-majoring in the sciences and the arts!

We can't stop it all from happening, but we welcome these types of changes for the most part and enjoy being right in the middle of it all! Of course, some changes are occurring all around us that are not positive and should not be welcomed by the minister on any level. The biggest change we must resist is the cultural tendency to ignore, change, discredit, and diminish biblical truth! More and more, real ministry requires us to stay loyal to biblical truth.

Called to Discernment

One of the greatest challenges of ministry is learning to distinguish between what is true and what is not. We must learn the art of spiritual discernment. Pastor John MacArthur writes:

> Discernment is the process of making careful distinctions in our thinking about truth. The discerning person is the one who draws a clear contrast between truth and error. . . . No one can be truly discerning without developing skill in separating divine truth from error.[2]

Such discernment must be grounded in a deep and accurate understating of the Word of God. Unless ministers become and stay loyal to biblical truth and learn to be discerning, there will be a deafening of conscience to the voice of the Holy Spirit. It is a change that is as swift as the change in technology, but it impacts peoples' lives more profoundly and permanently than the changes in technology. Therefore, we minister in order to counteract the cultural tendency to ignore, discredit, and diminish biblical truth!

Called to Minister in the Dark

The evil one is indeed wise and active in concocting some integrated, technical, scholarly attacks against Christianity. He cunningly disguises himself as an angel of light in order to deceive us (2 Cor 11:14–15). He disguises falsehood in truth. His schemes have infiltrated our colleges, universities, and churches. We as ministers need to be able to recognize this attack on biblical truth. One of the enemy's current strategies involves replacing *absolute truth* with *relative truth*.

Relative truth is something that is true to *some* people and *not* to others. Proponents of this position claim that something can be true today, but it may not have been true in the past, and it may not be true in the future. To some, truth is always subject to change and is based on the individual's perspective.

It is problematic to believe in relative truth because you are going to rely on your own heart and human, fallen, limited wisdom; then you are relying on a nonreliable source! "The heart is more deceitful than anything else, and desperately sick—who can understand it?" (Jer 17:9).

In addition, the entire concept of *declaring* that "all truth is relative" is logically and fatally flawed. This statement makes an absolute claim about all truth being relative. Relative truth is actually not truth at all. It is simply a subtle tool of the enemy to promote self and dethrone God in people's lives.

Absolute truth is something that *is true at all times and at all places.* Supporters of this correct position rightly claim that truth is true whether we believe it or not. In addition, truth is believed not to have been invented by a culture or by religious men but provided by the Creator of the world.

Dr Norman Geisler elaborates on the definition of absolute truth by deducing that "since God's moral character does not change, it follows that moral obligations flowing from His nature are absolute."[3]

The Bible Is the Source of Absolute Truth

God can be trusted because He is the true God (Jer 10:10) who cannot lie (Titus 1:2; Heb 6:18). Therefore, since the Bible is the Word of God (2 Tim 3:16–17; 1 Pet 1:20–21), it must also be true.

Your righteousness is an everlasting righteousness, and Your instruction is true. (Ps 119:142)

You are near, LORD, and all Your commands are true. (Ps 119:151)

The entirety of Your word is truth, and all Your righteous judgments endure forever. (Ps 119:160)

Jesus brings truth (John 1:17). Yet Jesus is much more than someone who *knows* the truth; He *is* the truth. "Jesus told him, 'I am the way, the truth, and the life. No one comes to the Father except through Me'" (John 14:6).

The simple yet profound reason we never equivocate from teaching and living the absolute truth of the Bible is because it is the only instrument that can regenerate, save, and transform a lost soul. God's truth is the only way to liberate a captive heart. Jesus promised:

"You will know the truth, and the truth will set you free." (John 8:32)

In ancient times the word translated "free" was used to describe a slave who was once shackled and dragged around by someone else but experienced an unlocking of the chains and was released from the control of the slave owner. Likewise, truth is the only thing that releases lost souls from bondage and allows them to experience freedom in Jesus Christ. Therefore, even though we minister in a culture to persons who believe that life-freeing truth is found within themselves, we must stay loyal to the truth. We must never cease to direct them to the source of truth, Jesus Christ and the Word of God.

A 2,000-Year-Old Prediction

We live in a world that has convoluted standards. But this shouldn't surprise us because this type of culture was actually predicted by the apostle Paul 2,000 years ago. He reminds us that we should not expect the problem ever to go away on its own. In fact the last days will usher in "difficult times" (2 Tim 3:1). People will be "always learning and never able to come to the knowledge of the truth" (2 Tim 3:7). They will in fact "resist the truth" (2 Tim 3:8). Resulting in "evil people and impostors" growing "worse, deceiving and being deceived" (2 Tim 3:13).

Fortunately Paul did not stop there. In the rest of the chapter, he provided us with a list of clear and concise directives on how to minister to the culture. These directives are so clear and understandable that further elaboration may tend to confuse their meaning.

> But as for you, continue in what you have learned and firmly believed, knowng those from whom you learned, and that from childhood you have known the sacred Scriptures, which are able to instruct you for salvation through faith in Christ Jesus. All Scripture is inspired by God and is profitable for teaching, for rebuking, for correcting, for training in righteousness, so that the man of God may be complete, equipped for every good work. (2 Tim 3:14–17)

Paul's solution to a world drowning in relative truth is the secure rock of the absolute truth of the Word of God. He told Timothy of six ways it

powerfully meets the needs of those swimming upstream against a culture a
drift in relative morality.

1. The Word of God will save you.
2. The Word of God will teach you all truth.
3. The Word of God will lovingly confront your sin.
4. The Word of God will correct any incorrect ideas of life.
5. The Word of God will guide you in every decision you make.
6. The Word of God will equip you to navigate through life with the
   proper perspective.

Pastor, author, and Bible teacher John MacArthur has dedicated his life to
teaching the Word of God. He is passionate about the supreme importance of
biblical truth:

> I've said this through the years, I continue to believe it more and more
> all the time. The most important reality in the world is divine truth.
> It's not just important for people who don't know Christ, who don't
> know God, who don't know Scripture. It is important for those
> who do.[4]

Living in the Light

The heart cry of every minister is to see a lost soul step out of the darkness
and accept the life-changing truth of Jesus Christ. Then one of the most amazing sights to behold is to see a person who has been changed by this truth grow
up spiritually. What is most memorable is to see a new believer grow so swiftly
because they hunger and thirst after righteousness. Their growth is contagious
as they passionately crave the Scriptures, memorize the Scriptures, and live out
the Scriptures in everyday life. It is the moment all ministers long to witness in
the lives of those to whom they minister.

This type of growth was exactly what Paul predicted 2,000 years ago!
The apostle Paul told Timothy, and all ministers, that if any believer, young or
old, craves the absolute truths of the Word of God, he/she will mature in the
Lord!

Let's take another look at 2 Tim 3:14–17. Paul tells us that, at the point of
salvation, we are considered children. But over time we develop into mature
Christians (*"man"* v. 17). So it begs the question, What matured us from being

spiritual infants/children in Christ into spiritual "men"? Just look at the verse in the middle (v. 16) to see what fuels our spiritual growth—the *Scriptures!*

The more the believer craves the Word of God, the more swiftly that believer will grow spiritually. In fact, the rate of growth for some new believers rivals the swift rate of change of technology. (You blink one day, and they have become full-time ministers themselves!)

Committed to Stand Firm

The Lord can swiftly change lives and develop them spiritually. But this type of growth occurs only when the truth of God speaks to a life.

This type of life change will not happen on its own. God's chief mode of delivering this truth to a dark world is through the life and message of a faithful minister who has committed never to waiver on believing and teaching the absolute truth of the Word of God.

We need more ministers committed to the Word of God. The question is, Are you going to be one of them?

What Now?

Do you find yourself being shocked by this description of the world?

Would you say that you exist within a Christian bubble that does not afford you too many opportunities to engage unbelievers with the gospel? If so, ask yourself if you placed yourself there by choice.

Have you purposely insulated yourself from any exposure to the unsaved world because you feel ill-equipped to minister effectively to them?

Do you sincerely love the people who are in desperate need of the gospel?

Are you tempted to give in to the relative philosophy of the world believing that it will be the best way to reach them for Christ?

Have you imbedded your heart into the Scriptures so that the truth of the Word of God comes naturally to you when you look upon all that is happening in the world today?

Have you prayed to God to solidify the truth in your heart and to make it burn with an unquenchable passion to see lost people come to Christ?

Ministry Is . . .

1. Believing and standing upon the absolute truth of the Word of God.
2. Understanding the philosophy of a dark world that embraces relative truth.
3. Passionately, carefully, and lovingly engaging a dark world with the truth.

⌒ Quotes ⌒

Absolute loyalty to the Truth must have priority in the life of the Christian worker. . . . All we possess we can sacrifice if need be, but the Truth we dare not sacrifice. We must never seek to bend it to our purpose, but must always bow to it.

—WATCHMEN NEE[5]

When churches, or individual Christians, lose their resolve to discern between sound doctrine and error, between good and evil, between truth and lies, they open themselves up to every kind of error.

—JOHN MACARTHUR[6]

The fact of the matter is that it is irresponsible and dangerous to attempt to do practical ministry apart from a sound theological base. The only proper basis for Christian living and pastoral ministry is biblical and theological.

—JAY ADAMS[7]

Notes

1. J. Falwell, in his final address to the student body of Liberty University on May 9, 2007.
2. J. MacArthur, *Fool's Gold* (Wheaton, IL: Crossway Books, 2005), 20.
3. N. Geisler, *Christian Ethics* (Grand Rapids, MI: Baker, 1989), 15.

4. J. MacArthur in the sermon, "The Christian's Priority: Luke 10:38–42," www.gty.org/Resources/Sermons/42–145.

5. W. Nee, *The Normal Christian Worker* (Hong Kong: Church Book Room, 1965), 125.

6. MacArthur, *Fool's Gold*, 15.

7. J. E. Adams, *Shepherding God's Flock* (Grand Rapids, MI: Baker, 1975), 1.

19

Living Up to Your Name

Ben Gutierrez

Parenting is fun, challenging, exhausting, and rewarding all at the same time. Rearing children provides a parent with memories that will last a lifetime. Challenges a parent ends up laughing about later (way later!) are the times the parent had to correct their child's behavior in public.

First-time parents are the most fun to observe. I mostly enjoy seeing them attempt to retrieve their curious child who has just learned to walk back into close vicinity of the parent. It usually goes something like this:

First, they usually attempt to summon them back by their nickname.

After no response . . . they call them by their "real" first name.

After no response . . . they usually try to entice the child to come join them in a certain activity that the child has enjoyed in the past.

After no response . . . one parent usually lunges for the child while the other parent restrains the lunging parent by stating that "our child has to learn to obey our words immediately."

After no response . . . the tone of their voice lowers as one parent usually adds a little more force, and they both recite the same command to return to them.

Then the child stops, turns, and looks at the parents.

The child smiles (cutely).

Then the child turns right back around.

After no response . . . they begin to take the matter a bit personal (as if the child is intentionally trying to embarrass the parent publicly) and in a low, firm tone immediately address the young child by a different title like "young man" or "young lady."

After no response . . . and no response . . . and no response . . .

The new parents resort to invoking the most classic, universal attempt known to all parents! All parents have found that once this time-tested attempt is deployed upon the child, they will most likely never cease using it. It will become their attempt of choice all the way through their child's high school years. It has been handed down from generation to generation and yields impressive results. Its powerful effect is unexplainable; nevertheless, it works! It is: The loud and bombastic reciting of the child's full and unaltered legal name (as registered with the Social Security Office) complete with suffix and hyphenations!

. . . and voilá, the child responds!

Don't ask me how, but nine out of ten parents agree that something about hearing his or her full legal name recited in public changes the child's attitude.

A Biblical Description of Ministers and Their Members

Interestingly, when God wants to reinforce a particular characteristic or attitude by which He would like the church to comply, He will change the word *church* in a particular passage of Scripture and refer to the church by a different name, a metaphorical name, in order to describe specifically how He would have us behave within the body of Christ. It's true. Fortunately, God doesn't do it just because we are being disobedient children. Actually, He does this in the Scriptures as a teaching tool for us so that we will really inculcate God's teaching about how we as believers should behave within the body of Christ.

This is a common practice in the Scriptures and should be duly noted when it occurs. When it does, we should ask ourselves, "What character is to be portrayed in this given situation?" It is a useful technique. God chooses particular names to teach us character, and often these names create a vivid picture in our minds of the attitude or action God wants from us.

Let's first take a look at an example of this technique used in the Bible to help us understand the amazing character of God. Have you ever thought about what the names of God *really* are in the Bible? Meaning, if you pay close attention to the names of God in the Bible, you quickly notice that they are not necessarily names of God at all, but *rather* they are *descriptions of His character* in that particular story, situation, or scenario in the Bible. Often the description will begin with the words, "The Lord our . . ." or "I am God who. . . ." Here are some examples to consider.

Descriptions ("Names") of God

"Jehovah Jireh" (Gen 22:14): "The LORD will provide"

This name of God was used when God provided Abraham a sacrifice instead of having to sacrifice his son Isaac. Abraham proclaimed the truth that God is a wonderful provider.

"Jehovah Rapha" (Exod 15:22–26): "I am the LORD who heals"

God's character was witnessed by Moses and the people when they were extremely thirsty during their wanderings after leaving Egypt. They finally found water in Marah, but it was too bitter to drink. So, Moses called out to the Lord for water to heal their dry, parched bodies. God performed a miracle in turning the bitter water into drinkable water. After the miracle God told Moses to "keep your eyes continually on me because I am *the God who heals* you."

"Jehovah Shalom" (Judg 6:24 NIV): "The LORD is peace"

Gideon attributed this description or "name" to God while he was hiding his crop from the Midianites and Amalekites. These foreigners were always ravaging and stealing the crops of the Israelites. During this time Gideon was having a pity party saying, "I know God wants me to fight them, but God has forsaken me!" So God Himself visited Gideon and said, "Peace to you. Don't be afraid, for you will not die" (v. 23). Gideon then asked if God could prove that He had actually visited him. So God agreed not to depart from Gideon until Gideon built an altar of worship to the Lord.

As promised, when the altar was completed, God increased the fire to consume the meat and unleavened bread. After God did this, He departed from Gideon. As soon as all this happened, Gideon declared, "So Gideon built an altar to the LORD there and called it Yahweh Shalom. It is in Ophrah of the Abiezrites until today" (v. 24). The name of the altar, "Yahweh Shalom" means "the Lord is peace."

Many more examples of God's character are depicted by the various "names" attributed to Him in the Bible. It makes for a wonderful study! When God in the Bible diverts from His normal pattern of referring to Himself as "the Lord" or "God" and adds descriptives such as "Provider" or "Healer" or "Peacemaker," then we should take note that He is describing how He will act toward us! This is how God manages our expectations of Him. This is who God is and how He will always act toward us.

In the same way, when God chooses to refer to us in ways other than as Christians or believers, we ought to take note that He is describing what he expects of us. He is doing this to reinforce the character that He requires of each member of His church.

Living Up to Your Name

As we have mentioned before, the goal of ministry is not merely to *do* church but to *be* the church. God wants us to live up to our name.

Let's take a look at these diversions from the norm in order to get a glimpse of how the Lord would have us conduct ourselves within the Church.

The Body of Christ: A Unified Fellowship

In the Bible sometimes the "Church" is called "the body of Christ." By calling us the word *body*, the Lord is reinforcing in our minds that His desire for us is that we all remain unified together under Him!

> He is also the head of the body, the church; He is the beginning, the firstborn from the dead, so that He might come to have first place in everything. (Col 1:18)

> But speaking the truth in love, let us grow in every way into Him who is the head—Christ. From Him the whole body, fitted and knit together by every supporting ligament, promotes the growth of the body for building up itself in love by the proper working of each individual part. (Eph 4:15–16)

> For the husband is the head of the wife as Christ is the head of the church. He is the Savior of the body. (Eph 5:23)

In Colossians, the apostle Paul intentionally used the word *body* to describe the church in Colossae because they were a little church off the beaten path that was getting severely attacked for their theology. Their culture hated them for believing that Jesus Christ is the only true sufficient Savior. So Paul was attempting to encourage the believers of this little church by saying, "Hey, hang in their together guys! Because you are all one body, and you need one another to get through this! So don't waste time arguing and fighting among yourselves about petty things because you all have to buddy-up and stay unified against this heresy!"

The Bride of Christ: A Faithful Fellowship

In the Bible sometimes the church is called the "bride" of Christ in order remind all believers that we must remain faithful to Him. Marriage analogies are myriad in the Bible as they are the most rich and vivid metaphors that could possibly be used to depict God's desired level of faithfulness. In the writings of 1 and 2 Corinthians, the apostle Paul was talking to a disobedient church (the church at Corinth). He likened their need to be faithful to God to how a husband and wife need to remain faithful to each other.

> For I am jealous over you with a godly jealousy, because I have promised you in marriage to one husband—to present a pure virgin to Christ. But I fear that, as the serpent deceived Eve by his cunning, your minds may be corrupted from a complete and pure devotion to Christ. (2 Cor 11:2–3)

Jeremiah states that not only is faithfulness a paramount characteristic of all believers, but that if there is to be unfaithfulness in our relationship with God, it will not be because the Lord has ever lost any affection for us! If there is unfaithfulness, it will always be a result of us moving away from him.

> Because of the LORD's faithful love we do not perish, for His mercies never end. They are new every morning; great is Your faithfulness! (Lam 3:22–23)

The Flock of God: A Dependent Fellowship

God often depicts the church as the flock of Christ in order to remind us that we should be continually dependent on Him just as sheep are totally dependent on the shepherd.

Both Acts 20:28 and 1 Pet 5:2–4 were written to the ministers of the Church to remind them that they are dependent on God and they should lead their churches also to depend on God.

> Be on guard for yourselves and for all the flock, among whom the Holy Spirit has appointed you as overseers, to shepherd the church of God, which He purchased with His own blood. (Acts 20:28)

Shepherd God's flock among you, not overseeing out of compulsion but freely, according to God's will; not for the money but eagerly; not lording it over those entrusted to you, but being examples to the flock. And when the chief Shepherd appears, you will receive the unfading crown of glory. (1 Pet 5:2–4)

Even the Lord Himself described His leadership oversight of the flock of God as a shepherd who is always leading His people with great care and trust:

So Jesus said again, "I assure you: I am the door of the sheep. All who came before Me are thieves and robbers, but the sheep didn't listen to them. I am the door. If anyone enters by Me, he will be saved and will come in and go out and find pasture. A thief comes only to steal and to kill and to destroy. I have come that they may have life and have it in abundance.

"I am the good shepherd. The good shepherd lays down his life for the sheep. The hired man, since he is not the shepherd and doesn't own the sheep, leaves them and runs away when he sees a wolf coming. The wolf then snatches and scatters them. This happens because he is a hired man and doesn't care about the sheep.

"I am the good shepherd. I know My own sheep, and they know Me, as the Father knows Me, and I know the Father. I lay down My life for the sheep. But I have other sheep that are not of this fold; I must bring them also, and they will listen to My voice. Then there will be one flock, one shepherd." (John 10:7–16)

The Family of God: A Supportive Fellowship

Another description of our necessary character is found in the words used to describe us as a family. Here the Lord is describing that He expects all of us to remain supportive of one another.

But to all who did receive Him, He gave them the right to be children of God, to those who believe in His name. (John 1:12)

So then you are no longer foreigners and strangers, but fellow citizens with the saints, and members of God's household. (Eph 2:19)

In life we need our family because times get tough. So too the church is a place you should expect to be comforted during the tragedies of life. Like a good family the church is a place where we can receive needed encouragement, support, and comfort. A good, supportive family makes you feel like you can make it another day.

Likewise, the church ought to be where people come in and say, "You know, life is pretty challenging right now, and I need your shoulder to cry on." The church should be a place in which we find solace that provides a much needed interval of peace within our daily struggle.

The Holy Priesthood: A Pure Body

A vivid description of a necessary characteristic is found in God's description of all believers as a "royal priesthood." In using these words, the Lord is telegraphing to us that He requires all believers to be pure and holy ministers before Him.

> But you are a chosen race, a royal priesthood, a holy nation, a people for His possession, so that you may proclaim the praises of the One who called you out of darkness into His marvelous light. Once you were not a people, but now you are God's people; you had not received mercy, but now you have received mercy. (1 Pet 2:9–10)

The type of purity God expects always comes from the heart:

> Who may ascend the mountain of the LORD? Who may stand in His holy place? The one who has clean hands and a pure heart. (Ps 24:3–4)

It is not that we have to be perfect because God acknowledges that we will need to experience forgiveness of our daily sins as we dwell upon the earth (1 John 1:9). But we are always to remember that God raises a pretty high bar for us to shoot for when it comes to personal holiness.

What Now? Are You Living Up to Your Name?

The goal of ministry is not merely to *do* church but to *be* the church. God wants us to live up to our name, the church, and all that it means.

Do you believe that visitors to your ministry quickly sense these characteristics? Remember that none of these characteristics will be true of your ministry if they are not first true of you. You and your ministry are inseparable.

Do you display unity with those around you, even when you don't fully agree? Are you pure? Would you be considered faithful? Does your prayer life reflect a strong dependence on God?

Are there one or two characteristics that you think you should hone in on now in order to solidify them in your own heart? Which characteristic(s) are you most proud of in your ministry? Most concerned about? Why?

I encourage all ministers regularly to assess their lives and ministries to see if these necessary characteristics are obvious and active within their own portion of the body of Christ.

Ministry Is . . .

1. Living up to your name, the Church.
2. Being the Church.
3. Maintaining unity, faithfulness, dependence, support, and purity within our ministries.
4. Revisiting and reexamining the spiritual climate of our own hearts and ministries to confirm that we have not slipped in any of these necessary characteristics.

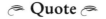 Quote

Don't go to church. Be the church.[1]

Note

1. Words on the back of the T-shirts used in the outreach marketing kit of the Faith in Action Campaign.

20 Keeping the Obedience Bar High

Ben Gutierrez

Often I am asked to identify the most important leadership principle that a ministry professor is able to teach his ministry students. Sometimes the question is posed in scenario form like, "If you had one final truth you could share with your students before you die, and you knew they would adopt it wholeheartedly, what one thing would you want them to understand about being a minister?"

Other times it is with a pad of paper and pencil in the interviewer's hand, seemingly eager to discover a hidden nugget of truth that has not yet been uttered before and they want to be the first to unearth and expose it to the rest of the kingdom. Still others who have felt their own ministry focus drifting away from what God would have them focus on have asked me the same question hoping to get refocused on what God would have them do. These are all fair questions, and it is understandable why they ask them.

Interestingly, I respond with the same answer every time I am asked. After I give my response, it is often met with the common response, "You know, I never thought about that!" Honestly, it has happened so much that I am starting to wonder if what I am saying is actually in the Bible! Yet the topic seems to be plastered all over the pages of the Bible. I find explicit and implicit statements supporting my answer along with descriptions of those who have both demonstrated this truth in their lives and those who have reaped the consequences of disregarding this truth. As I process it with the interviewer, I become even more

convinced that it is one of the most important lessons that a student studying to
be a wise minister can learn.

The one truth I wish I could cause every minister in the body of Christ to
agree to and inculcate in their lives and ministry is this: Ministers need to accept
the fact that they are held to a higher standard by virtue of their elevated level of
influence upon the body of Christ and they must live according to this standard!

It's All about Influence

A minister may have a wide range of skills and giftedness that he or she
deploys in any given week to persuade other believers to become mature. But
the minister's most powerful tool to effect change in another person's life, pro
or con, is their example.

> The highly influential medical missionary Albert Schweitzer observed,
> "Example is not the main thing influencing others. It is the only thing."[1]

> Missionary leader J. Oswald Sanders wrote, "Example is much more
> potent than precept."[2]

> Robert Coleman raises the banner of example when he said, "One living
> sermon is worth one hundred explanations."[3]

> Waylon Moore wisely concluded, "Since it takes a disciple to build other
> disciples, the chain of multiplication begins with you."[4]

In 1 Timothy, which is commonly labeled as a book on church organization, Paul said more about the minister's character and personal conduct as
a minister than the organizational structure of the church. Notice that Paul
emphasized to the younger minister, Timothy, the truth that people in ministry
are called to be examples to the flock.

> Command and teach these things. No one should despise your youth;
> instead, you should **be an example** to the believers in speech, in conduct,
> in love, in faith, in purity. Until I come, give your attention to public
> reading, exhortation, and teaching. Do not neglect the gift that is in you;
> it was given to you through prophecy, with the laying on of hands by
> the council of elders. Practice these things; be committed to them, so that
> your progress may be evident to all. Be conscientious about yourself and
> your teaching; persevere in these things, for by doing this you will save
> both yourself and your hearers. (1 Tim 4:11–16, bold added for emphasis)

Notice the flow of commands. First, Paul emphasizes the need to take great care in his personal life: "**Be an example** to the believers in speech, in conduct, in love, in faith, in purity" (v. 12). Second, after he instructs him to have his personal life in order, Paul then shifts to the subject of how Timothy should perform his formal ministerial duties: "Give your attention to public reading, exhortation, and teaching. Do not neglect the gift that is in you; it was given to you through prophecy, with the laying on of hands by the council of elders" (vv. 13–14). Third, Paul describes the scope of the impact that could potentially be made by a minister who uses his sphere of influence to affect change within the body of Christ: "Practice these things; be committed to them, so that your progress may be evident to all. Be conscientious about yourself and your teaching; persevere in these things, for by doing this you will save both yourself and your hearers" (vv. 15–16).

The logic is simple: Living the truth prior to preaching the truth will have the greatest influence on the people to whom you minister!

Paul prefaced this entire portion of Scripture with the command for Timothy to "command and teach these things" (1 Tim 4:11)! The apostle Paul was literally instructing Timothy to preach to people that their personal conduct will influence people to obey the truth and teach them how to use their personal influence to encourage obedience within the body of Christ.

Obedience on Display

Paul believed that teaching spirituality was so much more than lecturing behind a pulpit that he actually instructed the churches in which he ministered to watch him and model his actions. His offer to have the churches observe him was not offered out of pride or out of compulsion; rather he understood that it is incumbent upon a minister of the gospel to set the example of personal holiness.

To the church at Philippi, Paul instructed them to observe him: "Join in imitating me, brothers, and observe those who live according to the example you have in us" (Phil 3:17). To Timothy and the church at Ephesus, Paul offered himself once again to be the reference point of Christian conduct: "But as for you, continue in what you have learned and firmly believed, knowing those from whom you learned" (2 Tim 3:14). To the church of Corinth, Paul explicitly states that they should follow his example: "Just as I also try to please all people in all things, not seeking my own profit, but the profit of many, that they may be saved. Be imitators of me, as I also am of Christ" (1 Cor 10:33–11:1).

Paul was fine with the idea of being offered as an example of how to live out a biblical truth because he understood his role as a Christian leader. He understood that with the position of influence comes the heightened responsibility to use his influence. This understanding gave Paul a deep conviction to be a follower of Christ. Because he followed Christ, he could tell others to follow his example.

Likewise, we are to notice those who are not living according to the truth and not follow their example: "Now I implore you, brothers, watch out for those who cause dissensions and pitfalls contrary to the doctrine you have learned. Avoid them" (Rom 16:17).

God desires that all ministers back up their speech, sermons, devotionals, and their performance of all formal ministerial duties with a life that practices the truth *prior to* the preaching of it. Performance of duty without character is unacceptable to God.

Agree to Terms and Conditions

Every minister must accept the fact that the Lord expects us to live with a heightened sense of responsibility and be an example of how to conduct ourselves obediently before God while we minister to the body of Christ. Whether having oversight of a congregation at large or serving as a leader of a local church, every minister exhibits a heightened level of influence. As a result, we are responsible to maintain an honorable example at all times. If the minister chooses to adhere to this spiritual reality, the minister will be able to continue experiencing unique and special blessings. Unfortunately, if a minister tarnishes the influence by profoundly poor choices, then the God-ordained example of obedience is fractured. That minister will be the recipient of firm punishment from a loving yet holy God.

James, the pastor of the church in Jerusalem, provides an explicit caution to those who desire to enter into the ministry. Because even though as a minister you "desire a noble work" (1 Tim 3:1), you will also be held to a much higher standard:

> Not many should become teachers, my brothers, knowing that we will receive a **stricter judgment**. (Jas 3:1, bold added for emphasis)

Consider how the Amplified Translation attempts to capture the level of seriousness of this truth:

NOT MANY [of you] should become teachers (self-constituted censors and reprovers of others), my brethren, for you know that we [teachers] **will be judged by a higher standard and with greater severity [than other people; thus we assume the greater accountability and the more condemnation].** (Jas 3:1 AMP, bold added for emphasis)

Ministers are held to a higher standard by virtue of their elevated level of influence upon the body of Christ. Too many ministers haphazardly conduct themselves in their day-to-day lives without remaining on their guard. One unguarded lapse of judgment can deeply fracture the trust of the people and tarnish the example that is being observed. Unfortunately, in some cases, the minister is never able to recapture the influence that he once yielded and may even lose his role in ministry.

Be Careful

In the introduction to his book entitled *Top 10 Mistakes Leaders Make,* Hans Finzel supports this sobering reality when he says:

[O]ne of the sobering realities we must face when we take up the mantle of leadership [is] the greater our sphere of leadership influence, the more our impact on the world around us. . . . The more we lead, the greater the potential damage caused through our poor decisions and actions.[5]

Finzel further cautions the minister when he states:

The good you do can be destroyed by the precautions you fail to take. No matter how skilled or gifted you are as leaders, one or two glaring blind spots can ruin our influence.[6]

Ministers have to accept this reality just as readily as the minister welcomes the fact that he or she will experience some magnificent and unique blessings that ministers alone receive.

This One Thing I Do

Fortunately, there is nothing to worry about if one thing is true of you as a minister: Live each day controlled by the Holy Spirit. That's it. You see, high expectations to live righteously before God should not cause fear and trepidation. This is God's promise to His ministers:

> His divine power has given us everything required for life and godliness,
> through the knowledge of Him who called us by His own glory and
> goodness. By these He has given us very great and precious promises,
> so that through them you may share in the divine nature, escaping the
> corruption that is in the world because of evil desires. (2 Pet 1:3–4)

In other words, you can do what He is asking of you! God Himself will provide all the spiritual resources you need to do so. In giving us "everything required for life and godliness," we have the capacity to obey Him and exhibit the character required. The way we tap into His spiritual resources is to engage in prayer, spiritual thoughts, Scripture meditation, and intentional spiritual discussion as much as possible throughout the day. We can do most of these spiritual activities as we work, drive home, lie in bed, talk on the phone, take a walk, basically anywhere we are! The person whose mind is saturated with God's Word does not live in fear of damaging their spiritual influence because their mind is continually on guard and ready to deploy the spiritual resources provided by God.

Fulfilling Our Calling to Obey

We all have the calling to live a life of obedience. We have been changed by God to do so. God changed us, cleansed us, and saved our souls *in order to* get us in the proper condition to fulfill our calling to obey God.

Paul makes this clear when he describes our lives *prior to* salvation. There is one most notable characteristic of our lives prior to salvation: disobedience to God and His ways.

> And you were dead in your trespasses and sins in which you previously
> walked according to this worldly age, according to the ruler of the
> atmospheric domain, the spirit now working in the disobedient. We too
> all previously lived among them in our fleshly desires, carrying out the
> inclinations of our flesh and thoughts, and by nature we were children
> under wrath, as the others were also. (Eph 2:1–3)

Notice that prior to salvation, we either took small steps toward sin ("trespasses," v. 1) or we took flying leaps into sinful activity ("sins," v.1). We continually "walked" (v. 2) on this sinful path and resembled the character of the evil one himself ("according to the ruler of the atmospheric domain," v. 2). Then the passage comes right out and says that the life of the unbeliever is characterized by disobedience (v. 2) to God in all things. But no one can play the blame game and claim that the "devil made me do it" because we followed the desires of our own hearts, "inclinations of our flesh" (v. 3). As a result, we had no idea that we were walking on a path of destruction as "children under wrath" (v. 3). Prior to salvation, we were characterized by disobedience, and there was no way to break the pattern of sin.

But fortunately it does not stop there. The rest of the passage describes the beautiful transformation that God performed in our lives and the reason He changed us. He gave us the capacity to obey Him!

> But God, who is abundant in mercy, because of His great love that He
> had for us, made us alive with the Messiah even though we were dead in
> trespasses. By grace you are saved! . . . For we are His creation—created
> in Christ Jesus for good works, which God prepared ahead of time so
> that we should walk in them. (Eph 2:4–5,10)

When it is all said and done, the mandate to be an obedient minister is not a new and an overly oppressing requirement. Obedience is required of all believers. We were saved and taken off the path of disobedience and are now equipped spiritually to do what we were created to do—obey our great God and Savior Jesus Christ!

Mixed Emotions?

In dealing with this important subject of ministers being held to a higher standard, I find that I experience a swirl of emotions. It is as if the Spirit shouts, "Amen!" while our flesh shouts, "Not fair!" How about you?

Have you come to the realization that you are held to a higher standard as a minister in the body of Christ? How does that make you feel? Do you feel a twinge of apprehension? Resentment? Do you have a tendency to kick against this standard? Or have you asked the Lord to grant you the understanding to accept this expectation and prepare your heart to learn all the ways you can tap into His vast pool of resources to produce godliness in your life? Does this give you joy?

What Now?

Looking back over this week, what types of choices have you made? If the people who looked up to you were to emulate the actions, attitudes, choices, and decisions that you made this week, what type of people would they be like?

Would they be sources of encouragement and mercy? Would they be focused on righteousness and the Scriptures? Would you and I want to hang around them? Have you been able to demonstrate your love for the Lord by exhibiting righteousness, a passion for His Word, and praise for God?

Ultimately, even though His resources are available to you, they are only appropriated in your life if you choose to obey the Holy Spirit. So, what choice will you make today? Tonight? Tomorrow morning? This week?

Our heart's cry is for all ministers to make God-exalting choices every moment of every day in order to be a point of reference for those who desire to learn how to obey God for themselves!

Ministry Is . . .

1. Being an example.
2. Fulfilling my calling as a believer to obey God.
3. Understanding your heightened level of influence.
4. Greeting this reality with a passion and eagerness to meet His expectations for His glory.

☙ Quotes ☙

What the minister is, is far more important than what he is able to do, for what he is will give force to what he does. In the long run ministry is what we are as much as what we do.
—DAVID AND WARREN WEIRSBE[7]

Ministry is not an eight-to-five job, but a way of life.
—HENRI NOUWEN[8]

All ministry begins by following. Following God, that is. Each of the qualities on Paul's list [1 Timothy 3:1–7]—moral purity, hospitality, gentleness, sobriety, and so on—sprout from a nourishing, obedient relationship with Jesus.
—CHUCK SWINDOLL[9]

Notes

1. A. Schweiter, cited in P. Anderson and M. McKee, *Great Quotes from Great Leaders* (Franklin Lakes, NJ: Career Press, 1997), 35.

2. J. O. Sanders, *Spiritual Leadership* (Chicago, IL: Moody, 1967), 30.

3. R. Coleman cited in W. Moore, *Multiplying Disciples* (Colorado Springs, CO: NavPress, 1980), 10.

4. Ibid.

5. H. Finzel, *Top 10 Mistakes Leaders Make* (Colorado Springs, CO: Cook Communications, 2003), 12.

6. Ibid., 19.

7. D. Weirsbe and W. Weirsbe, *Making Sense of the Ministry* (Chicago, IL: Moody, 1983), 33.

8. H. Nouwen, *Creative Ministry* (Garden City, NY: Doubleday, 1971), xx.

9. C. Swindoll, *Excellence in Ministry* (Fullerton, CA: Insights for Living, 1996), 65.

Part 4

The Manner of Ministry

21

Turning Your Hurts into Helps

Dave Earley

God never wastes the gift of pain (Phil. 1:29). It is given to His ministers as He knows best, and its design is the consolation and salvation of our people.

—JOHN PIPER[1]

You Know Just What I Am Feeling

The year I turned 16 I had my summer well planned. I was determined to take my driver's education courses, get my driver's license, and chase girls the rest of the summer. Just as summer began, however, I found myself doubled over with a severe stomachache. It kept getting worse, and I ended up in the hospital having my ruptured appendix removed. Because of the severity of the situation, I was in the hospital recovering for nearly a week and then was limited for several more weeks, knocking me out of my driving course. While not totally torpedoing my plans, it was a severe setback.

As an immature teen, I wondered why God let it happen at that time. Several years later I got an answer. I was serving as an interim pastor. One Sunday afternoon I visited a church member in the hospital. He was coming out of surgery and, after a short visit, went to sleep. The room where he was staying had two beds. In the other bed was a 15-year-old young man lying uncomfortably in the bed. I introduced myself and tried to chat with him. He seemed rather disinterested. Then I looked him in the eye and said, "I bet I can guess why you are in here."

"No, you can't," he replied, looking at me skeptically.

"Give me one guess," I said. He agreed.

"You just had an operation, and I am guessing that you had your appendix removed."

"How did you know that?" he asked.

"Easy," I said, "I can tell by the way you are lying in the bed." Then I lifted up my shirt to show him my appendectomy scar and the scar from when I had my spleen removed. "I got this scar when I was 16 and this one when I was 13." He was impressed.

"So," he said nodding, "you know just what I am feeling."

From then on I had his attention. He opened up and told me all about himself. We had a great talk. Before I left, I led him to Christ.

When I got in my car to leave the hospital parking garage, the thought hit me: so this is one good reason I had appendicitis when I was 16. My suffering opened the door for expanded ministry.

The God of All Comfort

Called by many the greatest Christian of us all, Paul was a good and godly man who was a veteran of extreme hardship. He was persecuted for his faith, and few have suffered as much. He faced frequent imprisonments, skin-shredding whippings, bloody beatings, shipwreck, betrayal, sleeplessness, hunger, cold, nakedness, and the weighty stress of church leadership (2 Cor 11:23–29). He suffered so severely that he seriously doubted he could make it, and he mentally gave himself a death sentence. But God's grace proved sufficient (2 Cor 1:8–9).

Out of this experience, Paul learned one of the most valuable lessons anyone can learn in the school of severe sufferings and divine ministry training: The best person to help a sufferer is a veteran sufferer. Note what he said to some of his friends.

> Blessed be the God and Father of our Lord Jesus Christ, the Father of mercies and the God of all comfort. He comforts us in all our affliction, **so that** we may be able to comfort those who are in any kind of

affliction, through the comfort we ourselves receive from God. (2 Cor 1:3–4, bold added for emphasis)

Notice carefully what Paul wrote. We can paraphrase his words into three primary statements.

1. Our God is the Father of compassion and the God of all comfort.
2. When we suffer, our God comforts us.
3. God comforts us in our suffering so that we can comfort others.

When we suffer and learn to position ourselves to receive the comfort of God in our sorrow, we gain a priceless key that enables us to unlock hearts and minister to them more effectively. In a real sense suffering is a primary education and qualification for effective ministry. In some ways the more types of suffering we endure, the more types of people we can help. In commenting on this principle, one pastor wrote:

When a person has mastered the full curriculum of suffering—completed the course in dungeons and chains, in whips and scourgings, in shipwrecks and persecutions—then that person has received a master's degree in tribulation and is thoroughly qualified for the ministry of compassion.[2]

Has the Lord allowed you to be dragged through the valleys of sorrow and suffering? Have you ever felt crushing pressure and severe pain? Don't be resentful or regretful. Rejoice! Suffering is a prerequisite for more powerful ministry.

God Never Wastes a Hurt!

"God never wastes a hurt! In fact your greatest ministry will most likely come out of your greatest hurt. . . . God intentionally allows you to go through painful experiences to equip you for ministry to others," writes pastor and best-selling author Rick Warren.[3] He continues:

If you really desire to be used by God, you must understand a powerful truth: The very experiences that you have resented or regretted most in life—the ones you wanted to hide and forget—are the experiences God wants to use to help others. They are your ministry![4]

All of us have had setbacks and sorrows. Maybe you have had more than your share. Those painful points in our lives are the essence of our life message to others.

A Burden for Addicts

Recently I was the guest speaker at a church in Pennsylvania. After the service a lady named Bonnie told me her story. She began smoking pot and drinking alcohol at the age of 10. She soon advanced to harder, intravenous drugs. For 20 years she was bound by the painful, unrelenting chains of drug addiction, prostitution, and poverty.

Some caring Christian people reached down, pulled her out of the gutter, and set her on the right path. They helped her discover real freedom in Christ. Clean for eight years, she now has a vibrant ministry to others who are struggling to break the chains of addiction.

"My heart is for the lowest of the low, the dregs of society, the hopeless and the helpless because that's what I was," she said. "I want to help them just like someone else helped me. After all, who better to help an addict than an addict?"

Think about it, who better to help a sufferer than a sufferer? Who is more effective at ministering to someone with a chronic illness than someone who has had a chronic illness? Who better to encourage the children of divorce than someone who is the child of divorce? A woman who has had to endure an abusive husband may be the best person to minister to a battered wife. Who better to help a person with an eating disorder than someone who has had one? Our miseries can become our ministries.

Praying for Prodigals

You probably know of the world's most famous evangelist, Billy Graham. What you probably don't know is that two of his five children were spiritual wanderers, and they broke their parents' hearts. Billy's wife, Ruth Bell Graham prayed, watched, and waited for them to return to the fold. She used the pain she experienced to minister to others by writing a book, *Prodigals and Those Who Love Them.*

Ruth's writing shows deep understanding of the confusion and fear of the ones who wait for their prodigals to return. The power of the book is the fact that she was writing from her own painful experience and practice, not theory.

Because she had suffered the heartache of raising two prodigal children, she had the hard-earned credentials to minister to others with prodigals in their lives.

A Broken Heart in Every Pew

Ruth "Bunny" Graham is the daughter of the famous evangelist Billy and his wife, Ruth Bell Graham. Bunny, the daughter of one of the most famous Christians in American history, endured the pain and embarrassment of a divorce after her husband was unfaithful. Her children have taken her through many additional heartaches. She observed, "I know what it's like to sit in the pew with a broken heart."[5] With genuine candor and compassion, she tells her story in the book *In Every Pew Sits a Broken Heart.*

> My own story is not tidy. Nor is it simple. My story is messy and complicated and still being written. I have known betrayal, divorce, depression, and the consequences of bad judgment. I have struggled to parent my children through crisis pregnancy, drug use, and an eating disorder. I have known heart-break, desperation, fear, shame, and a profound sense of inadequacy. This is not the life I envisioned. Far from it.[6]

Out of her pain, Bunny developed a deep desire to help others. With wisdom only gleaned in the classroom of suffering and sorrow, she discovered a ministry in helping the hurting. Read her words slowly.

> My own plans for my life had been wrecked many times over, but it was not too late to join in on what God was doing. I knew I could serve others with compassion. . . . I was willing to touch hurting and broken people with the same grace God had shown me when I was hurting and broken.[7]

The Desert School of Ministry Training

Often we have a mistaken view of what qualifies us to minister effectively to others. Education is certainly helpful. Training is always good. Gifts are important. Godly character is essential. But we too often overlook the fact that in the loneliness of the wilderness and the difficulties of the desert God truly prepares us to minister to others.

After enjoying the thrill of successful ministry, cohosting a popular television show, writing books, and speaking and singing to large audiences,

Sheila Walsh fell apart and checked into a psychiatric hospital. She thought she checked in alone, but Jesus checked in with her. As she deeply experienced the love of God in her place of brokenness, He prepared her for much more effective ministry.

With deep understanding she writes: "You do not come out of the desert empty-handed but with a pocket full of gifts to share." One of the gifts she discovered in the desert was that she had a deeper, broader ministry than before. She says: "The amazing thing was my brokenness was a far greater bridge to others than my apparent wholeness had ever been."[8]

Looking back on the burdens and benefits of brokenheartedness, she wisely concluded:

> I now believe that God delights to use those of us who have had our
> hearts and wills broken in the desert, who understand that if we stood
> in front of the Red Sea and it parted we should get on our faces and
> worship, not call a press conference.[9]

"I Have Cerebral Palsy. What's Your Problem?"

The odds were cruelly stacked against young David Ring. He was born with cerebral palsy, an incurable set of neurological disorders that permanently affect body movement and muscle coordination. When he was nine, his father died. The family home burned to the ground a few years later. His mother died from cancer when he was only 14.

Orphaned and shuffled from family to family, David had nowhere definite to call home. He lived with continual humiliation and ridicule from other kids. But he met Christ as a teenager. Through Christ, David triumphed over his tremendous hardships. In Christ he discovered that he could be a victor instead of a victim.

Miraculously, God called him into a full-time ministry of evangelism, and in his early twenties David began to hold nearly 50 revival crusades a year. Today he speaks to an average of 100,000 people a year in a variety of venues. He also is married with four healthy children.

I first heard him speak over 20 years ago, and I have never forgotten his message. At first his slurred speech was irritating and difficult to understand. But like the rest of the audience, I was quickly captivated by his amazing story, positive attitude, and wonderful, self-deprecating sense of humor. He skillfully told his incredible story of overcoming such stiff odds. Then he looked at the audience and said, "I have cerebral palsy. What's your problem?"

All of our excuses for not serving God and all of our griping at our difficulties pale in comparison to what he has endured and still battles every day. His example of relying on Christ to rise above his overwhelming obstacles is an inspiration to all of us to rise above ours.[10]

Wounded Healers

In *The Wounded Healer*, Henri Nouwen argues that we heal others from our own wounds. He asks a profound question:

> Who can take away suffering without entering into it? The great illusion of leadership is to think that others can be led out of the desert by someone who has never been there.[11]

Through the empathy that comes from having been down the same road of suffering as another, we can minister more effectively than otherwise possible. Others can tell when we truly understand their pain and feel their hurt. A connection can be made. Trust can be built. Then real ministry can occur.

In describing the power of wounded healers, a young mother whose daughter died of sudden infant death syndrome shared:

> It's as though people who have lost someone precious speak a different language. I don't have to explain things. There is a clear understanding that is so comforting.[12]

Reflect and Learn

There is value in reviewing your life to understanding how it has shaped you. Forgotten experiences have little lasting benefit. We can rarely see the purpose in our pain and sorrow while it is happening. Only in hindsight can we see how our wise and loving God used our pain to produce our good.

One reason I keep a journal is to look at my life and extract the lessons I am learning. I go through a journal about every four months. I like to use the beginning of a new journal, or the beginning of a new year, to take the time to review what God was up to in the previous season. It is valuable to review how God has worked in the various defining moments of my life and consider some of the lessons I learned that might help others.

What Now? Turn Your Suffering into Your Story

For God to bring good out of your painful experiences, you need to share them. You have to stop covering them, and you must honestly admit your faults, fears, and failures. You must use painful past experiences as points of entry into the lives of fellow strugglers in need of ministry. You must not waste your pain but instead use it to encourage others. This will greatly enhance the fruitfulness of your ministry.

I suggest that you intentionally write up some of your painful experiences into your "suffering testimony." Your suffering testimony will include suffering you experienced innocently like a painful illness. It will also include pain that you brought upon yourself by poor choices such as an alcohol addiction.

1. My life seemed normal until . . .

Explain the occurrence(s) in your life where you were discouraged or challenged by a great burden. It can be something like a past addiction to drugs, alcohol, or pornography. It can also be an event like the death of a friend or family member, an illness, depression, or maybe the divorce of your parents. It does not have to be anything catastrophic or impressive, just an event of importance to you. This is not the time to be self-righteous. Rather, it is a time to be vulnerable and transparent.

2. I discovered hope and help in Jesus when . . .

As you recall the past occurrence in your life, explain in detail how God intervened. Use phrases that express emotions and feelings. Also recall Scripture verses and biblical stories that were helpful in meeting your needs.

3. I am glad I have a personal relationship with Jesus today because . . .

This is when you brag on Jesus! Explain how your life has changed for the better. However, be careful not to overexaggerate or to come off as if you have obtained perfection. Remember, the purpose of the suffering testimony is to use painful experiences to identify with others and create bridges to more effective ministry.

Immediate Application

Write out your suffering testimony by using the guidelines below:

1. My life seemed normal until . . .

2. I discovered hope and help in Jesus when . . .

3. I am glad I have a personal relationship with Jesus today because . . .

Ministry Is . . .

1. Enhanced and expanded by the affliction we endure.
2. Taking the encouragement we receive when we suffer and passing it on to others when they suffer.
3. Refusing to waste a hurt.
4. Not making excuses.

⮞ Quote ⮜

People are always more encouraged when we
share how God's grace helped us in weakness than
when we brag about our strengths.

—Rick Warren[13]

Notes

1. J. Piper, *Brothers We Are Not Professionals* (Nashville, TN: B&H Publishing, 2002), 167.

2. D. J. Kennedy, *Turn It into Gold* (Ann Arbor, MI: Vine Books, 1991), 34.

3. R. Warren, *The Purpose-Driven Life* (Grand Rapids, MI: Zondervan), 246–47.

4. Ibid., 247.

5. R. B. Graham, *In Every Pew Sits a Broken Heart* (Grand Rapids, MI: Zondervan, 2004), 12.

6. Ibid., 12–13.

7. Ibid., 168.

8. S. Walsh, "A Winter's Tale" in *The Desert Experience* (Nashville: Thomas Nelson, 2001) 181.

9. Ibid., 179.

10. D. Ring's full story is available on his Web site, http://www.davidring.org/biography.html.

11. H. Nouwen, *The Wounded Healer* (New York: Doubleday, 1979), 40.

12. M. Lattanzi-Licht, "Living with loss: Bereaved swim against tide of grief," 2001, Partnership for Caring, Inc. Distributed by Knight Ridder/Tribune Information Services, http://itrs.scu.edu/fow/pages/Course/C-14.html.

13. Warren, *The Purpose-Driven Life*, 247.

22

Partnering with the Holy Spirit

Dave Earley

The power of ministry is the Holy Spirit.
—DAVID AND WARREN WIERSBE[1]

Help Is on the Way

When I first started in ministry, I put a lot of pressure on myself to impact other people's lives. It was exhausting and frustrating. I could not lead anyone to Christ, make anyone more holy, more loving, or more joyful. I could not even make myself more holy, loving, or joyful. I found that in myself I lacked the necessary power to effect change in people's hearts and lives, including my own. What could I do?

The disciples faced a similar dilemma although they probably did not fully realize it. Jesus was going to be leaving them soon. Knowing they would severely struggle without Him nearby, He gave them a promise.

> And I will ask the Father, and He will give you another Counselor to be with you forever. He is the Spirit of truth. The world is unable to receive Him because it doesn't see Him or know Him. But you do know Him, because He remains with you and will be in you. (John 14:16–17)

"He will give you *another Counselor*." A Greek student will tell you that the word *another* means "another of the *same* kind." In other words this Counselor would be the same kind as Jesus. Just like Jesus, the Counselor is fully God. We generally refer to the Counselor as the Holy Spirit.

A Greek student also will tell you that the word *Counselor* is *parakletos*, which is a compound verb with the prefix *para* (alongside) and the verbal base *kaleo* (to call). So the Holy Spirit is called alongside of us. The word *parakletos* may also be translated "helper, comforter, advocate, aid."

This is good news. We do not have to try to be holy, loving, and joyful on our own. We do not have to try to make others holy, loving, or joyful in our own power. God the Holy Spirit does all of this through us.

Christian growth is simply a matter of cooperating with what the Holy Spirit wants to do in our lives. Christian ministry is simply partnering with what the Holy Spirit is already doing in the other person's life.

Meet the Most Important Person in Your Spiritual Life, the Holy Spirit

Some churches talk a great deal about the Holy Spirit. Others rarely do. While the Bible does speak more often about Jesus the Son and God the Father, it also has much to say about God the Holy Spirit. More than 100 names, titles, and descriptions of the Holy Spirit are listed in the Bible.[2] Let me give you a quick overview.

The Holy Spirit Is God

The Bible teaches the tri-unity of God. Historically Christians have believed in one God who expresses Himself in three persons. These three persons are God the Father, God the Son, and God the Holy Spirit. All three are equally God. The members of the Trinity are equal in nature, separate in person, but submissive in duty. The Holy Spirit has the exact same nature, attributes, and character as God the Father and God the Son.

When the Bible refers to the Holy Spirit, He is described as having attributes that are only found in God. The Holy Spirit is omnipresent (Ps 139:7). He is omniscient (1 Cor 2:10–11). He is omnipotent (Gen 1:2; Luke 1:35). He is eternal (Heb 9:14). He is holy (Luke 11:13). Beyond that, the Holy Spirit is frequently referred to as "God" (Gen 1:1–2; Luke 4:18; Acts 5:3–4; 2 Cor 3:18). He is equated with the Father and the Son (Matt 28:19–20). The early church fathers in the Athanasian creed stated, "We worship one God in Trinity and Trinity in unity, neither confounding the persons or dividing the substance."[3]

The Holy Spirit Is a Person

Some have mistakenly referred to the Holy Spirit as an "it." This could not be more inaccurate. The Holy Spirit is every bit as much a person as is God the Father or God the Son. He has intellect (Rom 8:27; 1 Cor 2:10–11; Eph 1:17), emotion (Eph 4:30), and will (1 Cor 12:11). He has creativity (Gen 1:2). He has love (Rom 15:30). Beyond that, He is referred to with personal pronouns (John 15:26; 16:13–14).

The Holy Spirit is also *not* a ghost who scares nonbelievers. He is *not* an impersonal force that zaps people. He *is* a person who pursues people and speaks to their hearts.

The Holy Spirit Carries Out God's Work on Earth Today

Although the Son and the Holy Spirit were evident in the Old Testament times, the Father was most dominant. Although the Father and the Spirit were involved in the work of the Son on earth, Jesus was front and center. Yet, since the day of Pentecost, the Holy Spirit is the person of the Godhead who is primary in God's work today.

Old Testament Times	Gospel Times	Current Times
1400 BC–4 BC	4 BC–AD 30	AD 30–Tribulation
God the Father	God the Son	God the Holy Spirit

Since the day of Pentecost in about AD 30, the Holy Spirit has been primary in God's work on this planet. The Bible tells us that Jesus sat down because His primary work was finished.

> [The Son] is the radiance of [God's] glory, the exact expression of His nature, and He sustains all things by His powerful word. After making purification for sins, He sat down at the right hand of the Majesty on high. (Heb 1:3)

When Jesus ascended to heaven, His saving work on earth was finished. But the sanctifying, empowering work of the Holy Spirit was just beginning. The noted pastor Charles Spurgeon observed, "Jesus Christ could cry out concerning his own work of salvation—'It is finished.' But the Holy Spirit cannot

say that. He still has more to do: and until the fulfillment of all things, when
the Son himself becomes subject to the Father, it will not be said by the Holy
Spirit, 'It is finished.'"[4]

The Holy Spirit is active in the lives of people today.

The Holy Spirit Is the Most Important Person in Your Spiritual Life

The work of the Holy Spirit does not end when a person gets saved. Any
spiritual progress is impossible in our old nature. If we make spiritual progress,
it must be accomplished in cooperation with the Holy Spirit.

> For those whose lives are according to the flesh think about the things
> of the flesh, but those whose lives are according to the Spirit, about the
> things of the Spirit. For the mind-set of the flesh is death, but the mind-
> set of the Spirit is life and peace. For the mind-set of the flesh is hostile
> to God because it does not submit itself to God's law, for it is unable to
> do so. Those whose lives are in the flesh are unable to please God. You,
> however, are not in the flesh, but in the Spirit, since the Spirit of God
> lives in you. But if anyone does not have the Spirit of Christ, he does not
> belong to Him. (Rom 8:5–9)

At salvation the work of the Holy Spirit expands as He makes us holy or
sanctified (1 Cor 6:11; 2 Thess 2:13). He produces in us virtues we could never
bring out on our own—love, joy, peace, patience, etc. (Gal 5:22–23). Spiritually
speaking, without Him we can do nothing.

Meet the Most Important Person in Your Ministry Life, the Holy Spirit

"If the Lord removed the Holy Spirit from this world, much of what we
are doing in the church would go right on and nobody would know the difference," write pastors David and Warren Wiersbe in their book *Making Sense of
the Ministry*.[5] "Too much ministry today depends on human personality, gim-
micks, good public relations, religious entertainment, and various techniques
borrowed from the world of show business," they continue. "It was the power
of the Holy Spirit that energized the early Christians, and you will need His
power to energize your life and ministry."[6]

Effective ministry begins today as you learn to spend time with God the
Holy Spirit by reading the Word, praying, yielding, obeying, worshipping,
avoiding sin, confessing unrighteousness. Learn to cultivate a good relationship

with the Holy Spirit, and you will discover the joy of being empowered by the Spirit to impact peoples' lives for Jesus.

Partnering with the Holy Spirit to Reach the Lost

The Holy Spirit wants people saved more than we do. He has supernatural power we do not have to convict lost people of sin, righteousness, and judgment. Because the Holy Spirit is omniscient, He knows exactly what is going on in lost people's lives and thoughts as we are talking with them. Only the Holy Spirit has the power to regenerate a lost person into a new creation in Jesus Christ. Therefore, it only makes sense that if we hope to evangelize anyone, we should rely on Him.

Anytime a person gives his or her life to Jesus Christ, it is never a solo operation. At least three persons are always involved. First is the nonbeliever who hears the gospel and receives Jesus by faith and repentance. Second is the person who shares the gospel with the nonbeliever—that would be us. Third is the Holy Spirit who applies the gospel to the understanding of the nonbeliever.

The Holy Spirit plays several primary roles in the conversion of the lost. First, He produces conviction. Jesus spoke of the Spirit's convicting the world of sin, righteousness, and judgment (John 16:8). Conviction is an awareness of guilt for one's own sins. Only God can produce such awareness. He uses believers to proclaim His truth about sin, but the Spirit must apply it to unbelieving men and women's hearts to produce conviction. Otherwise they would continue to deny their sinfulness and their need for a Savior.

Second, the Holy Spirit produces repentance. Repentance is a desire to turn from our sins once we have been convicted of them. God grants repentance (2 Tim 2:25) because men are incapable of repenting on their own (Acts 11:18).

Third, the Holy Spirit empowers the proclamation of the gospel. The Spirit empowers God's truth so it penetrates the unbeliever's mind and begins to do its saving work. He empowers both the proclaimer and the hearer. These works of the Spirit are necessary for effective proclamation and reception of divine truth (1 Thess 2:13). First Peter speaks of "those who preached the gospel . . . by the Holy Spirit" (1:12), and 1 John 5:6 says, "And the Spirit is the One who testifies, because the Spirit is the truth."

The Spirit's Power Is the Key Element in Effective Preaching

The Holy Spirit regenerates hearts. Jesus told Nicodemus in order to be born again he would have to be born *of the Spirit* (John 3:5–8). Paul said, "He saved us—not by works of righteousness that we had done, but according to His mercy, through the washing of regeneration and renewal by the Holy Spirit. This Spirit poured out on us abundantly through Jesus Christ our Savior" (Titus 3:5–6).

The key to being effective in evangelism is simply learning to cooperate with the Holy Spirit and share Christ's message with the person we are trying to reach. I am convinced that the times I have been least effective in evangelism have been those times when I either tried to go it alone, without being sensitive to the Holy Spirit, or worse, tried to be the Holy Spirit in the life of the lost person. Conversely, the times I have been most effective in evangelism are when I have tried to adjust my words and the pace in which I pressed the need to the leading of the Holy Spirit. If we want to be effective in the ministry of evangelism, we must stay attuned to and cooperative with the Holy Spirit.

I often ask Christians this question: "How many of you have ever shared the gospel with a lost person and found yourself saying things that were more clear and intelligent than you imagined you could?" They all nod their heads and answer yes. Why does this happen? The Holy Spirit actively partners with us when we share the gospel. Effective evangelism is simply cooperating with Him.

"My Name is Scott. I Used to Live in Columbus, Ohio, and I Love to Eat at Waffle House"

A few weeks ago I was speaking at a church in Pennsylvania. I was teaching through Luke 15:1–7 regarding Jesus' heart for lost people. I happened to tell two illustrations I had not planned on giving. They were not in my notes, but in the middle of my message, I found myself talking about a man named Scott in Columbus, Ohio. Later I found myself telling a story about a student doing servant evangelism at a Waffle House. I also had not planned on giving a "come forward and get saved" style of invitation, but I did. I was shocked by the 11 people who came forward, weeping as they gave their lives to Jesus. One of the men who came forward that morning approached me afterward.

"I need to talk to you," he said. He was an average-looking, middle-aged man. But I noticed that he had an odd smile on his face.

"Please do," I replied.

"I have never been to this church before," he began. "But I had to get saved today."

"What do you mean?" I asked.

"You see, *my* name is *Scott*, I used to live in *Columbus, Ohio*, and I loved to eat at *Waffle House*," he said slowly yet excitedly. "When you mentioned Columbus, Ohio, and Waffle House, you really had my attention. Then when you told about your friend *Scott* getting saved, God spoke to me and told me that I needed to stop running and get saved."

I was stunned.

"I have been to churches a few times, but it never made sense before. I guess I was not really listening. Today when you said Columbus, Ohio, Waffle House, and Scott, I knew I had to listen."

Think about it. Neither I nor the pastor of that church had ever met that man before.

But the Holy Spirit had.

Neither of us had any clue that he would be a guest at church that day.

But the Holy Spirit did.

I had no idea that using an illustration telling about evangelizing a man named Scott in Columbus, Ohio, or one about a student doing servant evangelism at a Waffle House would be key in getting this man's attention so he could hear the gospel and get saved. But the Holy Spirit did.

Effective ministry is partnering with the Holy Spirit in bringing people to Christ.

Partnering with the Holy Spirit to Help Others Grow in Christ

The Holy Spirit is already at work in the lives of everyone we are called to minister to. He is working in the lives of His children to transform them to be more like Jesus. Our job as ministers is to cooperate with Him as He works in our lives *and* partner with Him as He works in the lives of others.

Spiritual growth is not a Lone Ranger activity. Anytime a person grows in their walk with God, it is never a solo operation. At least three persons are always involved. First you and I share the Word of God. Second are those to whom we are ministering. They need to respond to the Word of God in faith and obedience. Third, the Holy Spirit applies the Word of God to the circumstances of their lives to bring about change in the life of the person to whom we are ministering.

I cannot change other people's lives for them. I must partner with the Holy Spirit as He works in them to bring about change in their lives. My job is simply to do my job. If I am leading a small group on a Tuesday night, or doing some counseling with a young believer on a Monday afternoon, or leading a worship-based prayer encounter on Wednesday night, or preaching to a large crowd on a Sunday morning, my responsibility is clearly, wisely, and graciously to share the Word of God. It is up to the other person or persons to respond as the Holy Spirit works.

Ministry becomes less intimidating, more joyful, and much more effective if we do our ministry with awareness of and empowerment by the Holy Spirit. He is already ahead of us working in people's lives. The Holy Spirit is what they need, and He does the work.

The Holy Spirit gives access to God the Father in prayer (Eph 2:18) and helps us pray (Rom 8:26–27). The Holy Spirit helps believers understand the truth of the Word of God and apply it to their lives (1 Cor 2:12–14; 2 Pet 1:21; 1 John 2:20,27).

Because He is God with and in us, He is everything we need for life and godliness. He also is everything needed by the people you are called to serve. When people are discouraged or brokenhearted, the Holy Spirit is the Comforter (John 14:16–17). When people need direction and understanding of truth, the Holy Spirit is the Teacher (John 14:26; 1 Cor 2:12; 2 Pet 1:21; 1 John 2:20,27). When people need guidance, He is the Guide (Rom 8:14). When they are weak, the Holy Spirit is the Power Giver (Luke 24:49; Eph 3:16; Acts 1:8).

The Holy Spirit is present, willing, and able to work in the lives of God's children. Effective ministry is cooperating with the Holy Spirit as *He* works in other people's lives.

"How Did You Know What I Was Going Through This Week?"

I cannot tell you the number of times someone has come up to me on a Sunday morning and said, "How did you know what I was going through this week?" or, "The whole time you were talking, it was as if you were talking straight to me." Whether I am teaching a large class of 500 college students or speaking at a church to 2,000 people, I hear it again and again. The truth is that I did not know what they were going through that week. But the Holy Spirit did. He applied the truth of the Word of God to their lives and situations as only He can.

Jesus Promised the Enabling Empowerment of the Holy Spirit

The last words a person says are often considered the most important. The last words of Jesus, the most important person who ever lived, are certainly to be considered some of the most significant words ever uttered on this planet. Interestingly they involve the promise of the Holy Spirit empowering us for global ministry.

But you will receive power when the Holy Spirit has come on you, and you will be My witnesses in Jerusalem, in all Judea and Samaria, and to the ends of the earth. (Acts 1:8)

Partner with the Holy Spirit

Effective ministry is actively cooperating with the Holy Spirit as He works in others' lives. When you do ministry, the Holy Spirit will give you wisdom you did not know you had. He also gives you sensitivity you could not possibly have on your own.

Ministry Is . . .

1. Recognizing the role the Holy Spirit plays in the lives of the people we are ministering to.
2. Valuing the Holy Spirit as the person of the Godhead who is primary in God's work today on planet Earth.
3. Partnering with the Holy Spirit in bringing people to Christ.
4. Actively cooperating with the Holy Spirit as He works in others' lives.
5. Relying on the Holy Spirit to give you wisdom and guidance you could never have on your own.

⌒ Quotes ⌒

*Spiritual ends can only be accomplished by spiritual
men using spiritual means.*
—J. OSWALD SANDERS[7]

*Ultimately, spiritual leadership comes as a result of the
working of the Holy Spirit. It is the Holy Spirit who
reveals God's will to people. It is the Holy Spirit who equips
people to lead others. It is the Holy Spirit who guides
leaders and authenticates their leadership before people.*

*It is, therefore, essential that leaders cultivate a deeply
personal and vibrant relationship with God as they
become the kind of leader God wants them to be.*

—HENRY AND RICHARD BLACKABY [8]

*Spirituality is not easy to define but its presence or absence
can easily be discerned. . . . It is the power to change the
atmosphere by one's presence, the unconscious influence which
makes Christ and spiritual things real to others.*

—J. OSWALD SANDERS [9]

*The anointing of the Holy Spirit helps me greatly when I
preach. I would never attempt to teach the truth of God by
my own power.*

—GEORGE MULLER [10]

*This one thing I know, brethren, . . . the Holy Spirit
must work all our works in us, and that without
him we can do nothing. . . . Only the Holy Spirit has
power over the hearts of men and women. . . .
We cannot reach the soul; but the Holy Spirit can.*

—C. H. SPURGEON [11]

Notes

1. D. Wiersbe and W. Wiersbe, *Making Sense of the Ministry* (Chicago: Moody Press, 1983), 45.

2. E. Towns, *The Names of the Holy Spirit* (Ventura, CA: Regal Books, 1994), 11.

3. P. Schaff, *The Creeds of Christendom* (New York: Harper Brothers, 1877), 1.4.5.

4. C. H. Spurgeon sermon, "The Power of the Holy Spirit," June 17, 1855, see http://www.biblebb.com/files/spurgeon/0030.htm.

5. D. and W. Wiersbe, *Making Sense of the Ministry,* 45.

6. Ibid.

7. J. O. Sanders, *Spiritual Leadership* (Chicago: Moody Press, 1967), 25.

8. H. Blackaby and R. Blackaby, *Spiritual Leadership* (Nashville, TN: B&H Publishing Group, 2002), 285–86.

9. Sanders, *Spiritual Leadership,* 25.

10. G. Muller, *The Autobiography of George Muller* (New Kensington, PA: Whitaker House, 1985), 35.

11. Spurgeon, "The Power of the Holy Spirit."

23

Engaging with Encouragement

Dave Earley and Ben Gutierrez

Therefore encourage one another and build each other up as you are already doing.

—1 Thessalonians 5:11

"I Got Nothing"

When we first got married, my wife and I (Ben) did a personality assessment, and she turned to me and said, "Look how high I am on mercy and encouragement! So, where are you on mercy and encouragement?" I looked at my chart to count the bubbled-in boxes I had filled out that registered as "encourager" and "mercy-giver." "Where are they?" I asked. "I can't find them." I turned my paper over, under, and upside down to find any boxes filled out that registered "mercy" or "encouragement." I turned to my wife and said, "I got nothin'." From that day I began to become a student of my wife as she taught me the value of mercy-giving and encouragement.

I observed my wife warm a friend's heart with her words. I witnessed how people would gravitate to her just to hear her point out a valuable characteristic about them. I noticed that she never got exhausted in offering encouragements.

In fact, it seemed to serve as fuel that made her thrive spiritually throughout the day.

I also saw the encouragement return to her in the form of others testifying of her when not around her. People would actually come to me out of a crowd just wanting me to know how much my wife had made a lasting impact upon their life. I could overhear people expressing their appreciation for her as I walked by a group of people in church. Mostly, I recall being greatly impressed at how many people profoundly respected her. My wife's testimony of encouragement persuaded me to cultivate that gift as much as possible.

So today I'm a softy compared to how I was many years ago. Now I receive immense joy in offering encouragements to my family, friends, coworkers, and fellow ministers. I am totally sold out to the fact that encouragement is the fuel that can ignite passion to serve, the power needed to endure to the end, and hope given to a soul about to throw in the towel. I love that God allows me to offer His life-altering words of encouragement to others!

The word *encouragement* seems to evoke a love/hate perception. In my personal ministry experiences, I find that most people either love encouraging people or loathe the thought of having to express encouragement to someone else. Some people attribute the value of encouragement as weightier than gold. Others tend to see it as something that will only send a negative message in some way, shape, or form. They are afraid that the person receiving such encouragement will never attempt to improve their performance because they have already received approval.

On more than one occasion, I have been told, "I don't really see the need to offer encouragement to a person for doing what he is supposed to be doing in the first place." Someone else asked me, "If it's their job and they're getting paid for it, why should I encourage them for doing it?" Once I actually had two parents tell me, "We don't offer any encouragement to our children for simply obeying what we say because that's what they know we want them to do."

But since I was raised in a similar home and have struggled to be an encourager as a result, I shared with them this truth, "You should affirm only what behaviors and actions you wish to continue. So, if 'standard' obedience and compliance are something you wish to continue, then you ought to encourage them like crazy!"

In one sense, effective ministry is not complex. Ministry is encouraging people.

We All Need Encouragement

I (Dave) train church planters. Not a week goes by without one of my guys calling or e-mailing. While the pressing issue is that they want a piece of advice, what I have learned is that what they really want and need from me is encouragement.

Stepping out to minister is a fearful thing. Everyone needs someone drawing alongside of him saying, "You can do it. Don't quit." Everyone needs someone who believes in him. Everyone needs encouragement.

I was a shy high school student. Yet my youth pastor kept encouraging and pushing me to get out of my comfort zone and minister. He made me share a testimony before the youth group. He "begged" me to be in the youth choir. He "twisted my arm" to give the devotional at a large youth gathering.

When I was getting ready to go to college, I was struggling to understand my future. My youth pastor had allowed me to get close enough to him to catch his heart to make a difference in people's lives. Because he had made the effort to deepen his relationship with me, I had been able to hear his prayers for people, see him minister to people, and watch him agonize over people. He had something I wanted. Yet I did not think I had what it would take to succeed in ministry. So when I sensed God speaking to me about going into ministry, he was the first person I sought out for confirmation. I will never forget when he said, "Dave, I believe that God will use you to make a difference for Him." I wonder if I would have become a pastor if it had not been for his encouragement. Everyone needs someone to believe in him.

When I was a college student, I sensed God calling me to plant a church. One of my professors expressed belief in my ability to plant a successful church. This was a giant encouragement that I desperately needed. I wonder if I would have become a church planter if it had not been for his encouragement. Everyone needs someone to believe in him.

Everyone needs encouragement. Effective ministers come alongside others and believe in them. They tell others when they are doing a good job. They help them any way they can. They lift them up by speaking highly of them in front of the group.

Much of ministry is encouraging people. Therefore, everyone is a candidate for your ministry because everyone needs encouragement.

God Wants You to Finish the Verse

Paul wrote to the young pastor Timothy to encourage him and to guide him as he led the important church at Ephesus. Second Timothy 4:2a is probably one of the most popular and valued verses by ministers who enjoy preaching, teaching, or sharing God's Word in any type of forum. We like it because it gives us the license to proclaim God's Word, do it all the time, and if needed, call out sin with all the authority of the Word of God: "proclaim the message; persist in it whether convenient or not; rebuke, correct" (2 Tim 4:2).

But the verse doesn't stop there! There's more to the verse. God wants us to finish the verse. Many people fulfill the first part of the verse because it is pretty much us doing all the work. We preach. We are ready. We convince and we rebuke. But the reason many don't practice the latter portion of the verse is because it causes us to have to focus on other people's learning curve: "and encourage with great patience and teaching" (2 Tim 4:2b).

The word "encourage" speaks of adding courage to someone who needs it. It literally means to have someone "come alongside of you" like a lawyer stands next to you and offers you protection, encouragement, guidance, and peace of mind. Paul joins it with the words *patience* and *teaching* He is saying that we are patiently to encourage and teach the person until the concept is understood. In order to encourage another person effectively, we must be invested in his life enough to know how he is doing.

Encouragement Only Happens Up Close

If we are to provide this life-sustaining encouragement, we can't always do it locked away and never seen by another human being all week long. It requires getting close and intimate with people. Of course, there are positions in which people can't walk the halls, utter 20 minute-long prayers with every member he meets, and kiss every baby with whom they come in contact. Time with people can be scheduled and arranged. But the point is that the time must be sufficient to engage in offering encouragement with your people.

Hans Finzel is a successful author, consultant, and expert in the field of leadership. He is also president of an international leadership development organization with associates in 65 countries worldwide. One chapter of his book, *Top 10 Mistakes Leaders Make*, really marked my (Ben) life. It is about the mistake of putting "paperwork ahead of people work." In it Finzel shares that as a young leader he was trying to serve his followers by taking care of all of their needs logistically. But he failed in one major area that he calls "the human element, that subjective, person-to-person contact so essential in ministry."[1] Quoting Henri J. Nouwen, Finzel states, "'I have always been complaining that my work was constantly interrupted, until I slowly discovered that my interruptions were my work."[2]

Finzel reminds us that regardless of what orientation one has in leadership style, task or people, effective leaders make room for people. He acknowledges that even though we may tend toward one style because of our personalities, we are not to use that as an excuse to ignore and avoid people. He concludes his chapter by testifying that "when all is said and done, the crowns of my achievements will not be the systems I managed, the things I wrote, the structures I built, but the people I personally, permanently influenced through direct contact."[3]

God wants you in the trenches with your ministry team. Express your care for them. Encourage them in the facets of their job they are doing well. Offer your thanks for their commitment to believe in the ministry in which you both colabor. Offer a prayer for them, their commitment to kingdom, and their family's commitment to be a part of their ministry.

Encouragement Can Take Many Forms

Encouragement is not a one-size-fits-all activity. A stirring pep talk may be needed on one occasion, but it may be totally inappropriate on another. Sometimes the performance of encouragement is the act of listening. Maybe it will be giving advice.

The most effective encouragers use more than one approach. They study the other individual's personality, spirit, temperament, and the current situation. Then the minister encourages accordingly. The onus is upon us as the minister to work on being well equipped to encourage the various members of the body of Christ.

> And we exhort you, brothers: warn those who are lazy, comfort the
> discouraged, help the weak, be patient with everyone.
> (1 Thess 5:14)

In this verse Paul encouraged the Thessalonians to use different strokes for different folks. Encouragement comes in different shapes, sizes, and colors in order to fit the need. The unruly person needs warning. The timid needs comfort. The weak should be uplifted. Everyone will require patience.

Through his letters Paul sprinkles little words of instruction that show us the many ways we can encourage others. Read through this list slowly and see where you can improve.

- "Love one another." (Rom 13:8)
- "Show family affection to one another with brotherly love." (Rom 12:10)
- "Outdo one another in showing honor." (Rom 12:10)
- "Be in agreement with one another. Do not be proud; instead, associate with the humble. Do not be wise in your own estimation." (Rom 12:16)
- "Therefore, let us no longer criticize one another." (Rom 14:13)
- "Therefore accept one another, just as the Messiah also accepted you." (Rom 15:7)
- Instruct one another. (Rom 15:4)
- "Have the same concern for each other." (1 Cor 12:25)
- "Serve one another through love." (Gal 5:13)
- "Carry one another's burdens." (Gal 6:2)
- "Accepting one another in love." (Eph 4:2)
- "And be kind and compassionate to one another, forgiving one another, just as God also forgave you in Christ." (Eph. 4:32)
- Speaking to one another in psalms, hymns, and spiritual songs, singing and making music from your heart to the Lord. (Eph 5:19)
- "Submitting to one another in the fear of Christ." (Eph 5:21)
- "Consider others as more important than yourselves." (Phil 2:3)
- "Forgiving one another." (Col 3:13)
- "Teaching and admonishing one another." (Col 3:16)
- "Overflow with love for one another." (1 Thess 3:12)
- "Build each other up." (1 Thess 5:11)

Rules for Relationships

Billy Hornsby is an effective ministry coach and a master at relationships. He has a way of turning everyone he meets into a close friend. In his little book *Relationship Intersections: 101 Rules for Relationships*, he shares a lifetime worth of insights into how to encourage others. Some of his "Relationship Rules" include:

1. Let your subordinates shine, if they shine bright enough it will reflect back on you.
2. Give the credit away. The man who takes credit away from someone else is a thief.
3. Listen long. Encouraging words that bestow grace are always a blessing, but listen first and listen long. Listen with your eyes and listen with your ears.
4. Never violate the confidence of a friend or an adversary.
5. Only speak negatively of ideas and actions, not people.
6. Never take advantage of another person's weakness.
7. Say "Thank you" often.
8. Don't offer criticism without giving a disclaimer.
9. Affirm people. Affirmation is the act of supporting and encouraging the efforts, gifts, self-worth, values and goals of the other person.
10. Never flatter. Sincere compliments are always welcome, but flattery is insincere.
11. Compliment a deed well done.
12. Forget all the past mistakes of your friend.
13. Don't correct adults in front of others.
14. Don't forget to reward accomplishment.
15. Praise character. Look for people who are faithful, attentive, on time, flexible, honest, truthful, caring, loving, humble, and polite.[4]

The wise pastor James reminded us that encouragement comes through listening. "My dearly loved brothers, understand this: everyone must be quick to hear, slow to speak, and slow to anger" (Jas 1:19).

Paul told the Romans that in order for listening to be effective, it must be active. We encourage others by empathizing when we listen to them. "Rejoice with those who rejoice; weep with those who weep" (Rom 12:15).

What Now? Making Your Ministry a Great Place to Work

Are you naturally prone to be an encourager? Or are your strengths in other areas and not in the area of encouragement? Have you ever attempted to become a more encouraging person? What is stopping you from trying to be an encouraging person?

Describe a time that you offered encouragement to a fellow believer who received with gratitude what you shared. How long ago was that encounter? Does the person still interact with you today, and are you reminded occasionally by this person that it really impacted his or her life?

Describe a time when someone offered you encouragement at just the right time. How did it make you feel? How long ago was that comment made to you? Do you still feel the positive impact of their words?

Have you ever experienced a season of drought with regard to receiving encouragement? How did it make you feel when no encouragement was coming your way? What types of questions did you raise in your head when you hadn't received encouragement? Did you wonder if you were viewed as a hard worker? Did you question if your friends were still your true friends anymore? Did you worry if you would continue to be used in your ministry position?

Take a moment to list some individuals you believe would be eternally impacted by your words of encouragement, and begin now thinking of what you could say to them and when the opportune time would be this week to share your thoughts with them.

Ask God for opportunities to make a positive impact with your encouraging words this week, and ask Him to use them to spark an excitement in their hearts to continue worshipping Him more passionately.

Ministry Is . . .

1. Going beyond the duties that are expected of us and ministering to others through our encouraging words.
2. Engaging the people to whom we minister and listening to them in order to understand how and when to apply words of encouragement.
3. Being thoroughly equipped to provide appropriate and unique encouragement to each individual in ministry.

⌒ Quotes ⌒

Christian organizations are sometimes the worst, because there is the attitude that: "They are working for the Lord, and He will reward them for their labors."

—HANS FINZEL[5]

A good leader learns to read the signs of upness and downness in the countenance of his people.

—HANS FINZEL[6]

Notes

1. H. Finzel, *Top 10 Mistakes People Make* (Colorado Springs, CO: D. C. Cook, 2002), 42.

2. Ibid., 41.

3. Ibid.

4. B. Hornsby, *Relationship Intersections: 101 Rules for Relationships* (Mount Pleasant, SC: Billy Hornsby Publishing, 2002).

5. Finzel, *Top 10 Mistakes People Make*, 55.

6. Ibid., 58.

24

Confronting Sin

Ben Gutierrez

Sadly, sometimes those we are ministering to in the body of Christ get caught up in sin. In may be immorality, or drunkenness, or pornography. It might be lying or cheating.

What happens when giving them encouragement is not enough? What do we do when godly affirmation, attention, and affection are not getting through? How should we respond when someone we care about is way offtrack? How do we handle it when a fellow believer is caught up in sin? What do we do about blatant sin in the body of Christ?

The answer to these questions is that the sin must be confronted. If we love people, we must love them enough to want what is best for them and for the body of Christ. This means that we must be willing to challenge them to face up to the sin in their life and deal with it. Sometimes mature ministry is confronting sin.

You don't do anybody any favors if you don't tell them their true condition. If you're a medical doctor and you know that their true condition physically is serious and you don't tell them, that's a kind of malpractice as well as a disregard for the worth and value of that person. Spiritually the same thing would be true if you understand the spiritual condition of a person is dangerous and you don't tell them. There are times when there is no real ministry without confronting sin.

The Attitude of Confrontation

Timothy served as the pastor of the church at Ephesus. No doubt some of his sheep wandered off into sin. For Timothy to serve effectively, he would need to confront them to make necessary changes in their lives. Paul understood this and gave the young pastor insight into the attitude he would need in order to confront effectively. "Preach the word! Be ready in season and out of season. Convince, rebuke, exhort, with all longsuffering and teaching" (2 Tim 4:2 NKJV).

If we take Paul's instructions apart, we can learn the type of spirit needed in order to confront effectively. "*Convince*" speaks of emphasizing the truth in a direct yet softened tone. "*Rebuke*" describes the fact that occasionally the person doing the confronting will need a forthright tone. "*Encourage*"—as you confront, you must offer genuine care and remind people that you are on their side! "*Great patience* " means that helping them will require not giving up unless they reject what God wants them to do." *Teaching*" implies always bringing truth to bear upon any situation.

In his letter to the Galatian church, Paul offered additional instruction on the spirit of those who are confronting another:

> Brothers, if someone is caught in any wrongdoing, you who are spiritual
> should restore such a person with a gentle spirit, watching out for
> yourselves so you won't be tempted also. (Gal 6:1)

"Restore such a person. " The word *restore* (*katartizo*) means "to repair." It's actually a medical term used of resetting fractures or mending bones, putting dislocated limbs back in place.

The idea then of dealing with sin in this way is certainly not to put people out. It's to restore them because they have so much value. And you do it in a spirit of gentleness. Never should this be harsh. Always it should be bathed in compassion, tenderness, sympathy, patience, and mercy because you understand your own sinfulness.

"Watching out for yourselves so you won't be tempted also"—nothing will make confrontation less effective and more explosive than a self-righteous attitude. They need to feel that you are not looking down on them or acting like you are better than them. You care about them and want to help them deal with something that is hurting them.

The word translated "gentle spirit" should be understood as meaning "a mild demeanor; not quick to arrogance or haughty thinking of oneself." It is interesting that Paul used the same word to describe the character of Jesus Christ Himself: "Now I, Paul, make a personal appeal to you by the gentleness and graciousness of Christ" (2 Cor 10:1).

Jesus, who unlike us had a reason to be self-righteous and could look down on others, did not. He dealt with people out of a spirit of gentleness.

Putting these verses together, we see that we must go into any confrontation with a Christlike attitude. We should make sure confrontation is done in the spirit of genuine humility and gentleness with the purpose of bringing truth to bear upon the situation. Occasionally we may have to be forceful in order to get the point across. But overall we should be enduringly patient and devoid of arrogance.

No one with a shepherd's heart really enjoys confronting sin. But if we love people, we will sometimes have no other choice. As we do so, remember this principle. You confront people in their sin because you deeply love them, but you should not deeply love confronting people!

You may know that you need to do it, and you may even have the skill set that allows you to confront with relative ease, but you should never fall in love with confronting. It should grieve you that it has to be done, and you should never relish the fact that you have to confront someone. So it is OK that you get nervous and anxious; I am glad you do! Still we realize that confrontation is a necessary act of ministry that we must prepare ourselves to do in order to lead a pure body of Christ.

The Approach to Confrontation

The Bible is explicit as to the protocol for confronting sin in the life of a brother or sister in Christ. Jesus gave us guidance as to the protocol of confronting a person with a concern we may have regarding their actions.

Step 1: One-on-One Confrontation

> If your brother sins against you, go and rebuke him in private. If he listens to you, you have won your brother. (Matt 18:15)

When you become aware of blatant and serious sin in the life of another believer, your first step is to approach individually. Approaching the person one on one dramatically reduces the chance for rumors to spread and demonstrates to the person that you are interested in resolution and spiritual healing and that you are not even remotely interested in spreading juicy gossip.

You should approach them with the appropriate spirit of concern, gentleness, humility, love, and truth. You should share how much you want God's best for them. You should make it clear that you do not enjoy what you are doing. Express to him or her that you are doing this because you love them so much.

One-on-one confrontation is the most nonthreatening form of confrontation and provides the most conducive environment by which confession can occur. Most people will break at this point, confess their sin, and repent. For someone not to confess at this level of confrontation is to show that they lack wisdom. It also will bring about additional embarrassment upon themselves in future encounters. For if confession is not made at this stage of the approach, then additional people must be summoned to speak to the situation.

Step 2: A Few-on-One Confrontation

> But if he won't listen, take one or two more with you, so that by the testimony of two or three witnesses every fact may be established. (Matt 18:16)

Sadly there are times when confession is not made in the nonthreatening environment of a dear friend and the sinner in the quietness of an empty room. Then it is required that one or two spiritual believers be summoned into the discussion to hear the continued discussion of the confrontation.

The purpose of doing this is to bring more pressure on the one caught in sin to repent. Having several people saying the same thing can open the person's eyes to a blind spot and awaken them to the seriousness of their sin.

Also, having a few other believers involved provides witnesses to the words spoken by both parties and testimony of the truth in the matter. If someone is caught up in sin and lacks wisdom and does not confess during the one-on-one confrontation, then the Scriptures tip us off that you may have a fight on your hands. As a result, you need even more people to testify to the truth of each person's testimony.

Sadly guilt-stricken sinners can turn on those who confront them. Usually in this situation the few additional people invited in on the conversation unfortunately end up needing to protect the initial confronter from the slander, hatred, and lies of the person who is being confronted. But make no mistake, spiritually discerning people will know the truth and be able to discern between truth and lies.

Step 3: Leadership-on-One Confrontation

> If he pays no attention to them, tell the church. (Matt 18:17a)

Sadly some refuse to respond to the gentle confrontation of a few caring believers. Refusal to adhere to the counsel of a few believers may be expected since he/she did not adhere to the counsel of their one close friend.

The next step is to bring the matter to someone in church leadership (a pastors, elder, or deacon). I believe this passage is talking about the church leadership as they would be addressing the issue with the gathered group of elders, pastors, or deacons *prior to* it coming before the entire church congregation without any notice, background, or prior critique by the spiritual leadership.

Unfortunately I have found that a sinning and rebellious believer usually avoids the invitation to bring everyone together for a myriad of reasons. Some avoid testifying once again in front of everyone together because they have spun their story. Or they simply do not want to address their sin in front of spiritual ministers who will undoubtedly confront their sin issues. Either way, the avoidance of this step is grounds enough to enact some level of discipline. But never forget, through this entire process we are praying for confession and repentance by bringing everyone together. Sadly, occasionally our prayerful hope is not realized.

Step 4: Church-on-One Confrontation

> But if he doesn't pay attention even to the church, let him be like an
> unbeliever and a tax collector to you. (Matt 18:17b)

If the person in sin refused to meet with the church leaders, or if leaders are not satisfied with the outcome of the meeting that took place with the one who has been found to be in sin, then the ministers have the responsibility to inform the church. At this point they are to inform the church that the believer in question has not repented of sin and thus has caused a fracturing in fellowship between him or her and the rest of body of Christ.

As a result, all succeeding interaction with the individual should be framed in such a way as to telegraph deep, abiding love for the sinning individual. But your love needs to be based on truth. Communicate that you love them so much, you must have a less intimate relationship with them until the individual repents. This must be communicated to the individual upon every encounter so that he or she will be reminded every time that he or she is loved by you and the members of the church. It must also be communicated whenever possible to the individual the camaraderie that you once enjoyed prior to their season of sin and nonrepentance will never be experienced again as long as he or she remains in their impenitent state.

This will be hard to do as it goes against our own human nature, but that's why it is the forth step of confrontation—only if needed. The Scriptures are clear as to the need for such a protocol. It is necessary to go through this demanding and time-consuming, biblical protocol if you indeed love and deeply care for the spiritual well-being of a fellow believer in Christ.

The Anticipated Outcome of Confrontation

As you know, Joseph and Mary had children after Jesus was born. These siblings of Jesus did not believe that He was the Messiah (John 7:5). In fact, they thought He was crazy. Yet after Jesus' resurrection, at least two of his half brothers, James and Jude, became fervent followers of Jesus. We assume that this is the result of loving confrontation by Jesus Himself. Both of them were compelled to exhort others to practice restoration, rescue, and retrieval of sinners.

Have mercy on some who doubt; save others by snatching them from the fire; on others have mercy in fear, hating even the garment defiled by the flesh. (Jude 22–23)

My brothers, if any among you strays from the truth, and someone turns him back, he should know that whoever turns a sinner from the error of his way will save his life from death and cover a multitude of sins. (Jas 5:19–20)

The Application of Confrontation

How do you feel about what you have just read? Do you think you can do this? Do you think you can manage this type of spirit as you, the minister, confront your precious people? I hope so.

But I have an even more important question. What if someone needs to confront *you* regarding a sin in your life? Maybe it is not something as serious as adultery or drug addiction, but perhaps you have some blind spots in some of your attitudes, actions, or words that are displeasing to Christ.

Do you think you can take this, too? Do you think you can accept a fellow believer confronting you in the tender spirit and per the biblical direction described in this chapter?

Ministers are not above being confronted by fellow leaders and members of their congregation. I have been lovingly confronted by friends and family members. At the moment of confrontation, I immediately attempt to rehearse the truth of the Bible verses presented in this chapter and fill my mind with His Word because the flesh despises instruction and sin *hates* to be exposed. But as long as the confrontation is done in the spirit that was described above and the motives of the confronter are pure, then I tell myself, "May the Lord be praised through this, and may I use this to be a better, more humble minister." It is indeed hard to take, but it is necessary for my spiritual growth as a minister.

Not to receive correction from a Spirit-led confronter is to deprive yourself of one of God's most loving ways to protect your life from a multitude of sins and further destruction from becoming a reality in your life (Jas 5:19–20). Ministry is more than confronting sin in the lives of others; it is being willing to allow others to confront sin in your own life. Beyond that, ministry is training others how to confront sin according to the pattern given to us by Jesus.

It Starts with You

We've talked about how to deal with a believer who has sinned. We have talked how logistically to confront the sinning believer, the protocol if repentance is not expressed, and the mercy that should surround such actions. But do you know who trains the congregation in this process? You do!

You give permission to your people to confront you in your sin. You educate them in the Scriptures so they will be guided in the words they say to you and to one another. You show them how and when to approach tenderly, patiently, or bluntly. You express your willingness to be placed under this type of scrutiny. You are the key to the faithful execution of this process!

Let me warn you. Your human flesh will not welcome such scrutiny. If you open your heart to the teachings of this particular chapter, your flesh will immediately begin to persuade you that you're crazy for even entertaining this advice. I can hear your flesh now:

> "What, are you nuts?! You can't trust your people. They're not educated like you are. They lack appropriate people skills. Are you actually going to place your reputation in the hands of mere parishioners of a church? There is no way you're going to listen to someone who has never

ministered before in his/her life! There's a reason why you're the minister
and they are not! So forget it. Go ahead and keep this *Ministry Is* book
on your shelf—it's an OK book—but you can forget this chapter. This is
where a textbook simply can't teach you about reality and real ministry!"

Remember, the flesh is always warring against the soul and spiritual things
(Rom 8). It will continue to scream and protest against what is true and God-
honoring. In fact, I can answer every protest that the flesh just raised above with
this reality. How your congregation responds will depend on you.

You teach and model for your congregation what it means to be biblically
literate, spiritually balanced, and trained to lovingly, patiently, and mercifully
confront you and fellow believers. Literally, you have the authority, influence, and responsibility to make sure your congregation handles confrontation
properly.

So, if you fear the above description of all the potential mishandling of the
confrontation moment, then start training them so they can take the truths of
the Word of God and translate these into practice. Commit sincerely to invest
in your people to make them seasoned ministers themselves to their families,
friends, and fellow believers. And by doing so, you'll have a culture of accountability in your congregation!

Open to It?

Do you think you can accept a fellow believer confronting you in the spirit
and direction that is talked about in this chapter?

Do you receive this discussion with thanksgiving because you acknowledge that God has put a safeguard in your life to keep you from making grave
mistakes? Or, in some warped way, has your flesh caused you to think, "Well,
if I ever got to the first step, I'd say [this]; then if it moved to the second step,
all I'd have to say is [this], etc."

Do you feel that you are above being confronted by any sin at anytime? Or
is your heart open to spiritual scrutiny for all the benefits it yields?

How you answer these questions in your heart will provide a clear commentary on your current spiritual state. If you welcome the spiritual scrutiny,
you have placed this much-needed protection around your mind, heart, and
soul. If you resent being confronted and feel accountability is only for the unrealistic idealist in the body of Christ, then it will be a commentary of pride that
the Scriptures promise will inevitably destroy your life and ministry.

So how open are you as a minister to accept loving and constructive criticism? My prayer is that you are free to accept it as well as committed lovingly to proceed with it if needed in the life of a fallen believer.

Ministry Is . . .

1. Confronting Jesus' way.
2. Following God's loving and wise direction when confronting sin.
3. Accepting spiritual advice and scrutiny for our spiritual well-being.
4. Training others how to confront sin in a biblical manner.

⇜ Quote ⇝

If you, in the church, are not willing to confront someone's sin, then you don't see them as having any value. Christ sees them as having value. He paid the infinite price for them, did He not? And He gives us the responsibility like any parent to go after our wandering children.

—John MacArthur[1]

Notes

1. J. MacArthur in the sermon "The Childlikeness of Believers: Confronting Sin, Matthew 18:15–20," www.gty.org/Resources/Sermons/90–348.

25

Balancing the Busyness

Ben Gutierrez

I'm busy."

We have all heard it thousands of times. It's the universal answer. It'll work as a response for virtually every formal, informal, casual, or courteous question that is posed to us. And no one ever questions it because they use it too! The conversations go something like this:

"How was your week?"

"Busy."

"Do you think you can make this weekend, or will you be busy?"

"I'm sorry; I think I'm busy on that day."

"Do you have a moment to talk right now?"

"Sorry, I'm a little busy right now."

"You have a phone call from your mother-in-law. What should I tell her?"

"I'm Busy!"

"Do you want to drop everything and play a round of golf?"

"Sure!"

OK, so it works for almost every question. But I think we would all agree that if that word was not in our vocabulary, we'd be in trouble because we use it all the time. We use it so often because we are so often very busy. Our world is spinning fast, and we seem to add tasks and responsibilities to our week on a daily basis.

Unfortunately, ministers are not immune from cultivating a busy schedule. According to a recent survey of 1,000 pastors conducted by LifeWay Research, almost two-thirds of all senior pastors work 50 or more hours each week while 8 percent pull 70-plus-hour workweeks. The survey also found that among full-time senior pastors, 42 percent work at least 60 hours a week.[1]

First Things First

Let's consider a scenario. One woman is working hard in the kitchen trying to prepare a big meal for her guests. Another lady is quietly sitting, listening, and learning. Which one is doing the right thing?

At one time in Jesus' ministry, He was put on the spot to make such a judgment call upon the weight and worth of doing a lot of ministry duties and tasks compared with doing nothing except sitting at the feet of Jesus and learning from Him. Two of His close friends, Martha and Mary, had chosen two different ministry objectives. Martha chose to slave in the kitchen and prepare the meal for Jesus and all of His disciples. But rather than assisting Martha in the kitchen (which would have been the customary thing to do), Mary chose to remain with the disciples to listen to Jesus' teaching. She was enthralled by it and seemingly would not break away for any reason.

It did not take long for Martha to disapprove of Mary's choice for practical reasons. Martha was busy. She had a lot to do in order to prepare for thirteen men, plus one sister, plus whoever else might be there. She was irritated that her sister was not helping her in the kitchen.

In all fairness to Martha, she certainly did not object to Mary's learning from Jesus. Martha loved Jesus as well. She simply saw a job that needed to be done, and she felt compelled to fulfill that responsibility. Hospitality was a major expectation in this culture, so for Martha to choose to prepare a fine, nourishing meal would have been considered an honorable thing to do.

Being frustrated, Martha burst out of the kitchen and made a direct request of the Lord Jesus. She insisted that He command her sister Mary (whom Martha might have already approached on many occasions to no avail) to join her in the kitchen to help her prepare the meal. She wanted Jesus to side with her and tell Mary to recognize that the duties of preparing the meal were of the utmost importance at this time. I doubt she was ready for Jesus' reply:

> While they were traveling, He entered a village, and a woman named Martha welcomed Him into her home. She had a sister named Mary, who also sat at the Lord's feet and was listening to what He said. But Martha was distracted by her many tasks, and she came up and asked, "Lord,

don't You care that my sister has left me to serve alone? So tell her to give me a hand."

The Lord answered her, "Martha, Martha, you are worried and upset about many things, but one thing is necessary. Mary has made the right choice, and it will not be taken away from her." (Luke 10:38–42)

What was the life lesson Jesus wanted to point out to Martha? At that particular time, Martha was too busy. When Jesus said that she was "distracted," he used a term that means "overly occupied," "pulled away," or "to be pulled away." This is the descriptive word for someone who is "too busy."

We often read this account and believe that it was the right time for a meal to be prepared or that Martha was following the appropriate protocol of preparing a meal. But by the tone of this word, it may have been that the meal wasn't called for another hour or two. In fact, Martha's frustration might have been self-imposed in a desire to prepare things in advance. Even then the Lord did not harshly rebuke her excellent desire to plan ahead. But the issue is that for some unstated reason Martha probably had her priorities backward and was missing out on what was most important at that time—communing with God Himself!

Three Realities about Communing with Jesus

There is certainly a place for the physical and logistical duties and tasks of ministry. If not, then why would God have granted His children so many spiritual gifts that focus on helping, serving, giving, and administration? Doing is vital to ministry and should be accomplished on time with excellence. This is not a chapter prescribing that we ignore the details and the doing of ministry and default to sitting in a corner and studying all day. A balance is needed. But in this particular situation with Mary and Martha, the doing somehow *replaced* time that should have been reserved for listening to the voice of God.

Notice three realities that Jesus makes in verse 42 about making sure you intentionally partition off and protect time to listen to the voice of God:

1. Communion with God Is Necessary

"*But one thing is necessary.*" Jesus pointed out that even though many things seemingly are necessary to accomplish in ministry, communion with God is the one thing that is needed. It functions as our life blood as believers. God reminds us that doing ministry without taking time to feed off His Holy Word will leave us frustrated and unfulfilled in ministry. To neglect listening to

Jesus through His words will focus on secondary duties rather than on what should be primary in our ministries.

Evangelist and Bible college founder Oswald Chambers keenly understood the value of spending time with the Lord in the midst of a busy ministry schedule. He wrote:

> The greatest competitor of true devotion to Jesus is the service we do for Him. It is easier to serve than to pour out our lives completely for Him. The goal of the call of God is His satisfaction, not simply that we should do something *for* Him. We are not sent to do battle for God, but to be used by God in His battles. Are we more devoted to service than we are to Jesus Christ Himself?[2]

In his sermon on Luke 10:38–42, John MacArthur states: "The single priority for all Christians is to hear the revealed Word of God because that is prior to every other spiritual duty, which is motivated by, informed by, and defined by Scripture. The story makes it so clear. Number one priority, hear what God has said."[3]

2. Communion with God Is the Best Choice

"Mary has made the right choice." Jesus reminds us that we should be able to discern between what is better and best. The most challenging task for all ministers is to discern the best decision for our lives. We settle for good, or beneficial, or safe and miss out on what is best. Jesus reminded us that communing with Him and His Holy Word is the best act of ministry that can ever be performed.

3. Communion with God Will Make a Lasting Impact

"And it will not be taken away from her." Jesus made a profound statement in this final phrase about the value of God's Word making an eternal impact on our lives as ministers. As ministers, we long to make an eternal impact for the kingdom in our community, country, and the world. We all long to see our friends, family, and fellow believers experience God in a life-changing way. We all want God to impact their lives in such a way that they never forget the moment for the rest of our lives. But we often try to make that impact by focusing on physical duties, tasks, and accomplishments to make that eternal mark on their lives. If we do this, they may never experience an eternal impact because we do not do what Jesus said that produces a lasting impact on our lives. Jesus said that partitioning, protecting, and devoting personal time to

prayer, devotion, and communion with God can make an eternal impact on anyone's life.

Recalling Encounters with God

I often ask my students, "What did you do in your ministries exactly six Sunday mornings ago?" Then I reinforce the fact that I want to know exactly and literally the duties they performed on the Sunday morning in question. Interestingly, I usually see a good number of hands raise immediately, but when they begin their response, they tend to provide generalities rather than specific responses. For example, I often hear, "Well, I usually get there early at around 7:45 a.m. or so. Then I always seem to take care of this [task] first. Then I usually go upstairs and . . ."

By this time I politely interrupt them and rephrase the question, "That's great that you have a routine, but are you able to pinpoint exactly what duties and physical tasks you specifically performed on that Sunday morning six weeks ago?" At this point they pause and look up the date and then try to recall what they did by first recalling if it was a special Sunday, what the pastor spoke on, who was/wasn't there, etc." In other words, they know they were there and active with responsibilities, but they have a difficult time rehearsing for me and the class what exactly they accomplished six Sundays ago.

"Me too," I quickly say. "If you were to ask me what I did approximately six Sundays ago, I too admit that I know I was there and was involved in doing ministry; but right off the top of my head, I can only recall in general what duties and tasks I most likely performed."

Then I quickly transition to another question. "How many of you remember a time you either listened to a pastor, Sunday school teacher, or someone else share a passage of Scripture that *so* moved you that you found yourself totally engrossed and impassioned in the teaching of the passage so that you couldn't help but contemplate what was shared well into the evening hours?"

Then I add, "Or better yet, how many of you remember a time when you were studying a portion of God's Word and your heart became so moved over what you were reading that you had to drop your pen and begin praising God because you could hardly sit down?" Hands begin to raise immediately with such excitement that it looks like I'm teaching a second-grade class of students who are saying with their gestures, "Oh, pick me! Pick me! Pick me!"

At this time I begin hearing some of the most glorious stories of how God's Word impacted their lives, and they do so specifically. In great detail they recall the first time they were exposed to a passage of Scripture that has since become their life verse. With contagious enthusiasm, they share how they experienced the Holy Spirit moving their hearts and were brought to tears as God's Word became so alive to them that they couldn't contain their praise. Some shared how they even stood up from their desk in their bedroom and began to shout praises to God! They share times of sincere confession where they knew God had totally forgiven them of their sins. Others share how they saw a lost loved one's heart break in front of their eyes as the minister simply read and reread a Bible verse without any elaboration. And when the students get on a roll, I often find myself fighting back tears because I too become so moved by the testimonies of how they were moved by the Scriptures.

The stories come one after another without pause. And then out of an immense amount of curiosity, I ask them quickly to shout out loud, "How many years ago did those specific encounters occur?" Immediately, I hear:

- "Three years ago!"
- "Four months ago!"
- "Two years ago!"
- "Eight years ago!"
- "Six weeks ago!"

Then a pause seems to strike us all profoundly. In the silence I ask them (rhetorically), "Now, what physical tasks did you do in ministry six weeks ago? And how long ago did the Scriptures make this level of impact on you?" Then I explain that I know what they are all feeling in their hearts by saying, "I think we know now what really makes an eternal impact in ministry—God's Word."

Spending Time with God in His Word

Spending time daily feasting on the Word of God is essential for maintaining effective ministry. Some general guidelines enhance any daily time spent with God's Word:

1. Have a set time. It may be first thing in the morning, late in the afternoon, or before you go to bed. The important issue is not when you take time but that you take time. It order to be consistent, it helps to have a standing appointment with God and His Word.

2. Block out an amount of time. This may be from 10 minutes to an hour. Reading three chapters a day takes approximately 15–30 minutes, depending on the length of the chapters. By reading three chapters a day, you can read through the Bible in a little over a year.

3. Have a place. Your place can be at the desk. Or in your favorite chair. Or in a coffee shop.

4. Follow a plan. Some people like to read all the way through the Bible. Others like to read the same chapters daily for a month. Others like to study a paragraph at a time..

5. Mark in your Bible or write in a notebook. What you note may be a sin you need to confess, a promise you need to claim, an example you need to fol-low, or a command you should keep. As you read, do not be afraid to under-line, circle, or mark key words, names, or verses in your Bible.

6. Read or study in different translations on occasion. You can get 22 differ-ent translations for free online (www.biblegateway.com).

7. Vary your "diet" by periodically switching from reading the Old Testament to the New and vice versa. It is all the Word of God.

Now What? Overwhelmed or Overjoyed?

Do you have any stories of how God impacted your life while listening to or studying His Word? If so, rehearse them out loud or with a friend. Take time to rejoice over them. Then say when that encounter occurred. And if there has been no encounter to that magnitude in the last year, ask yourself why you haven't experienced God that way in recent days?

Are you busy?

Are you too busy?

If you consider yourself "too busy," what do you believe is the cause of all your busyness? Is it simply a rough season in your life, or is it self-inflicted? Are there too many good and honorable irons in the fire that are actually keep-ing you from focusing on doing what is best?

Do you spin your wheels performing duties and tasks and calling it minis-try, or are you making sure that you are encountering God's Word during your ministry week? Are you convinced that this routine will make an eternal impact on your life? Will you take time to experience God's Word profoundly?

And, most importantly, are you a demanding taskmaster forcing your ministry team to perform so many tasks that it leaves no time for them to be impacted eternally by God's Word?

Ministry Is . . .

1. Intentionally partitioning, protecting, and devoting time to commune with Jesus.
2. Carefully examining ministry decisions to make sure the best option is always chosen.
3. Teaching your people the balance of doing ministry and communing with Jesus by your example.

Quote

In our Lord's life there was none of the pressure and the rushing of tremendous activity that we regard so highly today, and a disciple is to be like His Master. The central point of the kingdom of Jesus Christ is a personal relationship with Him, not public usefulness to others.

— OSWALD CHAMBERS[4]

Notes

1. M. Kelly, "LifeWay Research: Pastors' long work hours can come at the expense of people, ministry," January 5, 2010, http://www.lifeway.com/article/?id=169886.

2. O. Chambers, *My Utmost for His Highest, Updated Edition* (Grand Rapids, MI: Discovery House Publishers, 1992), January 18 entry, 18.

3. J. MacArthur in the sermon, "The Christian's Priority: Luke 10:38–42," www.gty.org/Resources/Sermons/42–145.

4. Chambers, *My Utmost for His Highest*, October 19 entry, 293.

26 Being Content Instead of Being Competitive

Ben Gutierrez and Dave Earley

"Will he ever learn?" I found myself saying to the pages of the Bible as I read and reread the account of Peter's restoration at the end of John's Gospel (John 21:19–22). Previously Jesus had recommissioned Peter to the ministry of shepherding spiritual sheep. Then Jesus warned him of the price to be paid, and He hit Peter with a stiff exhortation. Unfortunately, Peter gets off track . . . again.

> He asked him the third time, "Simon, son of John, do you love Me?"
> Peter was grieved that He asked him the third time, "Do you love Me?" He said, "Lord, You know everything! You know that I love You."
> "Feed My sheep," Jesus said. "I assure you: When you were young, you would tie your belt and walk wherever you wanted. But when you grow old, you will stretch out your hands and someone else will tie you and carry you where you don't want to go." He said this to signify by what kind of death he would glorify God. After saying this, He told him, "Follow Me!"
> So Peter turned around and saw the disciple Jesus loved following them. That disciple was the one who had leaned back against Jesus at the supper and asked, "Lord, who is the one that's going to betray You?" When Peter saw him, he said to Jesus, **"Lord—what about him?"** (John 21:17–21, bold added for emphasis)

"Lord—what about him?" Notice what Peter did. Peter turned around (literally) and said, in essence, "Wait a minute, Lord. If I'm expected to die in service for you, what about your servant John? He seems to be your favorite. Are you going to require that he die too, or will you let him live to see your coming? And if he is going to live to see your coming, that just doesn't seem fair to me!" How did Jesus respond? It wasn't pretty for Peter. "'If I want him to remain until I come,' Jesus answered, 'what is that to you? As for you, follow Me'" (John 21:22).

"What is that to you?" Another way of putting this is, "It is none of your business what I do with John!" Jesus immediately saw in Peter the natural tendency we all have to compare ourselves to and compete with other ministers. The Lord could not let this attitude go without addressing it. He was not going to sweep this under the carpet, overlook it, or ignore it. Jesus had to deal with Peter and his attitude. So He wasted no time in realigning Peter's focus!

"Follow Me." Notice that Jesus had used *two* simple words in His request of Peter in verse 19: "Follow Me." But when Peter got His eyes off of Jesus Christ (just like when he was sinking in the water after walking on the water) and began to worry about someone else, Jesus repeats His command to Peter with a little more intensity: "As for you, follow Me."

In His rebuke Jesus put more emphasis on Peter individually and specifically. Jesus had a personal and individual directive for Peter. Therefore, Peter should not even start down the path of worrying about what anybody else was doing in their ministry. Jesus wanted Peter to do what Jesus had called him to do, and He made that clear to him and to the other disciples.

The Reality of Comparison

Ministerial comparison was going on 2,000 years ago and continues today. You can see it exemplified throughout Scripture. The Corinthians fell in the trap of comparing one minister with another. But Paul refused to play their game.

> For we don't dare classify or compare ourselves with some who
> commend themselves. But in measuring themselves by themselves
> and comparing themselves to themselves, they lack understanding.
> (2 Cor 10:12)

This conviction in Paul makes me wonder if perhaps he had heard about the time Jesus had to confront Peter. It would not surprise me if Peter shared that story with Paul and many other disciples before he died. It is clear from Peter's letters that he learned a valuable lesson that day.

Too easily we fall into the trap of comparing our ministry with the ministry of someone else. For example, if their ministry is larger than ours, we fall into the trap of envying them. If ours is larger, it is easy for us to be proud. All of it is sickening and sinful.

The Reality of Competition

Closely linked to comparison is competition. Even the apostle Paul had to deal with other ministers who pulled no punches about how they believed their leadership should be followed and not the leadership of Paul.

Imagine. Paul was suffering in a Roman prison when he wrote his letter to the church at Philippi. In his letter he mentions that while some served out of pure motives, others were preaching the gospel out of a competitive spirit.

> Some, to be sure, some preach Christ out of envy and strife, but others out of good will. These do so out of love, knowing that I am appointed for the defense of the gospel; the others proclaim Christ out of rivalry, not sincerely, seeking to cause me anxiety in my imprisonment. (Phil 1:15–17)

A Remedy for Competition

Someone observed, "To love is to stop comparing." It is impossible to have a heart full of love for a Christian brother and still be envious or critical toward him at the same time. They are mutually exclusive. The Bible is clear that instead of spending our time and energy competing with and comparing ourselves to our Christian brothers and sisters, we are to love them.

Read slowly through this sampling of injunctions from the apostle Paul. As you do, ask God to give you a greater love for your colaborers in the gospel.

> Show family affection to one another with brotherly love. Outdo one another in showing honor. (Rom 12:10)

> Love does not envy. (1 Cor 13:4)

> Your every action must be done with love. (1 Cor 16:14)

But serve one another through love. (Gal 5:13)

Above all, put on love—the perfect bond of unity. (Col 3:14)

Now we ask you, brothers, to give recognition to those who labor among you and lead you in the Lord and admonish you, and to esteem them very highly in love because of their work. Be at peace among yourselves. (1 Thess 5:12–13)

No one should despise your youth; instead, you should be an example to the believers in speech, in conduct, in love, in faith, in purity. (1 Tim 4:12)

Now you, man of God, run from these things; but pursue righteousness, godliness, faith, love, endurance, and gentleness. (1 Tim 6:11)

The Result of Comparison and Competition

Comparison is the result of insecurity. Competition is a by-product of pride. Together, they become a cancer within the body of Christ and should be extracted swiftly before destruction can spread. Competitive spirits can easily lead to spreading false rumors and slandering other ministers.

Ministerial competition is a sin. It brings no value to the body of Christ, and it diverts our effort from performing the vital work of the ministry. Valuable time that could have been spent ministering to the precious, needy, and hungry is wasted.

Beyond that, it can hurt. Paul acknowledged that even though the Lord was in control of the matter, the ministerial competition hurt. In verse 16, Paul said that they are "seeking to cause me trouble in my imprisonment." The words "cause me" are also translated "to compound" or "to arouse." Therefore, Paul acknowledged that it was compounding his pain while he was in prison.

Remember the words of Jesus to Peter, "'If I want him to remain until I come,' Jesus answered, 'what is that to you? As for you, follow Me'" (John 21:22). Jesus is explaining that when He calls you for a specific purpose, you don't have to worry about what anyone else is doing. Don't begin listening to the lies of the evil one that you should be vitally interested in what is being said about you. Do not even start down the path of worrying about what anybody else is doing in their ministry. Jesus is saying, "I am your God! I am your Savior! I am your Creator! I am bigger than any Devil who suggests that his word is more profound and truthful than mine! My child, simply keep your eyes on Me and focus on my perfect and loving will for your life."

A Minister's Life Verse

Like most Christians, I (Ben) have a life verse that I use as a spiritual plumb line by which to measure all of my efforts and initiatives. I rehearse its message whenever I am tired in ministry and feel that I have nothing more to offer. And I find that the more I celebrate its truth, the easier it is to get back up and focus on why I became a minister in the first place—to bring joy and honor to the heart of God and to Him alone.

> Therefore, my dear brothers, be steadfast, immovable, always excelling in the Lord's work, knowing that your labor in the Lord is not in vain. (1 Cor 15:58)

Let me give you a quick explanation of some key words of this verse, and then I'll put the pieces together to help you apply this transforming verse. "My dear brothers" refers to all believers who have accepted Jesus Christ as their personal Savior (i.e., the "body of Christ"). This command is aimed squarely at believers and ministers.

"*Be steadfast*" means "to be seated" or "to stay in place."

"*Immovable*" means "to be rendered immobile, incapable of moving or going elsewhere." In essence, God is telling us not to move or even be able to move out of or from something.

"*Always excelling*" is a phrase that is expressing a superlative idea, meaning we are continually to be progressing, pursing, or growing by leaps and bounds.

This may sound confusing. On one hand, this verse teaches us that all believers have to be seated, stay in one place as if rendered immobile. But on the other hand, once we get to this one place, we start bouncing around! Does this seem odd? Hang in there with me, I'll explain in a moment.

"*Labor*" means to "work or toil to the point of exhaustion." So God is saying that you should not only get moving, but you should be so active that it brings you to the point of exhaustion. Almost like panting after running a hard race!

Confused? Wondering how can you be both "seated" and "rendered immobile" while "abounding"? It kind of sounds like God's Word is commanding us, "Don't move!" and at the same time, "Get moving!"

Let me attempt to put it all together. The words "steadfast" and "immovable" refer to how we should never leave the will of God—meaning don't you dare walk out outside of His will, His purpose for your life, or His mission for your ministry. But while you are smack-dab in the middle of God's will, start working like crazy! Work hard! Pray hard! Focus! Always be growing, developing, superseding, and abounding in your personal relationship with and service to Christ!

But here's the clincher: while you focus on being in the center of God's will, and while you worry about how you are doing in God's eyes, take confidence and be encouraged that your hard work and ministry are not "in vain" (i.e., without purpose, without value, or empty). Your work has profound purpose and depth of meaning!

Ministry is about settling into the will of God and working as hard as *you* can. We are to do this without needlessly comparing ourselves with or competing with anyone else. We need to do what *we* have been called to do.

Run Your Own Race

I (Dave) remember one year watching the Olympics on TV. I will never forget watching the drama as an athlete lost a race in the most frustrating manner. A runner was in the lead, but just before he reached the finish line, he turned his head to one side to check on his competition. In that split second another runner passed him on the other side. The tiny fraction of a second the first runner wasted in comparing himself with the others slowed him down enough to cost him the race.

The author of Hebrews understood the importance of staying focused as we race.

> Therefore since we also have such a large cloud of witnesses surrounding us, let us lay aside every weight and the sin that so easily ensnares us, and run with endurance the race that lies before us. (Heb 12:1)

Notice that each of us has a specific race marked out *for us*. The idea is that our particular course is unique as we follow Jesus. Just as no two fingerprints are identical, no two ministry courses are the same. We get in trouble when we compare ourselves with others and try to run the race the Lord has laid out for them. Instead we must run the race marked out for us.

Godliness with Contentment Is Great Gain

The fallen human heart says that you have to make sure you "watch out for yourself," "make your own mark," or "make a name for yourself" in order to make great strides in life. But God has a different remedy for success. Paul reminded Timothy that "godliness with contentment is a great gain." (1 Tim 6:6). Great gain is not found in pursuing human acknowledgment or achievement. Rather, it is pursuing godliness with a blind eye to external pressures or factors that appeal to you to replace God's way as the prime pursuit of your life.

When we get caught up in comparing ourselves with others we will always find someone who has it better than we do. When this happens, we will become discontent with our situation.

Strict focus on the task at hand and stubborn refusal to compare your situation with others will bring contentment. Don't believe me?

Read the words the apostle Paul wrote from a Roman prison:

> I don't say this out of need, for I have learned to be content in whatever circumstances I am. I know both how to have a little, and I know how to have a lot. In any and all circumstances I have learned the secret of being content—whether well-fed or hungry, whether in abundance or in need. I am able to do all things through Him who strengthens me. (Phil 4:11–13)

What Now? Are You Playing the Game?

Have you gotten sucked into the unending and unsatisfying game of ministry competitiveness? If so, how are things going for you? Do you find yourself exhausted or completely fulfilled? Do you feel that you can ever take a break from staying on top, or can you rest knowing that you are honoring God and that He will cause your ministry to succeed? Is what you do in ministry promoting the ministry of another minister? Is what you are doing tearing down and causing pain and frustration to another minister or ministry?

What if God were to walk up to you right now and ask you to articulate your true thoughts about other ministers and ministries within a 20-mile radius of yours? How would you answer? Are you filled with envy? Are you overly competitive?

Why don't you take a few moments and pray for the other Christ-centered ministries within a twenty-mile radius of you and your ministry. List them in the margin of this book. Ask the Lord to bless them in a very specific way that would reap eternal, spiritual blessings upon them and bring honor to God. Make this a regular part of your life!

Ministry Is . . .

1. Being content with who God made you to be and what God has called you to do.
2. Refusing to compete with or compare yourself to others in ministry.
3. Focusing on what God has for *you* and how He is dealing with *you* as a minister—and no one else.
4. Acknowledging that all ministers and ministries are under attack by the evil one.
5. Lifting up fellow Christ-centered ministries in fervent and sincere prayer.

⌒ Quotes ⌒

That's the way we sinners are wired. Compare. Compare. Compare. We crave to know how we stack up in comparison to others. There is some kind of high if we can just find someone less effective than we are. Ouch.

—John Piper[1]

Frequently I am asked this question, "What is the most discouraging thing in the ministry?" Two things are the most discouraging, distressing things in the ministry. Number one is people who know better acting as if they didn't. The second most discouraging thing in the ministry is being falsely accused, falsely accused by those who are your fellow preachers of Christ . . . who are your fellow servants of Christ but for some reason want to discredit and harm your ministry.

—John MacArthur[2]

Notes

1. J. Piper, "What Is That to You? You Follow Me!" article on Desiring God, http://www.desiringgod.org/ResourceLibrary/TasteAndSee/ByDate/2006/1837_What_Is_That_to_You_You_Follow_Me.

2. J. MacArthur from sermon, "Joy in Spite of Detractors: Philippians 1:15–18," http://www.gty.org/Resources/Sermons/50–58.

Part 5

The Methods of Ministry

27

Praying for Those You Serve

Dave Earley

> *Do you believe God wants to do more in the lives of the*
> *people around you than He is currently doing? Do you*
> *believe that God can do things bigger than you can? Are*
> *you convinced that God can do things faster than you can?*
> *Do you believe that God can do things better than you can?*
> *Would you say that what God does will last longer than the*
> *things you do?*
>
> —Dick Eastman[1]

Of course you do. God does do things bigger, faster, better, and more last-ing than we ever could. He usually does them in response to prayer. Therefore, we must be men and women of prayer who learn to pray powerfully and effectively for others.

A large part of effective ministry is intercessory prayer. The word *inter-cede* means "to go between." Used for prayer, it describes the act of going to God and pleading on behalf of another.[2] Prayer as a general term describes talking to God. Intercession is more specific. It describes coming to God *on behalf of another*. Therefore, while all intercession is prayer, not all prayer is intercession.[3]

Intercessory prayer seeks the best for others before the throne of God by bringing their needs to the One who has the answer. Intercessors go between God and man in prayer, bringing the concerns of poor and weak humans to our rich and powerful God.

Jesus Christ as Intercessor

Jesus lived intercession when He walked on this earth. He identified with us, stood in our stead, and He went to God the Father on our behalf. As a leader He prayed for His followers. In speaking of the 12 disciples, He said, "I pray for them" (John 17:9). In speaking of His then future followers, like us, He said, "I pray not only for these, but also for those who believe in Me through their message" (John 17:20). Even now in His exalted home in heaven, Jesus is the One who "has been raised; He also is at the right hand of God and intercedes for us" (Rom 8:34), and "He always lives to intercede" for us (Heb 7:25).

Moses as Intercessor

Moses had the impossible task of leading and providing for a nation of slaves in the wilderness for 40 years. His primary ministry as he led the Hebrews through the wilderness can be summarized in six simple words: "And Moses interceded for the people" (Num 21:7). Again and again in the books of Exodus and Numbers, we hear Moses crying out to God on behalf of His followers (Exod 17:4; Num 11:2; 14:13–19).

Samuel as Intercessor

Samuel led Israel as a prophet and intercessor. The people respected his role and begged him to pray for them: "The Israelites said to Samuel, 'Don't stop crying out to the LORD our God for us, so that He will save us from the hand of the Philistines'" (1 Sam 7:8). Samuel so prioritized intercession that he felt failing to pray for his people was sinful. He said to his people, "As for me, I vow that I will not sin against the LORD by ceasing to pray for you. I will teach you the good and right way" (1 Sam 12:23).

Paul as Intercessor

The apostle Paul had a busy ministry of pioneer missionary evangelism, disciple making, and church planting. Why was he so effective? What was the core of his ministry? If you read Paul's letters you will note a theme that appears again and again. In the midst of his activity, Paul lived a life of intercessory prayer for those he served.

For God, whom I serve with my spirit in [telling] the good news about
His Son, is my witness that I constantly mention you. (Rom 1:9)

I never stop giving thanks for you as I remember you in my prayers.
(Eph 1:16)

I give thanks to my God for every remembrance of you, always praying
with joy for all of you in my every prayer. (Phil 1:3–4)

We always thank God, the Father of our Lord Jesus Christ, when we
pray for you. . . . For this reason also, since the day we heard this,
we haven't stopped praying for you. We are asking that you may
be filled with the knowledge of His will in all wisdom and spiritual
understanding. (Col 1:3,9)

We always thank God for all of you, remembering you constantly in
our prayers. We recall, in the presence of our God and Father, your work
of faith, labor of love, and endurance of hope in our Lord Jesus Christ.
(1 Thess 1:2–3)

And in view of this, we always pray for you that our God will consider
you worthy of His calling, and will, by His power, fulfill every desire for
goodness and the work of faith. (2 Thess 1:11)

I thank God, whom I serve with a clear conscience as my forefathers
did, when I constantly remember you in my prayers night and day.
(2 Tim 1:3)

Nehemiah as Intercessor

In 586 BC Babylon's king, Nebuchadnezzar, invaded Jerusalem and sacked the city. When Jerusalem fell, the wall was broken down, and the temple, the royal palace, and the city were set on fire. All of the survivors, except for the poorest of the poor, were taken into captivity in Babylon.

Fifty years later, in 538 BC the Persian king, Cyrus, destroyed the Babylonian Empire. In that same year he issued a decree permitting the Jews to return to their native land. As a result, Zerubbabel led nearly 50,000 Jews back to settle in their homeland.

Some 80 years after this, in 458 BC, another return took place during the reign of Artaxerxes I, king of Persia. A scribe named Ezra led this return. This time over 5,700 people returned to the promised land. They worked to begin to rebuild the temple.

Yet, the city still lay in ruin and reproach because the protective wall that surrounded it was still broken down. In the ancient world a city without walls was a desperate and dangerous target for thieving marauders and military invaders. The situation was desperate, and when Nehemiah heard about it, he began to pray. "When I heard these words, I sat down and wept. I mourned for a number of days, fasting and praying before the God of heaven" (Neh 1:4).

Out of his intercessory prayer, the Lord called Nehemiah to go back to Jerusalem and rebuild the walls. A seemingly ordinary man led an untrained and fearful group of despairing and desolate former slaves to accomplish a nearly impossible engineering feat in record time against constant and severe opposition . . . *and* then experienced a major revival. Nehemiah was effective in ministry because he was effective in intercessory prayer.

Ministry Is Praying for Others

Although intercessory prayer is certainly not all there is to ministry, it definitely is the heart of effective ministry. Intercession also makes the other activities we perform—serving, witnessing, teaching, worshipping, disciple making, planning, leading—more effective.

Too many Christian workers and leaders pray too little, *and* too many Christian workers and leaders pray too little *for others*. This must change. Intercessory prayer is a primary tool used by effective Christian workers and leaders.

Missionary leader Wesley Duewel writes, "You have no greater ministry or no leadership more influential than intercession."[4] E. M. Bounds said, "Talking to men for God is a great thing. But talking to God for men is greater still."[5] S. D. Gordon said, "True prayer never stops in petition for one's self. It reaches out for others. Intercession is the climax of prayer."[6]

If we want to minister like Jesus, Moses, Samuel, Paul, or Nehemiah, we need to pray like Jesus, Moses, Samuel, Paul, and Nehemiah. Like them we must pray for our followers.

Keys to Powerful Intercession

Relentless Boldness

Abraham was a flawed but highly influential spiritual leader. He was the spiritual father of the faithful and the biological father of the Jews.

As you may recall, God and two angels had cloaked themselves in human form in order to visit Abraham and Sarah to tell Sarah that she would bear a child within a year. After dinner the three guests got up to leave, and the Lord confided in Abraham that they also were investigating the extreme wickedness of Sodom. Realizing that judgment is about to come, Abraham valiantly positioned himself between the Lord and Sodom. There he interceded on behalf of the people of Sodom.

> The men turned from there and went toward Sodom while Abraham remained standing before the LORD. Abraham stepped forward and said, "Will You really sweep away the righteous with the wicked? What if there are 50 righteous people in the city? Will You really sweep it away instead of sparing the place for the sake of the 50 righteous people who are in it? You could not possibly do such a thing: to kill the righteous with the wicked, treating the righteous and the wicked alike. You could not possibly do that! Won't the Judge of all the earth do what is just?" (Gen 18:22–25)

Notice his position—"standing before the LORD." That is a physical example of the spiritual positioning of an intercessor. Notice also that he gave God a definite challenge to respond to: "Will You really sweep away the righteous with the wicked?" (see 18:23). Further note that he appealed to the Lord's righteous and just character. "You could not possibly do such a thing: to kill the righteous with the wicked, treating the righteous and the wicked alike.

You could not possibly do that! Won't the Judge of all the earth do what is just?" (v. 25). God agreed with His servant and agreed with his request. "The LORD said, 'If at Sodom I find 50 righteous people in the city, I will spare the whole place for their sake'" (v. 26).

Abraham's intercessory prayers potentially saved an entire city! His bold directness made a difference. Yet Abraham was not through. He was not blind or naïve. He also knew the wicked nature of Sodom. He cared enough for the people of Sodom that he had to be sure of their deliverance. So he asked the Lord to spare Sodom again, this time for the sake of 45 righteous people. And God said yes!

> Then Abraham answered, "Since I have ventured to speak to the Lord —
> even though I am dust and ashes — suppose the 50 righteous lack five.
> Will you destroy the whole city for lack of five?" He replied, "I will not
> destroy it if I find 45 there." (Gen 18:27–28)

I probably would have stopped there, content to leave well enough alone. But not Abraham; he was relentlessly aggressive in his prayers. Four more times he sought God on behalf of Sodom. Each time he appealed for greater grace and mercy.

> Then he spoke to Him again, "Suppose 40 are found there?"
> He answered, "I will not do it on account of 40."
> Then he said, "Let the Lord not be angry, and I will speak further.
> Suppose 30 are found there?"
> He answered, "I will not do it if I find 30 there."
> Then he said, "Since I have ventured to speak to the Lord, suppose
> 20 are found there?"
> He replied, "I will not destroy it on account of 20."
> Then he said, "Let the Lord not be angry, and I will speak one more
> time. Suppose 10 are found there?"
> He answered, "I will not destroy it on account of 10."
> (Gen 18:29–32)

Amazing! One man's insistent prayers secured the safety of an entire city . . . if the city had a representation of a mere 10 righteous souls. It took faith to keep coming back to God and asking for more. It took serious concern for those people. It also took holy stubbornness, . . . and it worked. God agreed to Abraham's requests.

Unfortunately Abraham was overly optimistic in his view of Sodom. He must have assumed that surely his nephew Lot would have been able to convert a few others to join him on behalf of God and righteousness. But sadly Lot had failed to convert even his own wife. There were not even a handful of righteous people in Sodom. So it was destroyed.

But don't miss the bigger issue. Abraham's intercession had potentially spared Sodom from destruction. Persistent petition made a difference.

Sacrificial Selflessness

The Hebrews roaming in the wilderness were rebellious people. Their persistent sin infuriated the Lord. In Exodus 32, in a stunning announcement God offered to destroy the people and start over making Moses into a great nation.

> The LORD also said to Moses: "I have seen this people, and they are indeed a stiff-necked people. Now leave Me alone, so that My anger can burn against them and I can destroy them. Then I will make you into a great nation." (Exod 32:9–10)

If I were Moses, I might have been delighted. All of his whiny headaches would be gone *and* he could become the father of a nation—heady stuff for anyone to consider. But Moses did not even give it a moment's thought. He was a servant leader and a selfless intercessor. He immediately set out asking God to spare the people . . . and God did! (Exod 32:9–14). The Lord responds to selfless intercession.

In a parallel account given in Psalm 106, we see the power of selfless intercession beautifully summarized in one sentence.

> So He said He would have destroyed them— if Moses His chosen one had not stood before Him in the breach to turn His wrath away from destroying them. (Ps 106:23)

"If Moses . . . had not stood." Destruction would have come *had not Moses.* A nation would have been wiped off the face of the earth *had not Moses.* History would have been terribly altered *had not Moses.* Thousands would have died *had not Moses.*

The prayers of one selfless leader spared an entire nation from going into extinction. The intercession of a single man changed history for his people. The prayers of one made a big difference for many!

But why were the prayers of Moses so powerful? The secret is uncovered at the end of Exodus 32. Moses was not only selflessly willing to give up being the father and king of a great nation of his own, but he was willing to give up his own pass to paradise. Look carefully at his prayer.

So Moses returned to the LORD and said, "Oh, this people has committed
a great sin; they have made for themselves a god of gold. Now if You
would only forgive their sin. But if not, please erase me from the book
You have written." (Exod 32:31–32)

I am amazed at the sacrificial selflessness of Moses: "*Forgive their sin. But if
not, please erase me from the book.*" He was willing to lose his own reservation
in heaven if it would keep them from being destroyed. Amazing!

Great leaders are willing to sacrifice for their followers. Consider the heart
of the apostle Paul who cried, "For I could wish that I myself were cursed and
cut off from the Messiah for the benefit of my brothers, my countrymen by
physical descent" (Rom 9:3).

Dick Eastman is the president of a large mission agency, Every Home for
Christ. He also is a prayer warrior and catalyst. He has taught me much about
intercession. He writes, "An intercessor must bid farewell to self and welcome
the burdens of humanity."[7] Elsewhere he states, "As intercessors who bear our
crosses of sacrifice, we too stand between hurting humanity and a loving Father,
carrying their concerns to God."[8]

Brokenhearted Tears

Jesus had a huge heart for people. His heart is summed up in two words
"Jesus wept" (John 11:35). Consider how He became a man of sorrows and
acquainted with grief (Isa 53:3). Notice the tears tracing down His cheeks when
He contemplated the pain of the people: "As He approached and saw the city,
He wept over it" (Luke 19:41).

Jesus, the brokenhearted intercessor, shed tears for those He came to
serve.

When He saw the crowds, He felt compassion for them, because they
were weary and worn out, like sheep without a shepherd. (Matt 9:36)

During His earthly life, He offered prayers and appeals, with loud cries
and tears, to the One who was able to save Him from death, and He was
heard because of His reverence. (Heb 5:7)

There is no servant leadership without brokenhearted tears. God told the
prophet Joel that He wanted His spiritual servants to intercede for their people
with tears (Joel 2:17). He gave the same message through Isaiah (Isa 22:12).
When they refused to do so, God saw their selfishness as sin that "will never be
wiped out" (Isa 22:13–14).

A study of the great servant leaders in the Bible is a study in tears:

- David wept over insults to God's name (Ps 69:9–10).
- Isaiah wept over the plight of his enemies (Isa 6:9–11).
- Josiah wept for his people (2 Kgs 22:19).
- A crowd gathered as a result of Ezra's tears (Ezra 10:1–2).

The Weeping Prophet

One of the great servant intercessors is the prophet Jeremiah. Jeremiah has been labeled "the weeping prophet." Hear the deep burden in his words as he writes, "I am broken by the brokenness of my dear people. I mourn; horror has taken hold of me" (Jer 8:21) and, "If my head were water, my eyes a fountain of tears, I would weep day and night over the slain of my dear people." (Jer 9:1).

Out of anguished love he warned his people, "But if you will not listen, my innermost being will weep in secret because of your pride. My eyes will overflow with tears, for the LORD's flock has been taken captive" (Jer 13:17).

Jeremiah wrote another book of the Bible that, because of its tear-stained content, became widely known as Lamentations. In it he records God's grief over the sinfulness of His people and the destruction of Jerusalem. One of its astounding features is that the weeping of God results in tears streaming down Jeremiah's cheeks.

I weep because of these things; my eyes flow with tears. (Lam 1:16)

My eyes flow with streams of tears because of the destruction of my dear people. My eyes overflow unceasingly, without end, until the LORD looks down from heaven and sees. (Lam 3:48–50)

The Weeping Apostle

Paul's intercessory ministry is splattered with tears. He summarized his ministry in Ephesus by reminding the elders that he served "the Lord with all humility" *and "with tears"* and "for three years [he] did not stop warning each one of you with tears" (Acts 20:18–19,31). He told the Corinthians, "For out

of an extremely troubled and anguished heart I wrote to you with many tears"
(2 Cor 2:4).

The thought of his people, the Jews, not coming to Christ caused him to
write:

> I speak the truth in Christ—I am not lying; my conscience is testifying
> to me with the Holy Spirit—that I have intense sorrow and continual
> anguish in my heart. For I could wish that I myself were cursed and cut
> off from the Messiah for the benefit of my brothers, my countrymen by
> physical descent. They are Israelites, and to them belong the adoption,
> the glory, the covenants, the giving of the law, the temple service, and the
> promises. (Rom 9:1–4)

"Try Tears"

In more recent history the founder of the Salvation Army was a man of
tear-stained intercession. William Booth was an unconventional, controversial
zealot for Jesus. He lived the life of a spiritual soldier as the founder of the
Salvation Army and preached to the least of the least.

Two of his protégés set out to found a new work, only to meet with failure
and opposition. Frustrated and tired, they appealed to Booth to close the rescue
mission.

General Booth sent back a telegram with two words on it:

TRY TEARS

They followed his advice, and they witnessed a mighty revival.[9]

"God Give Me Souls or I Die"

One of the most challenging intercessors is the missionary John Hyde.
John served in India. Difficulties with hearing hindered learning the language,
and his early work was not noteworthy. His deficiencies drove him to desperate, tear-stained prayer. Soon he was spending whole nights in prayer. The
nationals called him "the man who never sleeps" because of his long seasons of
prayer and gave him the nickname of "Praying Hyde."

One year John dared to pray what was at that time considered an impossible request. He asked that during the coming year in India one soul would
be saved every day. Impossible, yet not to the man who sows in tears. That

year John prayed more than 400 people into God's kingdom. The next year he boldly doubled his goal to two souls a day. Eight hundred conversions were recorded that year. John's ferocious intercessions eventually opened the door for a great evangelistic revival to sweep down through the entire territory.

One of his biographers spoke of the holy power generated in Hyde's prayer closet. He said that to be near Hyde when he prayed was "to hear the sighing and the groaning, and to see the tears coursing down his dear face, to see his frame weakened by foodless days and sleepless nights, shaken by sobs as he pleads, 'O God give me souls or I die.'"[10]

Now What?

List the names of several people you believe the Lord especially wants you to pray for. Ask God to break your heart over them. Cry out to God for their spiritual needs daily until the Lord answers.   *Keith*

Prayer for each other

Ministry Is . . .

1. Praying for others.
2. Relentlessly bold intercession.
3. Selflessly offering sacrificial prayers on behalf of those we serve.
4. Tears.

Notes

1. D. Eastman, *No Easy Road* (Grand Rapids, MI: Baker Book House, 1971), 58.

2. Ibid., 57.

3. J. Wesley quoted by P. Wagner in *Prayer Shield* (Ventura, CA: Regal, 1992), 29.

4. W. Duewel, *Mighty Prevailing Prayer* (Grand Rapids, MI: Zondervan, 1990), 22.

5. E. M. Bounds, *Power Through Prayer* (CreateSpace, 2009), 27.

6. S. D. Gordon, *Quiet Talks on Prayer* (Grand Rapids, MI: Baker Book House, reprinted 1980), xxx.

7. D. Eastman, *Love on Its Knees* (Tarrytown, NY: Fleming Revell, 1989), 56.

8. Ibid., 17.

9. W. Duewel, *Revival Fires* (Grand Rapids, MI: Zondervan, 1995), 342–45.

10. F. McGraw, *Praying Hyde* (Minneapolis, MN: Bethany Fellowship, 1970), 16.

28

Mentoring and Multiplying Disciples

Dave Early

It all started in the bathroom. . . . Let me explain.

I was just beginning the second semester of my sophomore year of college. I enjoyed my classes and had learned how to spend quality time with the Lord every day. My ministry was serving as a youth intern in my church and coaching an eighth-grade basketball team of inner-city kids. Yet the Lord was speaking to me about something more—multiplication.

Over the Christmas break I had read a book about the power of spiritual mentoring and multiplication to change the world, and I wanted to get started. Yet where could I begin?

I began to pray every night that the Lord would give me one young man in whom I could pour my life. After two weeks of praying, I was asked to share in a college guys' prayer group about how to spend time with the Lord every day. Afterward Darrell sought me out and said, "I have never been consistent or effective at spending time with the Lord daily. I have a really busy schedule between school and work and never seemed to get everything done. Would you be willing to meet with me and help me?"

I realized that I was looking into the face of the answer to my prayer for someone to mentor spiritually. "Sure," I said. "When can we get together?"

After comparing schedules, we discovered that the only time we both had available was at 11:15 p.m. every night. That presented a problem. At that time our college was run more like a Christian boot camp with strictly enforced quiet hours and lights out. The only place you could talk and have a light on after 11:15 p.m. was the large dorm bathroom. So we agreed to meet the next night at 11:15 p.m.

The Bathroom Baptist Temple

The next night Darrell and I huddled in the corner of the Dorm 8 bathroom with our Bibles. He opened in prayer. We memorized a Bible verse together. I shared something I had learned from my quiet time that day. Then we prayed for each other and made a list of prayer requests.

It had been fun. It had been encouraging. We both were excited about what had taken place.

We jokingly decided to christen our new endeavor as the "Bathroom Baptist Temple."

Meeting with Darrell in that way was thrilling. I realized I had started the slow yet powerful path of spiritually multiplying my life. As I lay in bed that night thanking the Lord for what had taken place, I felt led to ask for another guy. So I did.

Darrell and I met faithfully every night in the Bathroom Baptist Temple. I prayed every night for another guy to join us. One evening, exactly two weeks after we began the Bathroom Baptist Temple, we had just sat down and opened our Bibles. A tall young man came over to us carrying a Bible.

He sat down and introduced himself. "Hey, my name is Tim," he said. "I live at the other end of the hall. I want to join the Bathroom Baptist Temple."

We were shocked. Neither of us could remember seeing him before and had no idea how he had even heard of the Bathroom Baptist Temple.

"Every night I brush my teeth down at the other end of the bathroom," Tim said. "For the last two weeks I have been listening to you guys. I need what you are doing. So I thought I'd ask."

Wow! We were astounded and excited. The Bathroom Baptist Temple had grown 50 percent in two weeks. That would make us the fastest-growing church in America!

Meeting with Darrell and Tim was thrilling. God was answering my prayer for laborers to send into the harvest. The slow yet powerful process of spiritually multiplying my life was taking shape. As I lay in bed that night thanking the Lord for what had taken place, I felt led to ask for another guy. So I did.

Tim, Darrell, and I met faithfully every night in the Bathroom Baptist Temple. I prayed every night for another guy to join us. One evening, exactly two weeks after Tim had joined the Bathroom Baptist Temple, we had just sat down and opened our Bibles. Tim opened in prayer. Then a short, curly-haired young man burst into the bathroom. He looked around and rushed over to us.

"I'm not too late, am I?" He asked.

"Too late for what?" I asked. I had never seen him before.

"Too late to join the Bathroom Baptist Temple," he said.

Skeptical, I asked, "How do you know about the Bathroom Baptist Temple?"

"Tim is my roommate," he said. "All he talks about anymore is the Bathroom Baptist Temple. He has changed so much in the last two weeks. Whatever you guys are doing, I want in on it."

So Tim's roommate Jim became a member of the Bathroom Baptist Temple that night. We had grown another 33 percent making us the fastest-growing church in Virginia.

As the semester went on, I kept praying, and God kept adding guys to the Bathroom Baptist Temple. Soon there were so many of us that the dorm leaders gave us our own room. We packed it out several nights a week for the rest of the semester. That was exciting, but what was even more exciting was that the Bathroom Baptist Temple was multiplied the next year as Darrell, Jim, and Tim led their own groups.

A few years later I took another one of my mentoring groups to Ohio and started a new church from scratch. There were 11 of us. Over the years those 11 multiplied into a church of 2,000, with over 125 groups that spun off five new daughter churches.

Make Disciples, the Example of Jesus

Jesus was the embodiment of what the world needs. Because of His evident love, unconditional grace, amazing words, and mighty deeds, huge crowds chased Him. They were desperately looking for food and healing, deliverance and direction, hope and truth.

> Jesus departed with His disciples to the sea, and a great multitude followed from Galilee, Judea, Jerusalem, Idumea, beyond the Jordan, and around Tyre and Sidon. The great multitude came to Him because they heard about everything He was doing. Then He told His disciples to have a small boat ready for Him, so the crowd would not crush Him.

Since He had healed many, all who had diseases were pressing toward
Him to touch Him. (Mark 3:7–10)

Jesus saw large crowds of people with deep and messy needs. He knew that
the crowds of thousands that followed Him represented a mere microcosm of
the millions worldwide who needed Him. How did He meet their needs?

Then He went up the mountain and summoned those He wanted,
and they came to Him. He also appointed 12—He also named them
apostles—to be with Him, to send them out to preach. (Mark 3:13–14)

Instead of working the crowd, Jesus invited a handful of men to join Him
in a three-year mentoring relationship. He withdrew from the many to focus
on a few so they could ultimately reach many more.

What is Christlike ministry? It is gathering a few so you can reach the
many.

Make Disciples, Change the World

Jesus Christ is, beyond a shadow of a doubt, the greatest revolutionary in
history. He literally changed the world. Important institutions for the world's
good such as churches, hospitals, orphanages, colleges, universities, mass produced books, the education of the masses, and the global literacy movement
can be traced back to Jesus! Our calendar, legal system, and the best aspects of
our culture can be traced back to Jesus. Over two billion people are Christians
today. Jesus changed the world.

How did a man who was a poor carpenter from a forsaken, enslaved nation
change the history of the world? He poured His life into a handful of men who
mentored and multiplied others until the message of Jesus covered the known
world.

Jesus left His disciples when He ascended into heaven. Yet the ministry of
Jesus has grown and multiplied many times over because they were multiplying
leaders. Since the day Jesus ascended into heaven, His ministry has exploded
around the world. In fact, it was imperative that He leave so that the Holy
Spirit would come and carry on His ministry through us (John 16:7–11).

What is world-changing ministry? It is mentoring and multiplying disciples with the truth of Jesus Christ in the power of His Holy Spirit. Think about
it. You can begin spiritually multiplying yourself today and start a dynamic
process that could reach beyond your generation and into the next century. It
can reach beyond a handful and eventually touch the world.

"Make Disciples"—the Last Words of Jesus

The last words and deeds of anyone's life are usually significant as they are an indication of the values and priorities of that person. For example, one of the last things my father did was have me sit down and write checks to the 20 church, ministry, and mission organizations he and my mother supported. They had a special account for some of these above-the-tithe gifts, and I was told to clean it out. As my father lay in the bed dying of cancer, he gave me detailed directions on how to invest eternally every last penny in that account. He said, "Give it all away." A few days later, he passed into glory.

A few days before Jesus ascended into glory, He gave some final instructions. Of all the words Jesus gave, these are especially important because of *when* He gave them: they were the last words He gave. They were also important because of *who* gave them—Jesus, who is God in the flesh. We should also note *who He gave them to*: His followers. Today we call these statements, these detailed instructions, the Great Commission.

> Go, therefore, and make disciples of all nations, baptizing them in the
> name of the Father and of the Son and of the Holy Spirit, teaching them
> to observe everything I have commanded you. And remember, I am with
> you always, to the end of the age. (Matt 28:19–20)

A Greek student will tell you the primary imperative of the Great Commission is the imperative verb "make disciples." The other words "go," "baptize," and "teach" modify and explain *how* we are to fulfill the big thing, which is "make disciples." In order to make this evident to English readers, I paraphrase Matt 28:18–20 as follows:

> This is the greatest challenge of your life . . . so take it seriously,
> As you are going into the culture
> MAKE DISCIPLES.
> Make disciples of people from every people group by baptizing them
> and staying with them in order to teach them to obey everything I have
> taught you.
> Then you will really experience my presence. (Matt 28:18–20, author
> paraphrase)

Note that scholars have titled these last words of Jesus as the Great *Commission*. The word *commission* is a military term meaning "an authoritative order, charge, or direction." It is used for a document conferring authority issued by the president of the United States to officers in the army, navy, and other military services. As an authoritative order, obedience is not an option. To disobey would be considered an act of treason. The one disobeying the commission would be subject to court martial.

No one who is refusing to obey can call himself a follower of Jesus. Since this order to "make disciples" was clearly given, it must not be disobeyed. Jesus' commission to evangelize the world by mentoring and multiplying disciples was not a suggestion to be considered but a command to be obeyed.

Multiply Your Life, Change the World

Leroy Eims, former director of the Navigators, shared an experience he had that drove home the power of multiplication to reach the world.

> Some time ago there was a display at the Museum of Science and Industry in Chicago. It featured a checkerboard with 1 grain of wheat on the first, 2 on the second, 4 on the third, then 8, 16, 32, 64, 128, etc. Somewhere down the board, there were so many grains of wheat on the square that some were spilling over into neighboring squares—so here the demonstration stopped. Above the checkerboard display was a question, "At this rate of doubling every square, how much grain would be on the checkerboards by the 64th square?"
>
> To find the answer to this riddle, you punched a button on the console in front of you, and the answer flashed on a little screen above the board:
>
> "Enough to cover the entire subcontinent of India 50 feet deep."[1]

If you want to make a huge impact, implement the power of multiplication. Walter Henrichsen noted, "Multiplication may be costly, and in the initial stages, much slower than addition, but in the long run, it is the most effective way of accomplishing Christ's Great Commission . . . and the only way."[2]

The *slow* process of discipling leaders who are multipliers is the *fastest* way to fulfill the Great Commission. The world is growing by multiplication, and the church is growing through addition. In order to catch up with and keep pace with the multiplying population of the world, we must multiply the multipliers.

I like the way Waylon Moore puts it, "When the church exhales disciples it inhales converts."[3] He further notes, "Disciple making has no prestige rating, no denominational category; but the results are consistently better than anything I have experienced in thirty years of working with people."[4]

Multiplying leaders is a seemingly small, slow, unappreciated process. But what is exciting to us ordinary people is that by using this small process of multiplication we can have a big impact. By using the slow process of multiplying leaders, we can reach the most people in the least amount of time. By practicing the principles of multiplying leaders, we can make an impact that thrills the heart of Jesus.

Make Disciples, Paul and Timothy

The apostle Paul was the product of spiritual mentoring and multiplication when Barnabas put him under his wing (Acts 9:27), gave him ministry experience in Antioch (Acts 11:19–30), and took Paul with him on a church-planting journey (Acts 13:3ff). Paul then became a mentoring multiplier into the lives of Luke, Titus, Silas, and Timothy as they ministered alongside him (see Acts 16ff). Paul later trusted Timothy enough to entrust him to lead the strategic church of Ephesus. To the young pastor Timothy, Paul wrote his important letters we now have titled 1 Timothy and 2 Timothy.

In 2 Timothy 2, Paul reminded his disciple of the necessity of mentoring multipliers. Read 2 Tim 2:2 carefully. See if you can observe the four generations of spiritual multiplication going in this passage. I will give you the first generation. Paul wrote this letter so the first generation is "me," speaking of Paul.

> And what **you** have heard from **me** in the presence of many witnesses, commit to **faithful** men who will be able to teach **others** also. (2 Tim 2:2, bold added for emphasis)

As I said, the first generation is Paul ("me"). He mentored the young man he wrote this letter to—Timothy ("you"). Timothy was to pass it on to a third generation ("faithful men"). They were to pass it on to a fourth generation ("others"). Paul emphasized to Timothy that in the midst of all of his many responsibilities as the lead pastor of a significant church, not to forget the main thing: make disciples and mentor multipliers.

Catch the Vision

In 1987, Cesar Fajardo had a small ministry with only 30 young people in his youth group. Yet he had a big dream. He took a photograph of the nearby indoor soccer stadium and hung the picture on the wall of his room. He began to dream and believe that God would one day fill it with young people. Today 18,000 young people line up on Saturday nights to get inside the same stadium for his youth worship service.

Within 12 years he had raised up a family of 8,000 youth cell group leaders for his church in Bogota, Columbia. His success began with a dream. His dream was built entirely on the process of mentoring and multiplying 12 disciples.

Cesar began to pour his life into 12 of his students who then became multiplying, disciple-making cell leaders. They met with him one night every week for Bible study, training, and prayer. At this point there were 12, plus Cesar, in the process.

His 12 young disciples committed to pray for their own 12 disciples. On another night of the week, they would meet with anyone who would meet with them for Bible study, training, and prayer. Soon more than 100 were in the process.

These third-generation disciples were each to strive to find their own group of 12 multiplying cell leaders, and so on. The 100 disciple makers multiplied to over 1,000, which eventually multiplied to the 18,000 who filled the stadium on Saturday nights.

Cesar went from a youth group of 30 to a young group of 18,000 because he connected a big dream with the power of mentoring multiplication. He states, "The vision must take hold of your life, and you must be able to transmit that vision."[5] The fulfillment of Cesar Fajardo's vision had eight simple, discernible elements.

1. He saw it. His dream was so vivid he could take a picture of it.
2. He saw it big. He saw an 18,000-seat auditorium full of students seeking God.
3. He saw it through the eyes of faith. He had only 30 kids, yet by faith he believed God would one day multiply 30 into a stadium full of young people.
4. He saw himself in the picture. He believed God could use him to make it happen.
5. He started where he was. He began to train the 12 he had in order to get to the 18,000 he did not have.
6. He diligently poured his life into raising up other leaders. The focus of his time, energy, and effort for a dozen years was training his 12 to multiply multipliers.

7. He kept focused on the dream over a long period of time. He stayed with it for 12 years until the dream became a reality.
8. God caused the growth. Today the stadium is full on Saturday nights.

How to Mentor Multipliers

In this chapter I have given examples of various aspects of mentoring and making disciples. Let me summarize them:

1. Pray for a few faithful people to pour your life into (Matt 9:37–38; 2 Tim. 2:2).
2. Spend as much time with them as you can (Mark 3:13–14). Meet with them as a group and one on one.
3. Pour into their lives the things the Lord is teaching you (2 Tim 2:2).
4. Allow them to do ministry alongside you (Acts 11:19–30; 13:3ff).
5. Push them to pour their lives into others (2 Tim 2:2).
6. Dream big.

There is no single method to mentor multiplying disciple makers. My favorite method is to train them to lead multiplying small groups. I started my church with one group, and it multiplied into 125 groups at our church and dozens of additional groups in our daughter churches.[6]

A Few Important Questions

Since the Great Commission is mentoring and making disciples, let me ask you: Who are you mentoring right now? Since mentoring and multiplying disciples was the example of Jesus and Paul, can you honestly say that you are following their example? Who is your "Timothy"? Who are your "twelve"? When and how are you pouring your life into them?

Three Final Questions

1. If not you, who?
2. If not here, where?
3. If not now, when?

Ministry Is . . .

1. Obeying Jesus' Great Commission of making disciples.
2. Following Jesus' example by practicing spiritual mentoring and multiplying.
3. Gathering a few so you can reach the many.

Notes

1. L. Eims, *The Lost Art of Disciple Making* (Grand Rapids, MI: Zondervan Publishing, 1980), 9.

2. W. A. Henrichsen, *Disciples Are Made—Not Born* (Wheaton, IL: Victor Books, 1979), 143.

3. W. B. Moore, *Multiplying Disciples* (Colorado Springs, CO: NavPress, 1981), 5.

4. Ibid., 30.

5. J. Comiskey, *Groups of 12* (Houston, TX: TOUCH Publications, 1999), 37.

6. For a detailed treatment of how to mentor multiplying small group leaders, see D. Earley, *Turning Members into Leaders* (Houston, TX: TOUCH Publications, 2003).

29

Leading Small Groups

Dave Earley

I love leading small groups! I have had the privilege of leading small groups and coaching small-group leaders consistently for 30 years.

I began as a 16-year-old public-school student. My friend and I started lunchtime Bible studies at our high school. They grew and multiplied until we were ministering to over 100 public high school students every day.

In college I started a discipleship group that spread over the campus. During my summer mission trips while in college, I got to start groups in little towns in England and in high-rise apartment buildings in New York City.

When I graduated, I started groups in rural Virginia. Then I was hired to train, write curriculum, and oversee 300 small-group leaders at a Christian university. Later I started a group in my basement that grew into a church with over 100 groups and several other churches.

Small groups will be a part of my life all of my life. Why? Small groups *are* big priorities. They were Jesus' primary ministry strategy. They were the foundational infrastructure of the early church. They meet deep human needs. They are a simple yet effective way to launch and multiply ministries. They can be the keys to explosive church evangelism and multiplication.

What Is a Small Group?

A healthy Christian small group is *a gathering of three to 15 people who meet regularly together for the purpose of spiritual growth and outreach.* Eight to 12 people is probably the optimum number for a small-group gathering.

When a group gets past 12 people consistently, then intimacy begins to diminish. Fewer than eight, and maintaining momentum became difficult.

Groups should gather together weekly, especially in the initial stages, as a sense of community develops. After true community has been reached, a week can be skipped here and there without the group's losing effectiveness. Of course, a group is more than a weekly meeting. It is more like a family, with members connecting throughout the week.

In the long run the most effective and healthy groups are linked to a local church. This gives the group an outlet for service and a connection with something larger than themselves. Being linked to a local church also keeps groups on track doctrinally.

My friend, Rod Dempsey, describes a healthy group as one with five distinguishing marks based on an acrostic for the word GROUP.

G: Guided by a Leader
R: Regular Meeting Times
O: Open God's Word
U: United in love
P: Prayer[1]

According to cell-group guru Joel Comiskey, healthy small groups should have a fourfold focus:

- Upward Focus: Knowing God
- Inward Focus: Knowing each other
- Outward Focus: Reaching out to those who do not know Jesus (with the goal of multiplying the group)
- Forward Focus: Raising up new small-group leaders[2]

Why Small Groups?

Small Groups Reflect the Image of God

Genesis 2:18 states, "It is not good for the man to be alone." From this text we clearly see that even before the fall, God said isolation is not the ideal state. Humanity needs to be in community with humanity.

In Gen 1:26, God said, "Let *Us* make man in *Our* image." Note the use of "Us" and "Our." They remind us that God has always existed as an eternal community of tri-unity. God is a plurality, as named elsewhere in the Scriptures as Father, Son and Holy Spirit. All are separate, yet all are vitally linked as one.

Genesis 1:27 states, "So God created man in His own image." Man being made in the image of God beckons back to the communal essence of God. As those created in the image of God, humanity has a deep, unique, embedded, relational identity. Yet instead of finding the fulfillment of our communal craving in ourselves, as God does, we find it in one another. In other words, we not only have a God-shaped void; we also have an others-shaped void etched into our hearts.

From these texts, Garth Icenogle draws a powerful conclusion as he writes, "God as Being exists in community. The natural and simple demonstration of God's communal image for humanity is the gathering together of small groups."[3]

Living in Community Is in Our DNA

Just as every person has a God-shaped void, we all also have a human-shaped void. We cannot be healthy or fully human without others. We will not be fulfilled until our relational void is filled.

Our relational hunger is an identifying mark of our humanity. Bill Donahue and Russ Robinson write, "God chose to embed in us a distinct kind of DNA. God created us all with a 'communal gene,' an inborn, intentional, inescapable part of what it means to be human." They continue:

> This relational DNA or "community gene" helps explain why churches
> need small groups. People don't come to church simply to satisfy
> spiritual needs. They come internally wired with a desire for connection.
> . . . Their hunger for togetherness is an inescapable mark of humanity."[4]

Living in True Community Is Beneficial

Solomon, the world's wisest man, observed that the benefits of interdependence are numerous. Accomplishment, help, warmth, and support are more accessible to those in community than those outside of it.

> Two are better than one because they have a good reward for their
> efforts. For if either falls, his companion can lift him up; but pity the one
> who falls without another to lift him up. Also, if two lie down together,
> they can keep warm; but how can one person alone keep warm? And if
> somebody overpowers one person, two can resist him. A cord of three
> strands is not easily broken. (Eccl 4:9–12)

A healthy small group has the power to create community and connected-ness. It can foster real fellowship. Biblical fellowship or *koinonia* involves par-ticipating in life with others to the point of knowing them, feeling their hurts, sharing their joys, and encouraging their hearts. Chuck Swindoll describes what happens when real fellowship occurs: "Fences come down. Masks come off. Welcome signs are hung outside the door. Keys to the doors of our lives are duplicated and distributed. Joys and sorrows are shared."[5]

Jesus Was a Small-Group Leader

Those who would be Jesus' disciples must practice His disciplines. If we want to live as Jesus lived, we must do as Jesus did. One of the main things Jesus did was invite a handful of men to gather together with Him in an intensive, ministry-focused small group (Mark 3:13–14).

Involvement in small-group life was a primary spiritual discipline in Jesus' life. Following Jesus today means following Him into the relationships of a small group. The question we ask is, "If Jesus, the Son of God, felt the need to be involved in leading a small group, *how much more* should you and I be involved in small groups?"

Small-group leadership was Jesus' ministry strategy. His pattern was gath-ering a few to transform the many. Jesus invested most of His time with 12 Jewish men so He could reach the entire world. The question we ask is, "If Jesus, the Son of God, chose strategically to minister by leading a small group, *how much more* should you and I?"

Living in Community Is an Answer to Jesus' Prayers

I pray not only for these, but also for those who believe in Me through their message. May they all be one, as You, Father, are in Me and I am in You. May they also be one in Us, so the world may believe You sent Me. (John 17:20–21)

The cry of Jesus' heart for His church was that we "may be one." Isn't such unity best facilitated in community? Theologian J. I. Packer believes as much when he writes: "How can God's one family, locally and denomination-ally separated, be enabled to look like one family? . . . By wisdom in structuring house-churches and small groups within congregations."[6]

Without Community We Are in Trouble

Dr. Lawrence J. Crabb is a clinical psychologist and serves as professor and distinguished scholar in residence at Colorado Christian University. He is a recognized authority on counseling and the Christian life. Crabb, after years of doing clinical counseling and training biblical counselors, writes:

> We have made a terrible mistake! For most of this century we have wrongly defined soul wounds as psychological disorders and delegated their treatment to trained specialists. Damaged psyches aren't the problem. The problem is disconnected souls. What we need is connection! What we need is a healing community![7]

Living lives of isolation has damaging results. Loneliness has been called "the most devastating illness of our day."[8] What can you do to help? You can lead a small group.

The Infrastructure of the Early Church Was Built on the Foundation of Home Groups

The early church of Jerusalem focused its corporate gatherings in two locales—the temple courts and the homes of the members.

> Every day in the temple complex, and in various homes, they continued teaching and proclaiming the good news that the Messiah is Jesus. (Acts 5:42, bold added for emphasis; see also Acts 2:46)

The early church met daily in the temple and *in various homes*. This makes sense as the first church building was not constructed until the second or third century AD. As the early church spread through the world, the primary meeting place was in the homes of the people. There they experienced fellowship.

Fellowship, or *koinonia*, was foundational for the early church in the first century and is equally important today. Asbury Seminary professor Howard Snyder observed, "It is my conviction that the koinonia of the Holy Spirit is most likely to be experienced when Christians meet together informally in small group fellowships."[9]

Healthy Churches Have Strong Small Groups

Christian Schwartz conducted the most comprehensive study ever attempted on the causes of church health and growth. The study included more than 1,000 churches in 32 countries on all five continents. The survey was completed by 30 members from each of the churches and resulted in 4.2 million responses. The goal was to discover the keys to church health and growth, regardless of culture or theological persuasion. Schwartz's findings indicate that church growth is the natural result of church health.

Schwartz discovered that of the eight quality characteristics of healthy, growing churches, the one universal principle that was the most important was small-group ministry. *The higher the value placed upon small groups, the healthier the church.*[10]

He emphasized that these must be holistic groups, those which go beyond just discussing Bible passages to applying its message to daily life. In these groups, members are able to bring up those issues and questions that are immediate personal concerns.

Well-known pollster George Barna reports that 70 percent of the senior pastors his organization surveyed stated that small-group ministry is "central to the overall success" of the church's ministry." He concluded, "Nothing is more important for ministry today than small groups."[11]

Healthy Christians Are in Small Groups

The apostle Paul's favorite term for the church was "the body of Christ." He taught that the church is in many ways similar to the physical body. Just as separate body parts combine to form one physical body, in like manner separate individuals become inseparable parts of Christ's body, the church. Paul emphasized that no single part could survive on its own. Every part relied on the others. The body functions best as a symphony of dependency. In 1 Cor 12:21 he stated plainly, "So the eye cannot say to the hand, 'I don't need you!' nor again the head to the feet, 'I don't need you!'"

John Ortberg notes, "We are created to draw life and nourishment from one another the way the roots of an oak tree draw life from the soil."[12]

Christian thinker and author Charles Colson seconds the motion when he states, "No Christian can grow strong and stand the pressures of this life unless he is surrounded by a small group of people who minister to him and build him up in the faith."[13]

The Largest Churches in the World Are All Small-Group Churches

The five largest churches in the world are all cell or small-group churches. They all trace their explosive growth and size to multiplying leaders and cell groups.

1. Yoido Full Gospel Church, Seoul, Korea; number of weekly attenders: 253,000
2. Yotabeche Methodist P. Church, Santiago, Chile: number of weekly attenders: 150,000
3. Deeper Life Bible Church, Lagos, Nigeria: number of weekly attenders: 120,000
4. Elim Church, San Salvador, El Salvador: number of weekly attenders: 117,000
5. Mision Carismatica Internacional, Bogota, Kolumbien: number of weekly attenders: 90,000[14]

The churches on the list above work on a simple system of multiplication. Small-group members reach out to their family and friends with the gospel. As they are saved, they become part of the small group. The small group grows through evangelism, and new leaders are developed. These new leaders multiply the group into new groups. One small group multiplies into two groups. Those two groups become four groups. Those four become eight, eight become 16, and 16 multiplies into 32. Multiplication keeps occurring until the church has hundreds of thousands of members.

The church I started in Ohio began with one group. Over the years that group grew and multiplied until we had 125 groups meeting each week with nearly 2,000 people involved, and we started five daughter churches. Each of these had many more small groups.

How to Lead Small Groups

Several years ago I wanted to help the leaders I was coaching know exactly what it would take for them to be more effective. I identified regular practices that seemed to make the difference between effectiveness and ineffectiveness.

The Habits of the Effective Small-Group Leader

Pray for group members daily. Daily prayer for themselves, their group meetings, and their group members is the most important task of the small-group leader. It is also the most powerful. A survey of small-group leaders revealed an interesting correlation between time spent in prayer and the multiplication of small groups. It revealed that those who spent 90 minutes or more in daily devotions multiplied their groups twice as much as those who spent less than half an hour.[15]

Invite new people to the group weekly. When it comes to inviting, there is one simple principle: *If you invite them, they will come.* According to Richard Price and Pat Springer:

> Experienced group leaders . . . realize that usually you have to personally invite twenty five people to get fifteen to agree to come. Of those fifteen, usually only eight to ten will actually show up, and of those, only five to seven will be regular attenders after a month or so.[16]

This research means you can grow a new group of 10 to 14 regular members in a year by inviting one new person each week! If a whole group catches the vision of inviting, a group can experience explosive growth.

Effective inviters realize that they need to saturate the situation in prayer. They are also careful to capitalize on the seasons of the soul. People have seasons of the soul when they are more open to the gospel. Most adults come to Christ, or come back to Christ, out of one of these seasons: death of a loved one; move to a new neighborhood, city, job, or school; divorce; marriage; family problems; major illness; and birth of a child. Each is a prime season for inviting.

Beyond that, effective inviters understand the power of relationship. They know that it is best to build a relationship *before* offering an invitation. In order to build a relationship, they invite people to coffee before they invite them to the group.

Contact group members regularly. Effective small-group leaders see that everyone in the group is contacted every week. This can be through phone calls, e-mails, texts, or personal conversations. Why? *If you contact them, they will keep coming.*

People drop out of groups because they do not feel cared for. Contacting tells them that you care enough to take the time to get in touch. It says that you care enough to find out why they were absent or what they think of the group. It says that you care enough to check on their prayer requests and to get to know them better.

Prepare for the group meeting. The most important element of preparation is personal preparation. You, as the leader, must strive to be as right with the Lord and with others as possible. Pray, fast, repent, worship, study, rest, and anything necessary to be prepared to lead. Nothing is more important than this.

Proper preparation of the atmosphere can make or break the meeting. The leader needs to have made sure that the atmosphere is prepared to make the group meeting as good as possible. This means the leader will be sure someone is responsible for the meeting location to make sure it is clean, comfortable, and spacious. They also make certain that the snack served before or after the meeting is going to be ready.

A good leader will prepare the agenda. The elements of a healthy group meeting cover the five practices of a healthy small group. We will discuss these practices in the next section.

Beyond that, the leader will prepare the Bible discussion. In studying a passage of the Bible, we must always ask three basic questions.

1. *What does this passage say?* Read the passage asking: "What does this passage seem to be saying? What is the author saying? Who wrote this passage? Who was he writing to? Why was he writing?"
2. *What does this passage mean?* Take each passage in chunks of phrases, sentences, or paragraphs. As you look at it, answer the question: "What did the author intend for this to mean to us today?" Try to paraphrase it in your own words.
3. *How can we apply this passage to our lives?* Interpretation without application leads to spiritual abortion, but interpretation with application leads to transformation.

Mentor an apprentice leader. If you want your group to grow and multiply, you must develop or mentor new leaders. Mentoring is cooperating with God in developing your understudy who will also become a highly effective small-group leader. It is letting go of ministry in order to let others minister.

Mentoring is also the most lasting part of the ministry of small-group leadership. I have led groups for 30 years. My most important legacy is not the groups I have led but the leaders I have developed, especially those who are continuing to minister to others. I count church leaders, pastors, church planters, and full-time missionaries among those I have had the privilege of mentoring. Their ministry has continued long after I have moved on to new areas of ministry.

Five Practices of a Healthy Small Group

The long-range effectiveness of a group revolves around some simple biblical disciplines practiced during group gatherings *and* flowing over into the week. The best quality about these practices is that they are doable. Any group can incorporate these practices into their weekly agenda and begin to see powerful results.

Applying these five practices will take any group to a new level. They are a path to group health and growth.

1. Welcome (community)
2. Worship
3. Word (Bible study and application)
4. Work (ministry)
5. Witness (evangelism)

Each of these five practices can serve as a part of your small group meeting agenda. For example:

- 7:00–7:15 p.m.: Welcome and Community—Greeting and icebreakers
- 7:15–7:25 p.m.: Worship—Two songs and prayer
- 7:25–8:00 p.m.: Word—Discussion based Bible study and application
- 8:00–8:10 p.m.: Work (ministry to one another)—Pray for one another
- 8:10–8:20 p.m.: Witness (evangelism and ministry to the lost)—Pray for the lost and strategize for outreach

Ministry Is . . .

1. Understanding the strategic and vital role of small groups.
2. Stepping up to leading a small group.
3. Effectively leading a small group through prayer, inviting, contacting, preparing, and mentoring.

Notes

1. D. Earley and R. Dempsey, *The Pocket Guide to Leading a Small Group* (Houston, TX: TOUCH®, 2007), 29–32.

2. J. Comiskey, *How to Lead a Great Small Group Meeting* (Houston, TX: TOUCH®, 2001), 13.

3. G. Icenogle, *Biblical Foundations of Small Group Ministry* (Downers Grove, IL: InterVarsity, 1994), 13.

4. B. Donahue and R. Robinson, *Building a Church of Small Groups* (Grand Rapids, MI: Zondervan, 2001), 24.

5. C. Swindoll, *Dropping Your Guard* (Waco, TX: Word, 1983), 22.

6. J. I. Packer, "The Church in Christian Thought," Department of Theology, Regent University, 1996.

7. L. Crabb, *Connecting* (Nashville, TN: Word Publications, 1997), 6.

8. Swindoll, *Dropping Your Guard*, 22.

9. H. Snyder, *The Problem of Wineskins Revisited* (Houston, TX: TOUCH®, 1996), 91.

10. C. Schwartz, *Natural Church Development: A Guide to Essential Qualities of Healthy Churches* (Carol Stream, IL: ChurchSmart Resources, 1996), 32.

11. G. Barna and M. Hatch, *Boiling Point: Monitoring Cultural Shifts in the 21st Century* (Ventura, CA: Regal Books, 2001), 248.

12. J. Ortberg, *Everyone Is Normal Till You Get to Know Them* (Grand Rapids, MI: Zondervan. 2002), 21.

13. C. Colson, *Kingdoms in Conflict* (Grand Rapids, MI: Zondervan, 1987).

14. W. Simson, "The Top 10 Churches in the World," July 30, 2004, http://www.simplychurch.com/2004/07/the_top_10_chur.html (accessed December 23, 2009).

15. J. Comiskey, *Home Group Cell Explosion* (Houston, TX: TOUCH®, 1998), 34.

16. R. Price and P. Springer, *Rapha's Handbook for Group Leaders* (Houston, TX: Rapha Publishing, 1991), 132.

30

Biblically Balanced Preaching and Teaching

Ben Gutierrez

Turn in your Bibles to . . ."

"Grab a Bible in the seat pocket in front of you and turn to . . ."

"I would like to direct your attention to the screens above as I read from God's Word."

"Pull out today's notes that you downloaded off the Internet."

"Turn in your iPods to . . ."

"Turn in your iPods? You have got to be crazy!"

"But there's something about carrying a physical book to church and flipping through the pages and writing notes."

I can't believe I actually said those words. Even though I personally still consider my first Bible that I was given in ministry as one of my most precious possessions, I am a convert to the age of technology. I have noticed that many in today's generation have actually hidden more of God's Word in their heart than I had at their age, and they have only owned a Bible on their iPod or computer! But what really calmed my spirit about which form of God's Word was more appropriate was when I watched people put their iPods to work while I was preaching. One time I made a statement about a particular Bible verse jump on their iPhones, and several students immediately read the verse in more than 20 translations, read three commentaries on the verse, and then cross-linked the verse grammatically and theologically to 10 other verses! All of this happened while I was commenting on that one verse. I quickly became a believer (and user) of technology while preaching my sermons!

We have more resources than ever before to be just like the Bereans who "welcomed the message with eagerness and examined the Scriptures daily to see if these things were so" (Acts 17:11). Admittedly, I was intimated that virtually every word I said would be checked and double-checked in a matter of seconds by dozens of people sitting in the auditorium! But now I actually value this level of access to Scripture and truth because it forces me to be sharp and thoroughly studied prior to preaching. If technology has affected preaching in any way, it most certainly has caused preachers to be prayed up and studied up prior to presenting God's Word.

Regardless of the technological device someone uses to research God's Word, the issue is what is *said* about the Word of God when we preach or teach. You will never have to fear the technologically savvy listener and their access to the massive pool of data as long as you have all of the necessary ingredients present in your teaching.

Ingredients of Biblically Balanced Preaching

In order to get a crystal clear description of the required ingredients of biblically balanced preaching, I want to examine one amazing verse to help us understand *exactly* what we are doing when we teach or preach the Word of God. In the apostle Paul's last chapter of the last letter he wrote in the Scriptures prior to his martyrdom, he felt compelled to reinforce the importance of preaching in the life of a minister. Notice the required ingredients that produce biblically balanced preaching: "Proclaim the message; persist in it whether convenient or not; rebuke, correct, and encourage with great patience and teaching" (2 Tim 4:2).

Proclaim

The word the apostle Paul used in his day is the word that means "formally preach" or simply "proclaim." It is an unqualified act that does not prescribe or connote any particular style, method, length of presentation, level of depth, or detail. Unfortunately, I find that when ministers-in-training are asked to preach, some of them tend to change the normal way they speak and divest from their pleasant personalities and morph into a verbose, smooth-talking, cliché-riddled speaker who shouts as if he is speaking in Madison Square Garden! This should not be your understanding of preaching. Preaching does not mean that the speaker is to be loud, quick-witted, or more brash and abrasive than other speakers. To safeguard from this unfortunate misunderstanding, it would be helpful to think of the word *proclaim* in this verse as simply an unqualified mandate (or command) that does not prescribe or connote any particular style, method, or length of talk.

Ministers are simply being commanded to tell God's message whether in a formal or informal setting when they preach. There is no fundamental problem with altering the description of a minister's "sermon" to "lesson," "talk," or "chat." Sure, the phrase "preaching at someone" has recently evolved into a negative connotation, but the description of the teaching is irrelevant. The issue is that the preacher proclaims exactly what God's Word says we are to proclaim.

The Message

The term the apostle Paul used in his day is the word that means "sayings," "truths," "principles," "concepts," and "teachings" of God found in the Bible. Therefore, the major concern for the preacher or teacher should be to make sure that he or she has a firm grasp on the accurate understanding of the truths, principles, concepts, and teachings of the Bible before they preach.

It does not mean that a preacher can never share how the truth affected his or her life, or how that truth has proven itself true or is evident in current events, or the speaker's opinion about how to apply the truth to the life of the listener. This is fine. What is meant by preaching "the Word" is that those opinions, thoughts, feelings, and recommendations are to be in perfect alignment with the Word of God. The speaker should never recommend an action that would cause the listener to reconsider the authority of the truth, nor should the speaker be considered as someone with more authority than the Scriptures.

A good way to understand biblically balanced preaching and teaching is to consider truth as a tabletop upon which the believer should place any life issue or question. Then the additional statements made by the minister through the sermon serve as the legs of the table. Therefore, the preacher of the Word should consider everything he says within his sermon, talk, lesson, or chat as ways to bring attention to, exalt, support, and prop up the truths of the Word of God! This is paramount to any other exercise when preparing to preach.

Be Ready in Season and Out of Season

This phrase provides the timing of preaching. It answers the question, *When* should I be a proclaimer of God's truth? And the answer is, when it is convenient or opportune ("in season") and also when it is not convenient or when it is an inopportune time ("out of season"). In essence, another important ingredient of biblically balanced preaching is committing to proclaiming God's truth all the time! There should never be a season of life, occasion, encounter, or situation where the minister does not bring truth to bear upon the situation.

Convince

This word implies that the preacher should clearly explain why certain acts are sinful, then lovingly correct and discipline a person if needed. It has a mentoring aspect to it, and it allows the preacher to draw conclusions about people's actions to help them stop sinning. The implications of preaching this way are important.

- There must be an acknowledgment of the specific sin being committed.
- The sin should be firmly addressed in a spirit of love.
- Clear guidance should be provided to help the person move past the sin and toward godliness.

Rebuke

Building on the word *convince*, this word takes the responsibility of the minister to discipline a sinning believer to the next level. This ingredient is necessary in preaching when the minister has to safeguard his people from obvious and blatant sin. It is often used when actions are clear-cut and there is no question as to the motive of the sinner.

Every minister must be prepared to perform such rebuke. But no minister should ever revel in exerting this level of spiritual authority upon another. Rebuke in a sermon should be used sparingly and not before you, the preacher, have personally experienced a season of prayer and fasting and pleading with the Lord as to how you should address the issue with your people. In my experience, if you seek the face of God first, you will most likely find the Lord will intensify the impact of a few sincerely spoken words spoken at an appropriate time.

Rebuke is an unfortunate yet necessary ingredient in preaching that must not be dismissed as "unproductive," "offensive," or "insensitive." Actually, to identify obvious sin that has entered the camp is one of the most loving things a preacher can do. And for a preacher to declare categorically that he will never condone such sharp, blunt speech about obvious sin will actually diminish the effectiveness of his preaching. However, balance is always required. If you find that your sermons are consistently heavy on rebuke and mostly point out the sins and impurities of your people, you will miss the opportunity to focus on the positive aspects of godliness. If this happens, your flock will be aware of their sin, but they will not have a clear direction to help them move past their sin.

Exhort

Encouragement is the most overlooked ingredient in effective preaching. It is the ingredient in preaching that propagates obedience in the lives of your people. Encouragement is to a soul as water is to a flower. Just as a flower starved of water withers quickly in the hot summer sun, your people will be harmed spiritually if they do not receive encouragement from you. If you don't share the encouragement that God provides, you will have exposed them to the merciless heat of life without any sustenance to make it through.

I am afraid that too many ministers are mostly negative when they preach. I have even noticed that if time is running short during their sermons, many ministers will choose to skip right over their prepared remarks of encouragement so that they are able to hit on the important content. God forbid! My prayer is that hope would always be considered a vital component of any preacher's sermon.

Long-suffering

The word the apostle Paul used in his day is the word meaning "self-restraining patience" or "enduring forbearance." In other words, the preacher should not expect to be able to preach something one time and expect everyone who attended the sermon to understand fully the teaching and immediately and unequivocally adopt it into their lives. It may not be due to disobedience as much as it is natural human nature to misunderstand, or perhaps they simply need to hear it again in order to get it. We all need to be patiently reminded of what God expects us to do.

Ministers are also in need of repetitious teaching. Consider how much patient repetition is needed at times before we finally get what our spouses really want us to buy them for their birthday! Better yet, how long does it take us before we get to the "honey do" chores for our spouses? We all need patient repetition to ensure that we consistently apply God's truth.

I'll never forget the moment I realized that I needed patient repetition in order to grasp a particular concept. I recall the time I joined my wife in taking our firstborn daughter to the pediatrician for her one-year checkup. We were escorted to the doctor's room in the back of the office and were asked to wait in the room until our doctor arrived. While we were waiting, our daughter became fussy and wiggly. So we did what every new parent does when a newborn child gets fussy: we gave her a bottle! I remember placing the bottle in our daughter's hands as she laid flat on her back on the examination table. "It worked!" We rejoiced as we sat on the bench waiting for the doctor.

I remember watching the doctor walk into the room, his eyes quickly moving to our daughter drinking the bottle while lying flat on her back on the table. He then sat down and turned to us and said, "Well, good morning. Oh, you know I don't usually recommend that young children lie flat on their backs while drinking milk. I have found that it can cause ear infections a little more quickly in some children." To which we replied, "Certainly, sir, we'll be mindful of that. Thank you."

We didn't budge an inch! For some reason we didn't walk over and pick up our child or elevate her back on a pillow. Nothing! In one ear and out the other! A few minutes later the doctor interrupted his normal line of "check up" questioning and once again said to us, "Let me pause right here and let you know that it's not recommended for young children of your daughter's age to lie flat on their backs to drink their milk. Studies have shown that it makes the ear canal more conducive to ear infections."

So, what did I do? Nothing! Rather, I turned to my wife and said, "Boy, honey, we have to remember that? Yeah, that sounds important." Then we turned back to the doctor to continue the interview. We never connected the dots as to what he was trying to teach us! We literally heard him say all that he said, and rather than responding appropriately, we just stared him in the eye with sincere appreciation for his kind recommendation. All the while our precious, pudgy daughter lay flat on her back going to town on her bottle.

So the doctor (probably thinking we're not too smart at this point) graciously continued with his standard list of questions. And then the doctor said the words, "You know, many physicians agree that when children drink milk while flat on their back. . . ." *Then it clicked!* "Oh my goodness," I thought to myself, "he's got to think I am the dumbest college professor *ever!*" "Say no more," I said, as I walked over and picked up our daughter and held her in my arms for the remainder of the appointment.

We had a good laugh over it. But it showed me something about me and ministers in general. That is, even the most trained, experience, and well-versed ministers still require patience in learning to apply a concept. Therefore, don't be too quick to criticize your people if they have to rehearse what you are teaching on a few occasions. We all need patient repetition to be our tutor in life.

Teaching

A vital and *required* ingredient of biblically balanced preaching is teaching. Preachers are *required* to be teachers! Biblically balanced preaching requires the preacher to proclaim the bottom-line truth of the Word of God and explain how believers can reach this conclusion for themselves. In essence, a biblically balanced preacher should equip his people to learn how to be like the Bereans in Acts 17 who have the skill to search the Scriptures for themselves, cross-reference other Scriptures, consider the genre of the particular text, and form a theology on their own. In this way they are equipped to determine if what they are being taught is consistent with the Scriptures. The only way your people will be equipped to do this is if you teach them how to draw conclusions based on what you are preaching!

So preach to equip! Do not preach simply to lecture or to satisfy your own personal desire to show off by presenting needless historical or grammatical facts that do not contribute to equipping your people. Your twofold goal in preaching should be to present the accurate, bottom-line message of the text *and* to teach in such a way that your people understand how you came up with your conclusions, thus showing them how they can come up with the same conclusions in their personal study apart from you.

Reminder: You Can't Preach the Word if You Don't Live the Word

It seems obvious, but it bears stating: you can't preach the Word of God if you don't live in the Word *and* let the Word live in you. Our friend Daniel Henderson, president of Strategic Renewal writes:

> Those in full-time vocational service can easily be "in the word" without the Word being in them. The Bible simply becomes a means to the end of saying something witty and insightful at the next event or church service. But in the long run, the process is much more important than the product. It is the process of "laboring[ing] in word and doctrine" (1 Tim 5:17 [sic]) that shapes character, out of which a life-changing message flows.[1]

Noted Bible expositor Haddon Robinson reminds us that the process of living in the Word is worth it. In speaking of the effort needed to prepare biblically balanced teaching, he writes: "Don't complain about the hours you are spending and the agony you experience. The people deserve all you can give them."[2]

John MacArthur is one of the best-known Bible teachers alive today. His expansive ministry and church are founded on the preaching of the Word of God. Regarding study, he writes, "Though I may preach only three hours a week, I study thirty."[3]

What Now?

Here are some questions to ponder:

1. Are you a biblically balanced teacher and preacher?
2. How much time do you spend in study to grasp the accurate message of the text you are going to preach?
3. Are any ingredients discussed in this chapter that are regularly absent from your proclamation of God's truth?
4. What do you think others say about your sermons, talks, or lessons? If you want to know, just look at the spirits of the people you have preached to for some time. Are they quick to judge, or do they encourage one another? Are they biblically literate, or are they unable to search the Scriptures without you in the room? Are they impatient people, or have they captured your patient spirit in your preaching?
5. Have you been tempted to prepare a sermon, talk, or lesson and focus more on scripting the clever language because you thought it may be the only way to keep the attention of your listeners rather than simply presenting the truth of the text?
6. Are the truths or Bible verses inserted within your sermon for the purpose of giving the sense of biblical validity? Or are they really there for the purpose of springboarding you into nothing more than a stand-up routine that props you, the preacher, up in the eyes of the listener?
7. Upon leaving the church, do people remember *your* words, jokes, antics, or opinions; or have you done all you can to brand the beauty and profundity of the Word of God upon their hearts?

Ministry Is . . .

1. Being a biblically balanced proclaimer of God's Word.
2. Involving every required ingredient in your preaching.
3. Patiently teaching through your preaching.

☞ Quotes ☜

Preaching is the chief human means God uses to dispense His grace.

—JOHN MACARTHUR[4]

The less the preacher comes between the Word and its hearers, the better.

—JOHN STOTT[5]

A shepherd who fails to feed his flock will not have a flock for long. The sheep will wander off to other fields or die of starvation. . . . The shepherd's goal is not to please the sheep, but feed them, not to tickle their ears but to nourish their souls. He is not to offer light snacks of milk, but substantial meals of solid biblical truth.

—JOHN MACARTHUR[6]

Notes

1. D. Henderson, *Defying Gravity: How to Survive the Storms of Pastoral Ministry* (Chicago, IL: Moody, 2010), 53.

2. H. Robinson, *Biblical Preaching* (Grand Rapids, MI: Baker Book House, 1980), 44.

3. J. MacArthur, *Pastoral Ministry* (Nashville, TN: Thomas Nelson, 2002), xiii.

4. Ibid.

5. J. R. W. Stott, *The Preacher's Portrait* (Grand Rapids, MI: Eerdmans, 1979), 30

6. MacArthur, *Pastoral Ministry*, 23.

31 Creating a Culture of Accountability

Ben Gutierrez

L ife is too tough to attempt to conquer it alone. We all need someone to get us through the challenges of life. When we go through a broken relationship, when the economy affects us profoundly, or when we experience the loss of a loved one, people coming alongside us seem to bring indescribable comfort. We value people who care for us and take time to listen and process our feelings with us! And sometimes what gets us through is just having a friend there for us. They don't have to do anything but just sit next to us, clasp our hand or put their arm around us, and listen.

Occasionally I am asked by ministers in training about the protocol of visiting someone in a hospital. They naturally ask the questions I once asked: "What do you do? How long do you stay? What should I say?" And with paper and pen in hand, they wait to receive the bullet-point list of do's and don'ts of hospital visitation. My initial response shocks some of them when I say, "Well, first you can joke about hospital food (especially the Jell-O). Or you can pull up a chair and watch TV with them. If that doesn't help, you can talk about the weather or a current event." Then the questions come. "Well, do you ever quote Scriptures, relate their situation to a foundational biblical doctrine, or bring Christian literature?" To which I reply, "Sure, if applicable. But the point is that sometimes the most poignant thing you can do is just to be there for them!"

Do I believe that truth can and should be brought to bear on every life situation? Absolutely. But there are times when *living* the truth makes a more profound impact than producing a lecture on that truth. When dealing with the practical challenges of life, people find comfort in having a spiritual person nearby simply to "do life" with them.

When it comes to a person's spiritual development, the same type of support system is needed. In our spiritual walk with Christ, we need others to be there for us. Therefore, this support system needs to be prepared, thoughtful, and tethered to the Word of God so it will support us with unshakable truth. This group that provides support, encouragement, and accountability is one of the most precious gifts we can provide a fellow believer.

Solomon, the world's wisest man, praised the powers of having others in our lives. He wrote:

> Two are better than one because they have a good reward for their efforts. For if either falls, his companion can lift him up; but pity the one who falls without another to lift him up. Also, if two lie down together, they can keep warm; but how can one person alone keep warm? And if somebody overpowers one person, two can resist him. A cord of three strands is not easily broken. (Eccl 4:9–12)

Notice the many benefits of having others in our lives. He speaks of increased productivity—"good reward"; added encouragement—"his companion can lift him up"; enhanced temperature—"how can one person alone keep warm"; and strong defense "two can resist him." Godly accountability is absolutely essential for those who hope to be all they can be for God. It can be one of the most valuable aspects of our spiritual lives!

We need accountability. The people we minister to need accountability as well. A wise minister will carefully create a culture of godly accountability for himself or herself and for those they serve.

What Accountability Looks Like

The apostle Paul writes Gal 6:1 for the specific purpose of teaching the congregations of Galatia how to restore fellow believers who have confessed their sin and are in need of spiritual strengthening. In doing so, we can glean some principles that inform us about how this environment of accountability works.

Brothers, if someone is caught in any wrongdoing, you who are spiritual
should restore such a person with a gentle spirit, watching out for
yourselves so you won't be tempted also. (Gal 6:1)

True Biblical Accountability Must Occur within the Body of Christ

Brothers is a term often used to depict the body of Christ. Therefore, true
biblical accountability must occur within the body of Christ. In other words
believers must help believers. The world is never able to provide the eternal,
spiritual, God-honoring, and life-changing counsel that a saved soul desperately needs. Only the Word of God is able to process, elucidate, and appropriately get to the root issues at the spiritual level that is called for by God.
Believers will only find true spiritual healing in the environment of the body
of Christ.

True Biblical Accountability Must Be Led by Spiritual Believers

The phrase "you who are spiritual" is an important qualifier when it comes
to forming a culture of accountability for your ministry. It is often an overlooked requirement that must be in place in your accountability structure
or the entire system will spiritually collapse. That is, even though true spiritual accountability must take place within the body of Christ, only believers
who are spiritual ought to take point in the accountability process of another
believer. This is not to say the majority of fellow believers are unable to check
up on their friends, be a sounding board for their loved ones, or listen to and
pray for their brothers and sisters in Christ. Of course they can and should. But
if you desire to cultivate an enduring culture of accountability in your ministry,
you must make sure every pocket of accountability that occurs in your sphere
of ministry is checking in and processing their previously discussed thoughts,
decisions, and challenges with someone who is considered spiritual.

So, what type of believer is considered *spiritual*? The word implies a
current and continual state of obedience and a life that is set apart for God.
Therefore, spiritual people are those who are currently demonstrating a pattern
of righteousness that has translated into obedience when around believers and
in their private, personal lives. These people are resolute in their commitment
to be faithful to the Word of God and are vigilant to fight against the evil one's
relentless attempts to tempt them to disobey God in the practical, daily decisions of life.[1]

This is particularly important for Christian leaders. Those who are facilitating the accountability process need to be aware that the temptations they will face are unique and a bit more intense in this environment of accountability. They will be tempted to gossip, become unnecessarily angry with other members, feel that they are holier than thou, or they may even be tempted by the same sins that weaker believers commit.

According to Gal 6:1 the spiritual person is to be more than just mindful that the temptation may be more profound upon him or her, but the leader is to remain on a heightened state of awareness of these temptations. The word *watching* in the phrase "watching out for yourselves so you won't be tempted also" draws upon an ancient word and describes an action that requires careful scrutiny of oneself in order to prevent temptation from getting a foothold.

Spiritual people understand how sin can enter the camp because they have remained observant to the ways sin subtly enters into their own lives. No one is serving as a Christian leader if they are not applying their keen spiritual discernment to speak to the spiritual root of all the issues, problems, motives, and discussions in their accountability group.

In addition, spiritual people will be tactful when dealing with the rest of the accountability members. Notice the verse says, "with a gentle spirit." Spiritual people will be sensitive to the fact that confessions of sin should not be met with a loud, screeching, and public rebuke of a penitent believer. Spiritual people will be careful to match the approach to the gravity of the situation. If you have been in ministry for any amount of time, you quickly hear of horrific encounters of ministers who have blasted sincerely penitent members of their church with such an over-the-top, abrasive tone that the members have left the church entirely based on the minister's lack of sensitivity. This is more than regrettable; it is shameful. For ministers to be unable to bridle their rage when dealing with a truly penitent believer is both regrettable and unconscionable and should not be considered spiritual. Instead, let's praise the Lord for His merciful offer to restore even the most seasoned of ministers to allow them to learn from their mistakes and become spiritual again!

True Biblical Accountability May Call for Imposed Safeguards

There may be times when the spiritual people within an accountability group must impose spiritual safeguards and prescribe spiritual activities for one who may have confessed their weakness in a certain area. This should be accepted as an act of love by the weaker member. This is the reason a culture of accountability is cultivated in the church—to strengthen fellow believers.

The word *restore* is an interesting word that adds vividness to the role of an accountability group. In the apostle Paul's day, the word was also used by the medical profession to describe a broken bone that had been set back into place. Therefore, an accountability group is there for the purpose of realigning and positioning the souls of the members into perfect alignment with God's Word. In doing so, it may only take a word of encouragement and a prayer offered on behalf of the member. Other times, it may be as involved as confronting and correcting believers in order to set them in the correct spiritual posture again. Upon recognizing that the person is rightly aligned spiritually, the accountability group may deem it necessary to prescribe certain spiritual activities and impose safeguards to the newly restored believer so that he or she doesn't give in to this same sin again. Here are some examples of what these safeguards could be:

- A list of Scriptures to read and discuss with a group member or family member.
- A list of locations to be avoided that promote certain sinful activities.
- Calling an accountability group member daily.
- Prohibiting access to the Internet unless in the presence of an accountability member who also tracks Internet surfing.
- Require more specific details when sins are confessed.

In essence, the accountability group places a "spiritual cast" around the weaker brother and limits his activity by dictating the amount of flexibility the weaker brother is granted. Then after the accountability group is able to witness progress and the beginning of a pattern of righteousness, they can grant a little more flexibility and a little less supervision. In this way we are removing a hard cast and placing a soft cast around the individual's soul with the goal that he regain his spiritual strength. When an enduring pattern of obedience and self-discipline is witnessed, then the accountability group is able to remove the cast of supervision. In this way the body of Christ will heal itself through true biblical accountability, which is the way God intended.

Thanks, but No Thanks

Being around supportive, God-focused believers is always a great joy for me. I enjoy engaging fellow believers as I visit their churches, homes, and ministries because I value intentional spiritual discussions and warm supportive fellowship. I wish everyone felt the same way about the support system we call the body of Christ. Unfortunately, some do not. After a brief time in and under the accountability group, they wrestle to get free from it.

Remember that the issue is *always* the heart! You can provide the most conducive environment for a person to experience pure worship, praise to God, and thorough accountability. But there will unfortunately be times when someone blatantly walks away from the spiritually rich environment you have provided for him or her. It will hurt. You will grieve deeply over their decision. In fact, the most difficult and discouraging seasons of ministry for me have been the times I observed a person in whom I poured my heart walk away from the faith. The pain hurts deeply. The emotions can move from anger to sadness to pity. These emotions surface frequently during the day, and they linger for a long time.

No minister is immune. Jesus lost some of His followers too. John depicts a mass defection (some believe it was hundreds of people): "From that moment many of His disciples turned back and no longer accompanied Him" (John 6:66).

The apostle Paul experienced defection of close coministers. He poured his life into a man named Demas and gave him one-on-one training. Unfortunately Demas followed his heart and left the spiritually rich environment Paul had given him.

Luke, the loved physician, and Demas greet you. (Col 4:14)

Epaphras, my fellow prisoner in Christ Jesus, greets you, and so do
Mark, Aristarchus, Demas, and Luke, my co-workers. (Phlm 23–24)

Make every effort to come to me soon, for Demas has deserted me,
because he loved this present world, and has gone to Thessalonica. (2 Tim 4:9–10)

So, in light of these defections, should we label our Lord Jesus Christ and the apostle Paul as "failures" in ministry? Of course not! Jesus and Paul fulfilled their responsibility to provide a spiritually rich environment that encouraged, trained, and facilitated spiritual intimacy and maturity.

If you, as a wise minister passionately produce an environment of godly accountability for those who are ministering with you, and they still choose to defect from the faith, you should not feel responsible for their choice. At the point of defection, you should find your consolation in the fact that you have fulfilled your responsibility as a minister. However, if they do walk away, don't think your job is over. You actually are required to continue one spiritual activity that you started with them the first day you began intentionally to meet with them; you continue to pray for them.

How It Works

We have discovered that the years where we have been intentional about finding an accountability partner, meeting regularly, and being utterly honest have been the years when we have enjoyed the greatest levels of personal growth and spiritual victory. We suggest that you try to touch base with your accountability partner at least once a week. Below is a list of sample questions you may ask each other each week.

Sample Accountability Questions

- Have you consistently been spending time with the Lord?
- Have you been morally pure in thought, word, and actions?
- Have you watched anything, read anything, looked at anything, or visited any Web site you would be embarrassed to watch with Jesus?
- Have you said, written, talked to, or touched anyone inappropriately?
- Have you honored and invested in your spouse?
- Have you lied about any of the above?

What Now?

How persuaded are you of the value of accountability in your ministry? Do you make it a priority to ensure that your ministry is known for having spiritual believers who provide accountability for all believers? Cultivating this culture of accountability must first be a priority in the heart of God's ministers in order to permeate the entire ministry.

Have you taken the time intentionally to pour your heart and life into a fellow believer within your ministry? Have you appointed spiritual leaders to become extensions of you in this regard? If so, how do your leaders match up to the biblical description of "spiritual"? Do they all align with the biblical description? If so, praise the Lord! If they don't, how did they get appointed to their leadership position? Did you inherit the leadership team from another minister? Did you choose the leaders out of desperation? Did you skip over the vetting process of your leaders in order to implement an accountability program swiftly? Consider your answers to these questions and make the necessary changes now to your ministry.

If a change is needed in your leadership team, what prohibits you from making the tough but necessary decision of shifting leadership responsibilities? Are you fearful of peoples' reactions, accusations, or personal embarrassment? Remember that any awkwardness or embarrassment may be due to a poor leadership decision in the past and should serve as a tender reminder to patiently and prayerfully appoint leaders within your ministry.

What about you personally? Are you a spiritual person? If asked to lead an accountability group, could you make the cut? If not, what spiritual issues would you need to address in order to mature spiritually? Have you solicited the help of an accountability team to come alongside you in order to support you and cheer you on?

Do you function in a gentle spirit, or are you more prone to lash out in rage even at the most sincere confession? Prior to reading this chapter, have you considered the repercussions of ministering to people with the wrong attitude?

If you do meet the requirements of a spiritual person, are you committed to leading members of the body of Christ to become spiritual people themselves?

Ministry Is . . .

1. Cultivating a culture of godly accountability for yourself *and* for those you serve.
2. Developing spiritual believers who are mature and who will become leaders of their own accountability groups.
3. Grieving over those who choose to defect from the faith and praying for them to return home.

⪧ Quotes ⪦

Genuine accountability is a mirror to the soul, providing vital feedback. . . . Accountability fuels proper perspective and encourages authentic purity.

—DANIEL HENDERSON[2]

One of the fastest roads to moral failure in ministry is a lack of accountability.

—MICHAEL TODD WILSON AND BRAD HOFFMAN[3]

Notes

1. For further discussion on misconceptions about being a godly person, see B. Gutierrez, "After Three: Know, Walk, Respond" (Bel Air, MD: Academx Publishing, 2010), 69–76.

2. D. Henderson, *Defying Gravity: How to Survive the Storms of Pastoral Ministry* (Chicago, IL: Moody Press, 2010), 91–92.

3. M. T. Wilson and B. Hoffman, *Preventing Ministry Failure* (Downers Grove, IL: Intervarsity Press, 2007), 45.

Conclusion

We've only just begun.

When we were young, those were the words of a song that dominated the radio waves. It was a song about the journey that begins at marriage. It speaks of walking and running and growth.

We've only just begun.

That's how we feel about this book. Even though we have walked you through 31 chapters about the meaning, motives, essentials, manner, and methods of ministry, there is so much more we could say.

We've only just begun.

That's how we want you to feel about ministry after reading this book. Ministry is a great adventure that you have just begun.

Index